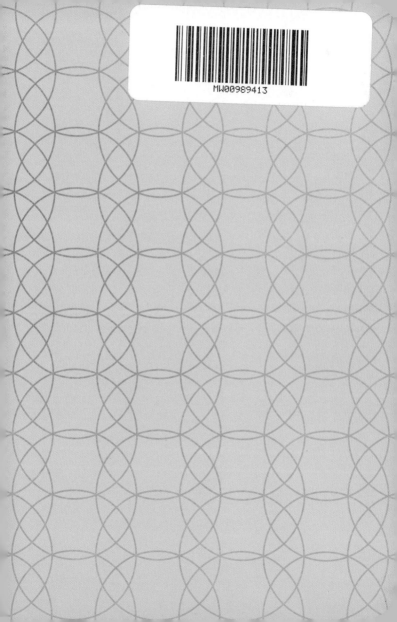

MW00989413

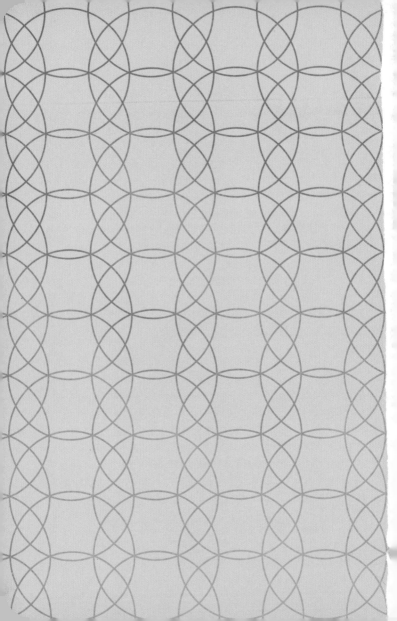

BRANCH
to hope

pause +pray

NEW HABITS
CREATE CHANGE

A 365-Day Devotional

BOBBIE COX

BroadStreet
PUBLISHING

BroadStreet Publishing® Group, LLC
Savage, Minnesota, USA
BroadStreetPublishing.com

Pause and Pray: New Habits Create Change

9781424568178 (faux leather)
9781424568185 (ebook)

Cover and interior by Garborg Design Works | garborgdesign.com
Tree graphics by Ashley Cox | A+B Designs

Printed in China

24 25 26 27 28 5 4 3 2 1

I dedicate this book to Ashley, my daughter, who devotedly makes me the best I can be, far beyond my capabilities. And to everyone with whom Jesus has woven into my life along life's journey. We've shared great moments, hurtful experiences, exciting celebrations, unfortunate betrayals, sweet memories, challenging product development ventures, and blessings that exceeded our imaginations. I am sincerely grateful to each of you, beyond what words can express.

Introduction

Are you frustrated with life, your irresponsible reactions, and the behavior of others? Are you searching for change yet don't know where to start? We can all fall into a rut of bad habits, and there never seems to be enough time to even think about change, much less maneuver one more task into our overscheduled life.

Change starts with you. You then affect others. One day, I was reading 2 Corinthians 1:11, which speaks of gathering in prayer together, and at that moment, I glanced at my watch; it was 1:11 p.m. The Lord whispered to me to text my prayer group, encouraging us to pause and pray together each day at 1:11 p.m. What started as a group text is now an app, Branch to Hope, bringing together thousands in daily prayer.

Like the challenge to pray at 1:11, this book contains three interactive features that will inspire you to develop a new lifestyle pattern. In addition, QR codes allow you to interact with the features in deeper ways.

- Galatians 5:22–23 speaks of the fruit of Jesus' Spirit: love, joy, peace, patience, kindness, goodness, faithfulness, gentleness, and self-control. Each devotion is color coded to a fruit of the Spirit. As you focus on one of the nine specific colors throughout the day, it will be a reminder of one of Jesus' characteristics, triggering a habit that helps you live more like Jesus.

- Each devotion contains a Scripture Whisper. This Scripture reference corresponds with the date. For example, January 1 features Genesis 1:1. Noticing the date on your phone, watch, calendar, or car dash will prompt you to change negative self-talk by weaving the verse through your thoughts.

- Most importantly, each day includes a message and prayer. By reading or listening to the devotion, you will realize that Jesus desires to walk alongside you and chitchat with you as your best friend. The prayers are written so that even if you're praying alone, you will be reminded that you're also praying with everyone who's reading this devotional.

These calls to action prompt lifestyle changes in the in-between moments: idling at a red light, waiting for an elevator, or standing in line. Some say it takes 21 days to make a habit. Therefore, spending 21 days on each characteristic of the fruit of the Spirit takes 189 days, so in six months, you will be living more like Jesus and improving your world.

Embracing this book with passionate intentionality will make your cry for change into a reality. A movement of change starts with one; let that be you!

January

Let's Embrace the Beginning

SCRIPTURE WHISPER

In the beginning, God created the heavens and the earth.
GENESIS 1:1 ESV

The first day of the New Year appropriately begins with our focus on the color red, signifying love. We should seek ways to show God's love, the foundation of the other fruit of Jesus' character. Our Scripture Whisper today reminds us that even in the beginning, God loved us enough to create us.

Satan's strategy is to disrupt the love in our relationships with God, our family, and our friends. Let's begin each day on the lookout for the Enemy's crafty strategies that interfere in our relationships so we can win the battle before Satan gains a foothold. By falling back on a lifestyle of living by the fruit of Jesus' Spirit, we can diffuse evil attempts and send them fleeing. Over time, when our automatic default flows toward Jesus, Satan will surrender in that area of our life. That door is slammed shut and sealed with the sacrificial blood of Jesus when we intentionally remain on guard. The benefits will include us experiencing less conflict, watching our relationships soar, and becoming more intimate in our daily relationship with Jesus.

Jesus of love, help our New Year's resolution to be making a habit of living a fruit of your Spirit each day.

Let's Not Run from Hardship

SCRIPTURE WHISPER

Consider it pure joy, my brothers and sisters, whenever you face trials of many kinds.

JAMES 1:2 NIV

Life's journey prepares us for what God created us to fulfill in his great plan. Circumstances and choices we make affect how our life unfolds. God loves us so much that he often corrects our course to better equip us for what's ahead. Rather than using our efforts to avoid hardships, we can ask God to navigate us through, and he will give lavishly.

Often, trials and hardships are out of our control because we live in a fallen world, but they are never out of God's control. God promises to take the experiences of those who love him and are called according to his purpose (Romans 8:28) and turn them into his blessings, far greater than we can hope or imagine (Ephesians 3:20).

Jesus of joy, we come to you today with a thirst to start this year renewed, aligning our desires with yours and realizing we need to approach the challenges, hardships, and trials of life differently, head-on. Help us always trust that you will lead the way and equip us for accomplishments for which you created us.

Scan To Branch Out

Let's Fellowship with Jesus

SCRIPTURE WHISPER

That which we have seen and heard declare we unto you, that ye also may have fellowship with us: and truly our fellowship is with the Father, and with his Son Jesus Christ.

1 JOHN 1:3 KJV

Fellowship with Jesus in a personal, intimate relationship is the pot of gold at the end of the rainbow; nothing is better as we navigate life on this earth. But why does it take a lifetime along the journey to realize this? It's because we live in a fallen world, and it is Satan's goal to disrupt our relationships with each other, which ultimately interferes with our relationship with God.

We must realize that when we accept Jesus in our hearts, we have the same power transferred from the cross to divert Satan's attempt and send his efforts straight into the pit of hell. All we must do is call on God to fight our battles. Satan cannot permanently reside in the presence of our Lord, so when we invite Jesus on the scene, victory is won in him.

Jesus of peace, fellowship with you brings meaning and value to your sacrifice and joy within our souls. Help us become intentional about spending more time with you each day.

Let's Partner with Jesus

SCRIPTURE WHISPER

God has something stored up for you in heaven, where it will never decay or be ruined or disappear.

1 PETER 1:4 CEV

We can be assured that if we have accepted Jesus as our Savior and have developed a personal relationship with him, our names will never be removed from the Book of Life. We will live in heaven for eternity, which our Scripture Whisper assures us.

Jesus calls us to spread that good news to others by following the fruit of his Spirit in our lifestyle. We are called to plant the seeds, and God will bountifully harvest them into his kingdom. It's a partnership, working daily with him as he arranges divine moments for us to advance his kingdom.

Jesus of patience, we thank you for the sacrifice you offered so that our names can be written in your Book of Life. Please help us never miss an opportunity to be your ambassadors by attracting others into your kingdom through our lifestyles so that hopeless souls don't have to navigate life on their own in this troubled land.

Scan To Branch Out

Let's Ask Jesus for Wisdom

SCRIPTURE WHISPER

If any of you lacks wisdom, let him ask from God, the One giving generously to all and not finding fault, and it will be given to him.

JAMES 1:5 BLB

It would be an unbelievable blessing to have a biblical counselor who lives by our side, precisely perceives the future, and has encountered every experience we could ever imagine. This counselor would know what's best for us, assisting us in every aspect of our lives. We do have such a counselor; it's the Holy Spirit.

So why do we not engage him? Why do we make choices and do life without his counsel? He has provided his Holy Word and prayer as his phone of communication, and he answers twenty-four seven.

Jesus of kindness, thank you that the Holy Spirit is accessible as our Counselor to guide us through life's challenges. Forgive us when we do life alone; that's our foolishness. We ask that we gain your wisdom in everything.

Scan To Branch Out

Let's Leave the Planning to Jesus

SCRIPTURE WHISPER

Let him ask in faith, with no doubting, for the one who doubts is like a wave of the sea that is driven and tossed by the wind.

JAMES 1:6 ESV

Aligning with the heart of God is a lifelong learning process and a recipe for answered prayers. God knows every detail of our lives, where he plans for us to reside, our career path, and our spouse. Rushing in with panicked prayer requests and quick decisions is not God's design. When we begin seeking God's plan, decisions of this magnitude come with ease and peace from the Lord as his perfect plan unfolds and the desires of his heart become our desires. Though things often happen differently than we envision, he has something arranged that is much more significant than we could ever imagine.

Those we encounter and those we were meant to miss will affect our lifelong journey and future. That applies to all decisions, significant life encounters, and small choices, too, whether at a red light, in line at the grocery store, or walking into a restaurant. Life is all about relationships, and God is the master planner.

Jesus of goodness, please mold our hearts' desires to align with your desires and focus our minds on the unfolding of your plan.

Scan To Branch Out

Let's Trust Jesus amid Trouble

SCRIPTURE WHISPER

The LORD is good, a strength and stronghold in the day of trouble; He knows [He recognizes, cares for, and understands fully] those who take refuge and trust in Him.
NAHUM 1:7 AMP

Nahum is such an overlooked book in the Bible. When was the last time you heard a verse quoted from the book of Nahum? Yet how powerful are these words in our Scripture Whisper, reminding us of the value of trusting in God?

When we are in trouble, he is our strength. When we feel weak and downhearted, he is our stronghold. When evil chases us down, we know the Lord is good. These words of Scripture assure us that God recognizes our troubles and knows what to do. He fully understands how to navigate us to the other side of trouble. We are blessed to be his children because we can call upon the one who will carry us through the storms of life.

Jesus of faithfulness, we are grateful that your promises were hidden in your Word centuries ago. They are full of encouragement that we can cling to today during troubled times. There's so much noise, distraction, and hopelessness surrounding us in the world; help us find that quiet solitude to reflect on your rich words and then share with others the value of trusting you.

Scan To Branch Out

Let's Know and Believe

SCRIPTURE WHISPER

Though you have not seen Him, you love Him; and though you do not see Him now, you believe in Him and rejoice with an inexpressible and glorious joy.

1 PETER 1:8 BSB

Faith is an unwavering confidence and clear expectation, just like we trust that the four legs of a chair will not fail us, a tall building's foundation will withstand its weight, and an invisible God is by our side leading the way.

But how can people live by faith if they do not have sufficient knowledge of God? We must welcome a personal relationship with God. That's our part, to come to know and depend on him as we journey through life. We must turn to his Word and pray for direction and guidance and strength, which increases our knowledge of God and our faith. Tragically, many believe in God's existence but do not live in an intimate relationship with him, as evidenced by their conduct and the downfall of our society's moral integrity and character.

Jesus of gentleness, help us ignite a revival for those who know of you but do not understand your gentle and tender character or your desire to lead them through the minefields of life. Equip us to be your light of hope and to trust in your plan with unwavering faith.

Scan To Branch Out

Let's Hang On with Jesus

SCRIPTURE WHISPER

You are receiving the end result of your faith,
the salvation of your souls.

1 Peter 1:9 NIV

Life's journey is a faith stretch. Every day, we encounter situations and experiences that challenge our faith. There's no doubt that Satan does not want us to live eternity in heaven, so he continually attempts to interrupt our daily walk with Jesus.

As we face circumstances and people who put us out on a limb, suspended from our fingertips in faith, it's encouraging to remember that we can look forward to a trouble-free life awaiting us in heaven. And that's what our Scripture Whisper is reminding us: "You are receiving the end result of your faith, the salvation of your souls." That should bring soothing warmth to our souls, an assurance we can cling to in troubled times.

Jesus of self-control, thank you for hanging on those limbs along with us. We know a safety net of your love will catch us when we encounter a faith stretch. We are incapable of hanging on with our own strength, and we are grateful that we can rest in your loving care.

Let's Produce Good Fruit

SCRIPTURE WHISPER

The way you live will always honor and please the Lord, and your lives will produce every kind of good fruit. All the while, you will grow as you learn to know God better and better.
COLOSSIANS 1:10 NLT

This is the road map of life we should follow daily. Just look at the rewards! And the Bible tells us that we can rest assured that our Father makes us strong enough to take part in life's challenges. This strength endures the unendurable and spills over into joy amid life's storms. Bright and beautiful days for which he has arranged for us ahead will unfold.

Approaching life with an expectation of the bright and beautiful should lift our souls as God completes his plan, giving us his spiritual wisdom and understanding, so even in the stormy days, life ahead can be nothing but bright and beautiful as we know God better.

Jesus of love, we ask that you help us be good stewards of your orchard, seeking ways to plant seeds of hope in lives you arrange for us to encounter each day. We ask that we become thirsty for your knowledge, wisdom, and understanding so that we can fulfill your plan with ease throughout our lives.

Let's Pause and Pray

SCRIPTURE WHISPER

You join in helping us by your prayers. Then many will give thanks on our behalf for the gift that came to us through the prayers of many.

2 Corinthians 1:11 csb

The verse that started my ministry Branch to Hope is 2 Corinthians 1:11, making January 11 our signature day. This Scripture Whisper is the seed that inspired the gathering of people to pray for each other and our country at 1:11 p.m. every day. This small effort sprouted and blossomed into our Branch to Hope movement, which promotes the power of prayer in unity while bringing hope to the hopeless.

With his whispers into our spirits, our Lord guides us to pray throughout the day. As he drops someone on our heart, let's pause, pray, and let them know we are praying for them. Often our prayers are needed at that very moment, in his perfect timing, and the ones we pray for become encouraged because they see that prayer makes a difference.

Jesus of joy, thank you for your nudge to pray. The greatest gift is to partner with you in prayer. As you flash someone across our thoughts, help us never miss those opportunities to pause and pray. Give us a thirst to be devoted and diligent prayer ambassadors when you whisper needs into our hearts.

Scan To Branch Out

Let's Endure Testing

SCRIPTURE WHISPER

God blesses those who patiently endure testing and temptation. Afterward they will receive the crown of life that God has promised to those who love him.

JAMES 1:12 NLT

Everyone wants a blessing, but unfortunately, it's often something tangible, something worldly that we desire. A true blessing, however, is a God-given gift to bless others from the blessings of Jesus living through us. A blessing, in the eyes of Christ's followers, is kingdom victory. Blessings are meant to be experienced, enjoyed, and shared through the goodness of God. They are intended to bring about internal change within us and influence those we encounter.

Often trials open the door to God's blessings. Paul said to embrace trials and receive them joyfully, praying for wisdom and expecting to be more equipped to be a blessing in Christ's likeness. As a result, trials prepare us to live the fruit of his Spirit, encouraging us to recognize that we are blessed to be a blessing so we can share with others the fruit of blessings along our path.

Jesus of peace, we ask for your wisdom and strength to persevere under trials so we can encourage others. That is your promise, and we are grateful when you can use us for your kingdom's victory.

Scan To Branch Out

Let's Live Rescued

SCRIPTURE WHISPER

He has rescued us and has drawn us to Himself from the dominion of darkness, and has transferred us to the kingdom of His beloved Son.

COLOSSIANS 1:13 AMP

Let's pause and reflect on the heart of God. He offered his Son, Jesus Christ, to purchase us from the rule of Satan because of Adam and Eve's fall to the slavery of evil. We were all born as slaves to sin, but God so desired to have a daily relationship with his children that he paid the price for each of us with his life. The cost of our freedom was God's only Son, and believing in him is an entrance to heaven.

Many think they must work for their freedom through good works, living as slaves to themselves without understanding that their freedom is found only in Jesus. Seeing the life of Jesus living through us can open their heart of understanding and set them free.

Jesus of patience, help us be your voice of freedom in this world of darkness so that others can find freedom in your sacrifice, rescuing us from the kingdom of darkness and bringing us into your kingdom of hope.

Let's Rely On God

SCRIPTURE WHISPER

The Word became flesh and dwelt among us. We observed his glory, the glory as the one and only Son from the Father, full of grace and truth.

JOHN 1:14 CSB

Jesus relied on his Father when he was in need. We have the same Father. With an outstretched hand and compassionate heart, he waits for us to ask for guidance as Jesus did. Why is it so hard for us to do that? Why do we try to do life on our own without calling on him to carry us through?

The lure of Satan supersedes when we allow our free will to take over instead of surrendering to the only one who knows the future and wants the very best for us. Jesus encountered Satan's tug throughout his walk on earth. Yet he trusted his Father to lead the way around the pitfalls of life. The Father never had to pull him out of the pits, though, because Jesus never fell into the pit. Our Lord suffered and died so that we never have to fall in either; he provided a way around Satan's pit and will lead the way for us too.

Jesus of kindness, you understand the pitfalls and paved the way around them. You give us a stable path should we choose to follow in your footsteps. Help us depend on you every step of the way.

Scan To Branch Out

Let's Embrace the Time

SCRIPTURE WHISPER

He said, "The time has come, and God's kingdom is near. Change the way you think and act, and believe the Good News."

Mark 1:15 GW

The time has come to be a light in the darkness. By changing our thoughts and actions that are not in alignment with the ways of Jesus, we can live by the fruit of his Spirit for others to see. In this troubled world, the light of Jesus shines brighter. Time seems to indicate that the coming of the Lord is soon; it's time for us to be ambassadors for his good news of salvation by the way we live.

Jesus of goodness, help us during these times to be aware of the importance of leading others into your kingdom. We do not know what tomorrow brings or when it may be too late. It's the way we live that will draw others to you. Help us be all that you desire us to be to reach the lost and hopeless every day along our journey; as we plant seeds, you harvest hearts.

Scan To Branch Out

Let's Start Again

SCRIPTURE WHISPER

From his abundance we have all received one gracious blessing after another.

JOHN 1:16 NLT

How often do we ignore the blessings that our Lord arranges each moment? He is behind the scenes orchestrating things for which we fail to give thanks. Let's join in a season of starting again, making better choices, living more meaningfully, and giving thanks and appreciation for the many things that bless us, which we too often ignore.

Why do we complain when God showers us with grace on top of grace every day? The blessings from the simple things in life bring more value than the self-imposed complications that tend to capture our focus.

Jesus of faithfulness, we come to you today asking you to help us notice the blessings that make a difference in our lives and that we so often take for granted. Help us smile more at others and give affirmation that we appreciate them for the little things they do for us every day. And Lord, we thank you in the unity of our prayer today for the gift of your sacrifice and for the many things you do in the moments of our day that protect us and bless us along life's journey.

Scan To Branch Out

Let's Always Face the Son

SCRIPTURE WHISPER

Every good gift and every perfect gift is from above, and cometh down from the Father of lights, with whom is no variableness, neither shadow of turning.

JAMES 1:17 KJV

Have you ever thought about why the earth becomes dark even though the sun always shines? It's because the earth keeps turning. Similarly, we so often turn our backs on the bright light of Jesus, failing to live out his shining light. He never changes; we do.

God continuously shines his goodness, truth, gentleness, and grace on us, and we must intentionally turn toward him, not away from him. The evil forces attempt to cast a shadow to camouflage the light of Jesus within us. It's up to us to keep our focus on the brightness of the Son.

Jesus of gentleness, we are grateful for your bright, shining light. You continually stretch out your hand to take us through the dark moments of our lives. The pull of Satan is as dynamic as we allow it to be, and it is weakened when we refuse it. Please help us refrain from turning to the darkness and, instead, focus on your light.

Scan To Branch Out

Let's Withdraw Our Inheritance

SCRIPTURE WHISPER

I pray that the eyes of your heart may be enlightened in order that you may know the hope to which he has called you, the riches of his glorious inheritance in his holy people.
EPHESIANS 1:18 NIV

God navigates our lives through the maze of life experiences amid our own free-will choices. He leads us in extraordinary ways along life's journey and equips us to live out the plan he uniquely created for us.

There is a bank of spiritual blessings for those adopted into the family of God. God lovingly customizes our lives for a purpose. So we are spiritually wealthy; we just need to open the Bible bank of promises and, in faith, take out a withdrawal. Many Christians live spiritually poor lives while sitting on a pile of blessings. We are spiritually impoverished when we refuse to believe God's promises or to activate our blessings through faith.

Jesus of self-control, we pray that the eyes of our hearts will be enlightened so we recognize the hope of our calling, understand the wealth of your glorious inheritance by reading your Word, and activate your promises through faith.

Scan To Branch Out

Let's Be Heartfelt Listeners

SCRIPTURE WHISPER

Understand this, my dear brothers and sisters: You must all
be quick to listen, slow to speak, and slow to get angry.

JAMES 1:19 NLT

We should listen with sincerity to learn others' stories; life
is all about stories. There's a lot of meaning between the
lines, and when we are "quick to listen," that meaning reveals
much about how we can support one another. And when we
listen through the heart of Jesus, we are less likely to speak
in haste or anger while we listen compassionately for the
meaning of others' stories.

Everyone interprets things differently, from everyday
humdrum to life-altering events. We're all on a unique
journey that no one else has traveled, and our different
experiences provide varied interpretations of life. That's what
makes our individual stories so unique. Let's become better
listeners and hear others through the heart of Jesus.

Jesus of love, we ask that you help us listen to others through
your heart. We pray for the discernment to perceive heart
cries between the lines so we can be a vessel of hope and
help those who need a compassionate heart. And help us sift
our words through your filter so that we live a lifestyle that
emulates you.

Scan To Branch Out

Let's Share God's Wisdom

SCRIPTURE WHISPER

Wisdom shouts in the street, she raises her voice in the markets.
PROVERBS 1:20 AMP

Wisdom is available and accessible to anyone, but it requires that we ask and get out of God's way. The world's wisdom and God's wisdom are vastly different. We learn at an early age and spend our cumulative years learning, but that doesn't equate to wisdom. Wisdom is gained little by little as we journey along life. It's human nature to make choices on our own, and it's a continual tug-of-war battle, but Satan knows he has lost us when we surrender our will to the wisdom of God.

God's wisdom requires less effort—surrendering our ways to his ways, defaulting our choices to his wisdom—yet we seem to make that a lifelong training session too. Our stubborn will and Satan's interference keep us in a vortex that discourages us from surrendering to the wisdom of God.

Jesus of joy, we humbly ask your forgiveness for living in a vortex of our own choices and for allowing Satan to interfere in our asking you for wisdom. It is such a blessed gift that we can turn to you. There's no need for worry, fret, concern, or confusion; your wisdom is all we need.

Scan To Branch Out

Let's Live for Jesus

SCRIPTURE WHISPER

To me to live is Christ, and to die is gain.

PHILIPPIANS 1:21 KJV

When we make Jesus our reason to live, joy permeates our atmosphere everywhere we go. No matter the circumstances, if we choose joy when we feel like screaming, crying, or giving up, the Spirit of God floods in and blankets us with an indescribable peace that all will be alright. His promise to take what Satan meant for harm and turn it into good for those who love him and are called according to his purpose will manifest. It's that simple. We must call on him instead of cracking open the door to Satan.

And then dying to our flesh and the ways of the world ensures eternal life and a life on earth that rises above the worries and woes we might face. Intentionally making a habit of living in the character of Jesus allows us to leave drama behind and lifts us above the trivial frustrations of life.

Jesus of peace, help us make you the focus of our moments, replacing worldly distractions with time spent with you, emulating your character as your ambassadors, permeating the world with your light, and overtaking the darkness of the hopeless.

Scan To Branch Out

Let's Not Just Listen

SCRIPTURE WHISPER

Don't just listen to God's word. You must do what it says.
Otherwise, you are only fooling yourselves.

JAMES 1:22 NLT

God is the giver of all good things and is looking for every
opportunity to bless us. But we often have difficulty trusting
and receiving good things, even when those things come
from God. Satan is the master deceiver and attempts to trick
us and camouflage God's truth.

The frustration is that we not only have trouble
recognizing God's work in our lives, but we also don't always
respond to God's still, small voice of direction and gentle
guidance; we allow the world's noise to overpower and
overtake our hearing. We often hear the Scriptures but don't
listen, and we fail to put them to use. James tells us to live
out God's Word every day.

Jesus of patience, we ask for keen ears to hear your voice
and fertile hearts to store the truth of your Word. We hope
to understand your promises and intentionally live out your
Word throughout our lives. Your Word is a gift, the lamp
to our feet, a road map with clear direction to fulfill your
plan. Remind us that we may be the only biblical interaction
someone ever encounters.

Scan To Branch Out

Let's Make Jesus Our Navigator

SCRIPTURE WHISPER

If you respond to my warning, then I will pour out my spirit on you and teach you my words.

PROVERBS 1:23 CSB

Jesus desires to help us navigate our lives around the land mines, infusing joy, peace, and gentleness into our life. That's why he suffered in such agony to win our souls away from Satan's chaotic life of turmoil. God provides the ability to live well and make good decisions as we depend on him, who is never stingy when it comes to counseling those who seek him. But when we try to go it alone, trouble lurks around the corner.

We must be intentionally anchored in a single-minded commitment to God. Those who depend only on their own judgment are like those lost on the seas, carried away by any wave or picked up by any wind. Those who half-heartedly obey Jesus while swimming after their own whims never find peace. But those anchored in a genuine commitment to seeking God's counsel will live in the palm of God's gentleness.

Jesus of kindness, forgive us for failing to turn to you and instead favoring Satan in our decisions, choices, and ways. Help us intentionally seek your wise counsel and form a habit of always turning to you for our choices.

Scan To Branch Out

Let's Binge on Jesus

SCRIPTURE WHISPER

The Scriptures say, "Humans wither like grass, and their glory fades like wild flowers. Grass dries up, and flowers fall to the ground."

1 Peter 1:24 cev

When we are born again, we receive a divine seed that is imperishable, but it requires nourishment. Our sinful, self-centered nature will take over if we let it, causing our spiritual life to become malnourished, withered like grass, and fading like wildflowers. To be physically healthy, we must consume nutritious foods while avoiding what is unwholesome. The same principle is true in the spiritual realm: we need to feed on the Word of God.

Babies know when they're hungry and cry out for milk. As born-again believers, we should thirst for the Word of God, but instead, we often remain malnourished. While babies eat regularly throughout the day, many Christians binge on Scripture only on Sunday and expect it to last all week. For the rest of the week, they consume worldly junk food, which won't produce growth. Let's change our diet and steadily consume the Word of God.

Jesus of goodness, forgive us when we choose trivial things to consume our time rather than choosing to be nourished by you. Give us an insatiable desire throughout the day to pick up the Bible, a source of your nourishment, more than we pick up our phones.

Let's Live in God's Protection

SCRIPTURE WHISPER

The one who peers into the perfect law of liberty and fixes his attention there, and does not become a forgetful listener but one who lives it out—he will be blessed in what he does.
JAMES 1:25 NET

Obedience to God's law is for our protection, and he promises that he will shower the blessings of his favor upon our life of obedience. Many feel that obedience to God means giving up their freedom to have fun, but what is fun about the consequences of sin? Not following God's voice means following Satan's voice, which leads to eternal destruction. Why is it so hard for us to put into action the ways of God, who is compassionately waiting to navigate us away from Satan's lure?

When we open the eyes of our hearts, embracing the beautiful truth found in obedience to God's laws, we gain liberty and freedom. We avoid many distractions, heartaches, and frustrations when we realize the joy, peace, and contentment found in God.

Jesus of faithfulness, why do we complicate life when you make it so easy to depend on you to navigate us through the minefields of Satan's traps? Forgive us when we do life on our own and favor Satan instead of surrendering our moments into your care.

Scan To Branch Out

Let's Make Our Words Powerful

SCRIPTURE WHISPER

If you claim to be religious but don't control your tongue, you are fooling yourself, and your religion is worthless.
JAMES 1:26 NLT

As Christ's followers, we should implement into our lives on Monday the words we hear on Sunday. Others should hear our faith through our Jesus-inspired word choices, gentle tone, and topics of conversations. Our compassion and love for Jesus should showcase his message through the way we live and speak.

As followers of Jesus, we should demonstrate a mastery of our tongues by talking less and listening more. If our religion is to be genuine, we must communicate with a compassionate heart, especially with those who can do nothing for us in return; that's what Jesus did for us. We must never allow the world to influence our behavior and tarnish the testimony Jesus is building through us for others to see. Instead, our lifestyle should sprinkle seeds of his grace and goodness.

Jesus of gentleness, help us live in the mirror of your character by controlling our tongues and using your word choices, knowing that our lives will influence those who don't know you. Allow us to model an attraction to your forgiveness as we are reborn into your kingdom.

Let's Remain Humble

SCRIPTURE WHISPER

God has chosen what is foolish in the world to shame the wise, and God has chosen what is weak in the world to shame the strong.

1 Corinthians 1:27 csb

The worldly way is to seek people who have achieved popularity, success, and notability, but God chose the foolish and weak to shame the elite of the world who live apart from his saving grace. He chose fishermen, tax collectors, carpenters, and the persecuted to speak his message to the world.

God uses those with low self-esteem, those from humble beginnings, those who have endured a lifetime of extreme struggles, those who are bullied and don't fit in, and those who are ridiculed by the crowd. These are ready ambassadors for God's kingdom unlike those of high stature who refuse to humble themselves or elevate Christ on their stage of life. Since many eyes are on them, it's a tragedy when they choose not to portray humility.

Jesus of self-control, help us remain humble in your strength. We are chosen to be your light although we may seem foolish to those drowning in their popularity, success, and notability. We will be elevated and blessed as you use us to captivate their hearts and help them recognize that their only hope for eternal salvation is in you.

Scan To Branch Out

Let's Live Highly Favored

SCRIPTURE WHISPER

The angel appeared to her and said, "Greetings, you who are highly favored! The Lord is with you."
LUKE 1:28 BSB

The word *favor* describes someone who has been granted special treatment or attention. The verse above from Luke refers to the time the angel Gabriel told Mary that she would be the mother of the Son of God; she was favored.

We, too, are offered a life of favor. Numerous stories from the Bible show us insight, and so many promises in Scripture show us how to claim favor from God as his children. Still, Satan attempts to make us feel unworthy and undeserving because of our sins, but Jesus eradicated our sins on the cross, rendering us clean and white as snow in his eyes, worthy of favor because of his sacrifice.

Jesus of love, we are grateful that we are highly favored in your eyes. You see our sins no more, past, present, or future, so why do we allow Satan to conjure up a feeling of unworthiness? When we do, it's as if we nail you to the cross repeatedly. Please forgive us. Help us live worthy of your suffering, see ourselves favored in your amazing grace, and walk in the atmosphere of favor as your goodness and magnificence shine through our lives.

Scan To Branch Out

Let's Be Seed Bearers

SCRIPTURE WHISPER

God said, "Look! I have given you every seed-bearing plant throughout the earth and all the fruit trees for your food."
GENESIS 1:29 NLT

Jesus has provided every seed-bearing plant for the nourishment of our physical bodies. He has also provided spiritual food for us to grow branches and to spread fruit from his Spirit for the lost and weary people we encounter in our lives.

If we don't eat the fruit he supplies, we aren't nourished. Just like if we don't plant seeds of hope in Jesus throughout our days, then the fruit in our lives withers and dies. It must germinate from our intention to live like Jesus, which we learn how to do by devoting time to God's Word, prayer, and worship. Otherwise, God's masterful creation in each of our lives is in vain, and Jesus suffered in agony and died an inhumane death for nothing.

Jesus of joy, we pray that we become more rooted in your Word so that we scatter seeds wherever we go. Help us expect that the fruit of your Spirit will permeate the lives of others. Jesus, may we never miss an opportunity to plant seeds for you to harvest lost and hopeless souls into your heavenly home.

Scan To Branch Out

Let's Strengthen Our Faith

SCRIPTURE WHISPER

God has united you with Christ Jesus. For our benefit God
made him to be wisdom itself. Christ made us right with
God; he made us pure and holy, and he freed us from sin.
1 Corinthians 1:30 NLT

Jesus suffered agony to set us free from sin and render us
shameless and guilt-free. But how often do we allow fear and
worry to grip us and keep us from the freedom God gifted to
us as his children? We fight a constant battle against fear and
guilt as Satan creeps into our thoughts to hijack our peace
amid the storms. God has answered our prayerful cries and
rescued us when things seemed hopeless. Remembering
this is the greatest way to strengthen our faith and break the
chains of bondage over worry.

We are teachers of faith in Jesus by the ways our joy
and peace prevail through the stormy days of life. But rest
assured that tomorrow the Son will rise in the light of
his glory and grace, and we can boldly expect him to do
miracles again.

Jesus of peace, thank you for making us pure, holy, and
freed from sin as you work to manifest miracles and do what
seems impossible, touching lives and drawing us into your
kingdom. Create a testimony through us.

Let's Love the Next Generation

SCRIPTURE WHISPER

God looked at everything he had made, and he was very pleased. Evening passed and morning came—that was the sixth day.

GENESIS 1:31 GNT

God saw everything that he had made and said it was very good. In the same way, I feel inspired to embrace children, grandchildren, nieces, and nephews, and everyone in the younger generations. They enrich our lives with a special blessing of love. I pray we all embrace as very good the creation God weaved into young people. Let's look for the goodness in them, which we so often take for granted, by loving them in their trials and difficulties of life and being pleased by the way God uniquely created them.

No one but Jesus will ever be faultless; we have all failed throughout our journeys, and God still sees us as very good. Let's extend that to others, especially the children in our lives, whether young or now adults, seeing the goodness in them. Let's rejoice in and encourage their strengths, gifts, and talents as they navigate through unchartered waters that come with generational changes.

Jesus of patience, we pray that we see everything you made as very good. There is no room for offenses or unforgiveness; help us love like you.

February

Let's Become Unified in Prayer

SCRIPTURE WHISPER

First of all, then, I urge that supplications, prayers,
intercessions, and thanksgivings be made for all people.
1 TIMOTHY 2:1 ESV

In 2023, when a twenty-four-year-old football player lost
consciousness on the field during a high-profile NFL game,
both teams surrounded him in a wall of prayer. The entire
country began praying as medics worked to revive the player,
the news media focused on the prayers of the onlookers, and
a sports newscaster stopped the broadcast to pray.

God turned what Satan meant for harm into a clear
example that prayer is what our country turns to during
tragedies, displaying to the world that prayer makes a
difference. And it did, for not only was this young man's life
spared and restored, but many lives throughout our country
changed. We cannot deny it. No matter the attempts to shut
God out, America's impulse is to turn to the unity of prayer
in times of need.

Jesus of kindness, we pray that we shine your light brightly.
Help us become the lens of change that will bring you back
into focus for our country. May we develop a renewed
awareness that prayer makes a difference, transforms
lives, and can restore our world. Ignite a revival
through the tragedies happening all around so
the world can see that our hope is rooted in you.

Let's Chitchat with Jesus

SCRIPTURE WHISPER

"I cried out to the LORD in my great trouble, and he answered me. I called to you from the land of the dead, and LORD, you heard me!"

JONAH 2:2 NLT

When spending the day with a friend, we typically have a lot of chitchat and little silence. So if the Lord is by our side while journeying through life, why don't we chitchat with him all day? Jesus longs for a personal relationship with us. He suffered in such agony on the cross to wipe away our sins so that we can be in his presence.

There are times to be alone with him in quiet, focused prayer, but there are also times when we're with people and can still be engaged in prayer. He hears not just our audible prayers, but he also hears our prayerful thoughts. The desire of his heart is that we journey through our days in joyful communication with him. And then, when circumstances become tense and challenging, we can engage him to intervene because our communication with him is ongoing.

Jesus of goodness, thank you for answering our prayers. What comes next may not be what we envision, but it is always what's best for us to transform hearts and draw others into your kingdom.

Scan To Branch Out

Let's Live Humbly

SCRIPTURE WHISPER

Do nothing out of selfish ambition or vain conceit.
Rather, in humility value others above yourselves.

PHILIPPIANS 2:3 NIV

Christ modeled humility and treated others as if they were more significant than himself. We should do likewise. However, Satan is the master of selfishness, pride, and self-centered ambition, and he lurks in every opportunity to instill a prideful, selfish nature into our lives. A prideful nature often stems from insecurity in the lives of those who are searching for their identity, trying to be someone they are not, or living a life of confusion. They somehow feel living a life of pride and arrogance is a way to camouflage these internal insecurities.

A worldly view prompts anger and frustration when we encounter prideful people. But from Jesus' perspective, we must display a gentle spirit and see these people through Christ's eyes. Deep-seated hurt, pain, and a troubled spirit live within those with a prideful nature. Let's model humility. Brokenness is the way to rise into the identity God created for us.

Jesus of faithfulness, help us mirror your character in how we live so that others understand that living in humility, putting others first, and being a servant for you will raise their lives above the turmoil and chaos of this world.

Scan To Branch Out

Let's Have Servants' Hearts

SCRIPTURE WHISPER

Don't look out only for your own interests,
but take an interest in others, too.
PHILIPPIANS 2:4 NLT

When we have a servant's heart and seek ways to care for others' needs and interests, our lives take on new meaning. We find our lives more fulfilled, invigorated, and vibrant when we serve more each day. The results are so rewarding when we know we made a difference in others' lives. Then our own lives are enhanced with a pure satisfaction that surpasses our understanding.

We are blessed by Jesus to be a blessing. When we bless others, God is behind the scenes blessing us in ways that money can't buy. We often take for granted the blessings bestowed upon us in the little favors and sweet moments God provides throughout our days. He protects and navigates us around land mines, and we often don't even realize he has prevented harm from coming to us. Let's be aware of the quietly hidden blessings and never fail to give him praise.

Jesus of gentleness, help us be ambassadors of your servant's heart and be open to ways of modeling your love. Nothing speaks louder to hopeless souls than an outstretched heart of kindness, a smile, and a gentle gesture that says, "I care." Help us penetrate their soul with your love.

Scan To Branch Out

Let's Adopt Jesus' Attitude

SCRIPTURE WHISPER

Adopt the same attitude as that of Christ Jesus.

PHILIPPIANS 2:5 CSB

Jesus emptied himself and took on the form of a servant. He didn't stop being God as he took on human flesh and became a servant to humanity. He didn't allow his deity to stop him from expressing his humanity. He was entirely God and fully man.

Jesus could serve because he knew who he was. Being a servant often feels threatening to us when we aren't anchored in who we are, children of the highest God. It's the goal of Satan to make us insecure in our identity. Jesus knew his position as the Son of God; we, too, must never fail to be secure in our identity as children of our almighty Father.

Serving becomes uncomfortable when we are unsure of who we are. We fear losing our identity and believe that serving is beneath us. We think we are vulnerable and will be taken advantage of if we lower ourselves by serving others. But that's insecurity and questioning who we are in Christ. Let's live in the security of Jesus' arms.

Jesus of self-control, we want to live with the attitude of your heart and mindset. Help us anchor our hearts in your love and grace and draw others to you.

Scan To Branch Out

Let's Make Jesus Our Cornerstone

SCRIPTURE WHISPER

This is why it says in Scripture: "Look! I am laying a chosen, precious cornerstone in Zion. The one who believes in him will never be ashamed."

1 PETER 2:6 ISV

There is only one cornerstone: Jesus, the foundation of God's kingdom. And if we follow Jesus, the layout of our lives will be straightened just like a cornerstone straightens stones in masonry.

Let's ask ourselves who or what we have made the cornerstone of our lives. Does it seem like our life is crooked, out of alignment, and always leaning toward one disaster or drama after another? Maybe it's time to reevaluate our focus to see what may have replaced Jesus as the cornerstone of our lives. He longs to be our master stonemason. That's what he's waiting on.

Jesus of love, thank you for being our cornerstone. Forgive us for the stones we have allowed Satan to sneak in. Help us do our part, handing over the chisel so you can remove those stones that are a facade, a false foundation, and a foothold of evil. Instead, help us depend on you to rebuild the cornerstone of your love with your hand-picked stone into the foundation of our lives.

Scan To Branch Out

Let's Live Jesus' Character

SCRIPTURE WHISPER

He will give eternal life to everyone who has patiently done what is good in the hope of receiving glory, honor, and life that lasts forever.

ROMANS 2:7 CEV

Jesus provided a beautiful road map for us to follow by making a habit of living the fruit of his Spirit; we will reap what we sow, and what goes around comes around.

When we long for love, let's love more. When we long for joy, let's be joyful. When we need peace in our lives, let's create an atmosphere of peace. When others are impatient, let's be patient. When we need a dose of kindness, let's be kinder, especially to those with hardened hearts. When we need others to be good to us, let's share the goodness of Jesus' nature. When we feel betrayed and long for others' faithfulness, let's be faithful. When we feel the brunt of harshness and need the warmth of gentleness, let's be gentler. And when we need others to exert more self-control, let's show how Jesus is in control of our emotions.

Jesus of joy, help us recognize that going against the Golden Rule is living life backward, producing weeds that choke out the fruit. Instead, help us live fruitful lives for you.

Scan To Branch Out

Let's Live Gracefully

SCRIPTURE WHISPER

By grace you have been saved through faith,
and that not of yourselves; it is the gift of God.
EPHESIANS 2:8 WEB

We often fail to live as beautiful examples of grace, with love that stoops to forgive with a tender embrace. That's a vivid picture of Jesus, his unconditional love so profoundly displayed. When we're helpless, he bends down, gently and tenderly, to embrace us out of our misery and into his everlasting care.

This he promises, but we must intentionally invite him to live through us with his continual forgiving and loving grace. But also, we must stoop down and forgive ourselves for those sins for which he suffered and died. He has forgiven and forgotten our sins, and so must we. We can't embrace the goodness of his grace until we forget the former things, no longer dwelling on the past. Otherwise we continue nailing him to the cross. Let's live gracefully forgiven.

Jesus of peace, thank you for your grace and for reminding us in today's Scripture Whisper of your forgiveness and unconditional love. Help us live gracefully so others are drawn into your kingdom by the gift of your love and grace.

Scan To Branch Out

Let's Anticipate Greatness Ahead

SCRIPTURE WHISPER

As it is written, "What no eye has seen, nor ear heard, nor the heart of man imagined, what God has prepared for those who love him."

1 Corinthians 2:9 esv

God offers a glimpse of what he has prepared for us not just for our eternal life in heaven but also for today. He has provided a pathway of joy and peace for those who love him and dedicate their time to living in his care and allowing him to work through their lives.

Where Jesus is, Satan cannot abide. That's even more reason to walk hand in hand with the one who loves us unconditionally and suffered inhumanely to forgive and forget our sins, past, present, and future. God has arranged the very best for us, individually and uniquely, to fulfill our desires as they align with his. God has provided his inspired, written Word, and through the Word of God, the Holy Spirit reveals mysteries that illuminate a lifestyle we can emulate by applying Scripture to our own personal experiences so that we can fulfill his plan.

Jesus of patience, make our hearts thirst for your Word as we invite the Holy Spirit to reveal what we cannot understand. We anticipate the greatness you have provided and prepared for us, your children.

Scan To Branch Out

Let's Embrace Our Authority

SCRIPTURE WHISPER

Ye are complete in him, which is the head of all principality and power.

COLOSSIANS 2:10 KJV

Satan's goal is to tear us down, confuse our identity, and keep us questioning who we are in Christ. But when we give our hearts to Jesus, surrendering our sinful ways to his forgiveness, he overcomes every power and authority, and Satan is defeated. Yes, evil forces still attempt to interrupt God's plan, but as our Scripture Whisper reconfirms, in Christ, we have the power and authority to shut down the forces of evil because Jesus lives within us.

Adopting Jesus' blueprint of life creates a barrier against Satan's intrusion. Living the fruit of the Spirit in our daily walk results in victory because of the power of Jesus living within us. Whenever we're tempted to give in to Satan's schemes, remember that Jesus has already won.

Jesus of kindness, help us always remember that your death on the cross transferred your power and authority to us, your children, to shut down the evil forces. We call on you to fill the atmosphere with your presence.

Scan To Branch Out

Let's Show No Favoritism

SCRIPTURE WHISPER

God shows no partiality [no arbitrary favoritism; with Him
one person is not more important than another].
ROMANS 2:11 AMP

It doesn't matter to God what your life experiences have
been, which neighborhood you're from, what your parents
taught you, or what schools you attended. God sees us as his
unique creation, designed specifically for his plan to fulfill
what no one else can do.

When we embrace the way God does things, we see
wonderful results, including a joyful peace that surpasses
understanding. There's no automatic stamp of approval;
God is not swayed by what others say about us or what we
think about ourselves. He has made up his mind to love us
unconditionally and without favoritism.

Jesus of goodness, thank you for seeing us impartially.
It doesn't matter who we have become; you still love us
unconditionally. Give us an insatiable desire to become what
you uniquely designed us to be, shutting out the ways of the
world and embracing the fruit of your Spirit. The benefits
are supernatural as we live hand in hand with you. Forgive
us for the times we have failed to put our moments in your
hands; help us do our part to influence others
into your presence by modeling your character.

Scan To Branch Out

Let's Course Correct with Jesus

SCRIPTURE WHISPER

"May the LORD reward your efforts! May your acts of kindness be repaid fully by the LORD God of Israel, from whom you have sought protection."
RUTH 2:12 NET

We often forget to pause to realize the blessings Jesus provides along our daily journey. God always remembers the good things we do on his behalf, the seeds we plant, and the moments of obedience when we reject the tug toward worldly ways. Though we may not notice every time he blesses us, those blessings change the trajectory of our lives and the lives of those around us. Those moments of favor can correct our course in the slightest ways to help us reach our place of destiny.

Envision a pilot who sets the airplane control slightly off course, navigating that aircraft to a different destination. Something similar happens to us when we manage our life without involving the master air traffic controller. We will never reach the destiny he intended, and in the best scenario, we will travel the long way around the world to reach our goal.

Jesus of faithfulness, thank you for the moments of favor that you sprinkle in our lives and forgive us for taking for granted the ways you direct and bless our lives.

Scan To Branch Out

Let's Please God

SCRIPTURE WHISPER

God is working in you, giving you the desire
and the power to do what pleases him.

PHILIPPIANS 2:13 NLT

This Scripture Whisper contains powerful words for our
spiritual growth, which we so often quote yet which often
remain dormant. Paul instructed us to work to show the
results of our rebirth in Christ. This does not mean that we
have to work for our salvation, which we receive by the grace
of God through faith in Jesus. What we do once we are saved
is our choice: to fulfill God's plan through our lives or to
choose to allow Satan to veer us off God's path. We are called
to live worthy of Christ's suffering by placing our decisions
in God's hands, glorifying him in all we do.

God brings into our lives circumstances that require us
to make choices between his ways or Satan's. Our obedience
is based not on our willpower but on God's power working in
us. Grumbling and arguing prompt adverse reactions, discord,
and dissension, interfering and hindering our obedience.
Scripture tells us, instead, to do what pleases the Lord.

Jesus of gentleness, help us become more diligent and
devoted to pleasing you and help our desires align with
yours. The rewards will be more than we can
hope or imagine.

Let's Put Faith into Action

SCRIPTURE WHISPER

My friends, what good is it for one of you to say that you have faith if your actions do not prove it? Can that faith save you?
JAMES 2:14 GNT

Many people misunderstand or were incorrectly taught that good works are the way to salvation. However, the Bible says that our works are because of our salvation. Salvation is based on God's gift, his Son's sacrifice for our sins, and on his grace when we invite him into our lives. Our faith is reflected in the condition of our hearts. We should desire to do good works to please Jesus, healing broken hearts and hopeless lives and bringing people into his unconditional, loving embrace for comfort through challenging days.

It's up to us to remain empty of the world so others are attracted to us when our lifestyles show Jesus' character. Do we live complacently, praying for others' needs instead of working to fill them? There are no works apart from faith and no faith apart from works. Faith and works fit together, hand in glove.

Jesus of self-control, pure genuine faith is known by the fruit of your Spirit living through us. Help us make a difference by being a blessing for others as you bless us along the way.

Scan To Branch Out

Let's Live Free of Shame

SCRIPTURE WHISPER

Do your best to present yourself to God as one approved, a worker who does not need to be ashamed and who correctly handles the word of truth.

2 Timothy 2:15 niv

Shame is one of the tools of Satan, distracting us by focusing our attention on pleasing ourselves and other people rather than on satisfying God, living with him in an intimate relationship, and doing his work together. We are his ambassadors, called to demonstrate the true meaning of the gospel through the way we live. Through our reactions and responses, we reveal that the Holy Spirit is living within us. God has equipped us with his Word, our road map of life.

There are many false prophets, wolves in sheep's clothing, that confuse the Word of God. It is our duty to stand firm and correct any false teaching. We can identify counterfeit currency through our knowledge of the real thing; we can identify false teaching by embracing his Word, which opens our hearts to the truth. Let's thirst for God's wisdom, live the truth of God's Word, and be blessed with his approval.

Jesus of love, help us understand the purity of your truth and never be ashamed to speak out when we hear false teaching or confusion, instead emulating a lifestyle of your truth.

Scan To Branch Out

Let's Live by Jesus' Design

SCRIPTURE WHISPER

All that is in the world—the desires of the flesh and the desires of the eyes and pride of life—is not from the Father but is from the world.

1 JOHN 2:16 ESV

John gave us a checklist of the things that are not of God: the lust and cravings that Satan dangles along our path, the longings of our eyes, the boastful pride and confidence in our own behavior, and the dependence on earthly things. We should instead look to God, who gives us the answers for how to live according to his design.

How can we establish a radar within our spirit that goes off when we are tempted to fall into Satan's trap? By learning God's ways modeled by Jesus. As we become more familiar with his character, that alarm in our soul will sound when we encounter what is not of God, and with God's help, we can slam shut and seal the door on Satan's trap.

Jesus of joy, please sound an internal alarm when our eyes stray and our pride and worldly desires tempt us. Draw us like a magnet to your Word a few moments here and there throughout the day, just like picking up the phone for a little chat with you, Lord.

Scan To Branch Out

Let's Encourage Others' Hearts

Peace

SCRIPTURE WHISPER

May He encourage your hearts and may He strengthen them
in every good work and word.
2 Thessalonians 2:17 BLB

We should constantly be aware that the coming of the Lord
could be any day so we never become complacent about
drawing people into the kingdom of God. We may be the
way God has planned for someone to hear of the hope of
salvation, eternal life, and Jesus.

Let us not miss opportunities that Jesus puts before us.
God has well designed the intersection of lives, positioning
divine appointments throughout our day. The Holy Spirit
helps our lifestyle to be Christlike, and when people sense
the Spirit of the Lord within us, the Holy Spirit does the rest,
bringing in the harvest.

Jesus of peace, we come to you today and ask to be your
ambassadors of encouragement. We pray to strengthen
others' hearts and to help them get on course through the
power of your grace. Help us never miss an opportunity to
encourage as you arrange divine appointments throughout
our days, weaving our lives together in your masterful
design. We want to make a habit of living the fruit of your
Spirit, allowing your love to shine through.

Scan To Branch Out

Let's Display Authentic Faith

SCRIPTURE WHISPER

Someone may say, "You have faith, and I have actions." Show me your faith without any actions, and I will show you my faith by my actions.

JAMES 2:18 ISV

To understand the strength of our faith, we must look at what we do. Faith is complete trust in someone or something. Whom do we trust? Where does our focus turn when things get rough? Do we depend on man or ourselves to jump in and rescue the day, or do we depend on God, in whom our faith should abide? God should be our default, automatic, go-to helper. We should rest our care on him who cares deeply, loves unconditionally, forgives, and forgets our sins.

In the Hall of Faith, found in Hebrews 11, God's inspired Word repeatedly describes how faith is manifested and accomplished. We must demonstrate pure and authentic faith by the way we live.

Jesus of patience, forgive us when we favor Satan instead of reaching for you to guide us through the muddy waters of life. Help us strengthen our faith by recounting the many Bible stories of wavering people whom you restored by your compassionate, gentle, miraculous promises, proving you are faithful.

Scan To Branch Out

Let's End Our Unrighteousness

SCRIPTURE WHISPER

God's solid foundation still stands. It has this inscription on it: "The Lord knows those who belong to him," and "Everyone who calls on the name of the Lord must turn away from evil."

2 TIMOTHY 2:19 ISV

God is intimately acquainted with his children, knowing every detail about us. As devoted followers, let's learn more about God's desires for our lives so we can do what is beneficial for his kingdom, attracting the lost and hopeless souls seeking refuge in him in troubled days.

Turning away from our sinful ways is evidence that the life of Jesus has transformed the condition of our hearts. He has been so patient on the sidelines, waiting for us to stop living on our own and instead to start embracing the life he uniquely designed for us to live in alignment with him. God calls us to be willing vessels that he can work through. Let's be his ambassadors for the specific tasks he created for us.

Jesus of kindness, we are etched in your heart with a seal. Thank you for the special privilege that we can call upon you twenty-four seven and boldly expect your supernatural intervention.

Scan To Branch Out

Let's Pause and Praise Jesus

SCRIPTURE WHISPER

The shepherds went back, singing praises to God for all they had heard and seen; it had been just as the angel had told them.
LUKE 2:20 GNT

Luke's account of the Christmas story is relevant every day. The shepherds, ordinary people like us, experienced the Spirit of the Lord and began to praise and glorify God for the blessings they had just encountered.

How about us? How often do we take for granted the experiences that God arranges for us each day? Do we pause to praise him for being in the details? Too many times we do not realize all that God does behind the scenes as he changes the trajectory of our lives. He prevents moments of hardship and bestows blessings. The more we pause to reflect on the moments of goodness, when God came through again, the more our hearts will rejoice in the miraculous Spirit of Jesus. Let's be more aware of the divine moments throughout our day and pause to thank him with grateful hearts.

Jesus of goodness, just as the shepherds glorified you for the miraculous experience in which they were involved, help us be aware of the miraculous moments you weave into our daily lives.

Scan To Branch Out

Let's Ask for Jesus' Help

SCRIPTURE WHISPER

"The Lord will save everyone who asks for his help."
ACTS 2:21 CEV

In this world of confusion and chaos, what a gift and blessing it is to be free and at peace when we call upon the name of the Lord. The purpose of his suffering and death and the resurrection of his life was so that we could be set free and live in peace, cultivating an intimate and daily relationship with our Lord.

What thoughts, feelings, and images come to mind when you think of Jesus? The character of his Spirit when he walked this earth is the image we should engrave on our hearts and mirror in our lives. Knowing who Jesus is gives us confidence to ask for his help, which he offers us with freedom and peace that surpass any understanding.

Jesus of faithfulness, as your ambassadors, we ask that we carry the image of your character so that others can be drawn to you and liberated in your freedom of peace. How we live our lives impacts how brightly your light shines within us. We pray that our heart's desire is to become empty of the world so that your loving brilliance shines brighter every day.

Scan To Branch Out

Let's Remodel God's Home

SCRIPTURE WHISPER

In him you too are being built together to become a dwelling in which God lives by his Spirit.

EPHESIANS 2:22 NIV

Our Creator used the apostles and prophets for the foundation of the church. Now he is using us, brick by brick, stone by stone, with Jesus as the cornerstone that holds all the parts together. We are each a holy temple built by God, in which he is quite at home. Our life journey is the building of a place within us that the Holy Spirit can call his home and accomplish what he plans to fulfill through each of our lives. We are an ongoing remodel, tearing out the old worldly ways to be rebuilt into a fresh, new home for the Spirit of Jesus to live.

Our responsibility is to stay refreshed through his Word and seek ways to accelerate the remodel so the Holy Spirit can accomplish immeasurable work through his home within us, more than we could ever hope or imagine.

Jesus of gentleness, our life journey is a continual remodel of our spiritual temple. Help us not to interfere with your plan but to do our part by living in the fruit of your Spirit to accelerate your work within us.

Scan To Branch Out

Let's Rejoice as God's Friend

SCRIPTURE WHISPER

The scripture was fulfilled that says, "Now Abraham believed God and it was counted to him for righteousness," and he was called God's friend.

JAMES 2:23 NET

Being called God's friend is an indescribable gift made possible by the sacrifice of our Lord, who eradicated our sins so that we could be accepted as righteous. Faith believes the things not seen will come to pass in the care of God. It's like falling off the cliff and expecting that God is at the bottom to catch us. However, if we pull the parachute cord of doubt halfway down, that's not faith.

This seems to be our life journey, repeatedly falling just a little farther before pulling the rescue cord. With each jump, we stretch our faith. Finally, we come to the day when we jump off the cliff without the parachute. That's faith!

Jesus of self-control, we believe that what seems impossible is possible when we cast our cares on you. No matter how bleak our circumstances, you are always there to catch us since you promise to never leave us or forsake us. We declare the safety net of doubt is destroyed. Satan has lost his grip, and victory is won!

Scan To Branch Out

Let's Teach

SCRIPTURE WHISPER

A servant of the Lord must not quarrel but must be kind to everyone, be able to teach, and be patient with difficult people.
2 TIMOTHY 2:24 NLT

Our Scripture Whisper today reminds us that we must not be quarrelsome or resentful; instead, we are to be kind to everyone. When we model Christlike behavior, people are more likely to listen as we teach the truth, and "perhaps God will change those people's hearts" (v. 25).

When we act differently than the world expects, even astonishing other believers, everyone takes notice. When we choose Jesus' self-control during challenging situations and live in kindness, we open the door for people to see the truth of Jesus living through us. Our Christlike actions are like a magnet of curiosity, drawing others to investigate how Jesus can turn a volatile moment into an atmosphere of gentle peace. He chooses to live and be seen through us. Let's be available for him every day.

Jesus of love, as we come to you today, we ask you to shower us with your kindness. When we encounter quarrelsome situations and opportunities to be resentful, we hope to be surrounded by your spirit of kindness, teaching others about living in relationship with you and bringing hope to their hopeless hearts and faith into their world.

Scan To Branch Out

Let's Find Our Joy in Jesus

SCRIPTURE WHISPER

Apart from him who can eat or who can have enjoyment?
ECCLESIASTES 2:25 ESV

Where do we find our enjoyment? It's a sobering question to ponder as we reflect on how we spend our time. When we have free time, where do we attach our focus? God provides many things for our enjoyment on earth: the overwhelming canvas of nature, the love of others as we share in relationships, seeds that manifest into delicious meals, tender moments of service that make a difference in others' lives. These are just a few things that bring us divinely arranged enjoyment. Are we including Jesus in our enjoyment, turning to him for life's meaning?

Life can be predictable, causing us to feel trapped in a rut every day. Watch out. That's fertile ground for Satan's attempts to disrupt God's plan in our lives. Let's pause and analyze the cause of our enjoyment. Is it temporary, fleeting with no future? Or is it long-lasting and meaningful, bringing value to our existence and value to others' lives?

Jesus of joy, the depth of our enjoyment is directly related to our inclusion of you to heighten our moments of joy and fulfillment. Thank you for the enjoyment of being used by you.

Scan To Branch Out

Let's Receive Good Gifts

SCRIPTURE WHISPER

To the man that pleaseth him God giveth wisdom, and knowledge, and joy; but to the sinner he giveth travail, to gather and to heap up, that he may give to him that pleaseth God. This also is vanity and a striving after wind.

ECCLESIASTES 2:26 ASV

God gives us wisdom and the knowledge of himself to direct our ways as we seek him and live a life that is good in his sight. God gives us knowledge—which includes the understanding of his grace, his gifts, and his goodness—to discern the ways he intends for our lives to unfold. God gives us joy and peace as we invite the presence of his Spirit into our days.

But to the sinner, he gives a life of labor, disappointment, and distress. Because the sinner is an enemy to God, the wealth of the wicked is laid up for the just. When we remember the sorrows of our life before Christ, let's pray for those who have not yet turned to God for wisdom, knowledge, and joy.

Jesus of peace, we want to please you in every way. Help us become all you intend and fulfill your purpose so joy fills our lives.

Scan To Branch Out

Let's Tighten Our Grip

SCRIPTURE WHISPER

The anointing that you received from him abides in you, and you have no need that anyone should teach you. But as his anointing teaches you about everything, and is true, and is no lie—just as it has taught you, abide in him.

1 JOHN 2:27 ESV

The Word of God is our cell phone to God and constant communication line to Jesus. It has been preserved throughout history to teach us the ways of God and assure us that we are living the truth. Having God Almighty teaching us everything we need to know is quite astonishing. Pause and think about that. Why do we often ignore his presence and make choices on our own?

Satan is always attempting to separate our hand from God's, but God never releases his grip. We are the ones who let go. Jesus calls us to have a firm grip, but he will never interfere with our free will when we choose to remove our hand from his.

Jesus of patience, your hand is always outstretched to guide us along the path and around the pitfalls of Satan's traps. Help us tighten our grip, knowing you will lead the way and we are safe in the clutch of your hand.

Scan To Branch Out

Let's Find Contentment in Jesus

SCRIPTURE WHISPER

"He has shown me the path to life,
and he makes me glad by being near me."
ACTS 2:28 CEV

The pursuit of contentment is a lifelong journey ending only in being near Jesus. It's rare that we find anyone genuinely content with their condition in life. The Bible has a great deal to say about contentment, being satisfied with what we have, who we are, and where the days ahead are taking us. Jesus tells us the lack of contentment puts us in the same category as those who do not know God and are apart from his presence. We all long for contentment; it's simply being near to Jesus.

Are we the master of our choices? Are we continuing to run toward areas that keep us apart from God? Let's start seeking contentment by inviting Jesus into our hearts. The rewards will be beyond measure, like a little taste of heaven while on this earth, when we seek our contentment in the care of Jesus.

Jesus of kindness, forgive us when we worry and fret. We strive for contentment in worldly matters that have no lasting value, and that's why we find ourselves discontent. Help us find contentment abundantly in your care.

Scan To Branch Out

March

Let's Embrace Change

SCRIPTURE WHISPER

To every thing there is a season, and a time to every purpose under the heaven.

ECCLESIASTES 3:1 KJV

Nothing is forever; life is a cycle of seasons like the change of semesters in the academic world. We are to learn from past seasons, embracing the things that bring value and meaning and leaving behind what has no place in our days ahead.

Unfortunately, Satan often tries to sneak in as our seasons of life change. He packs our suitcase full of guilt and shame, anger and frustration, blame and regret, all burdens from past seasons. His motive is to weigh us down with baggage that keeps us chained to the past, preventing us from flourishing in the new season ahead that God has predestined.

Our challenge is recognizing when our season is changing. God uses nature to give us signs of our new season awaiting, like fall-colored leaves and blossoms in the spring; we just need to listen to his signs of change and welcome them. He has our next season prepared, full of divine moments headed toward the fulfillment of his plan.

Jesus of goodness, help us not to resist change and to no longer carry the baggage from one season to the next. Instead, let us bring only lessons we have learned and sweet memories that have meaning and value.

Let's Live Jesus' Words

SCRIPTURE WHISPER

You yourselves are our letter, written on our hearts,
known and read by everyone.

2 CORINTHIANS 3:2 NIV

We have the opportunity to imprint the heart of Jesus on those around us, helping them to discover the love of Christ. All who cross our paths each day, those whom God divinely arranged to intersect our lives, see our lifestyle. The way we live, the choices we make, and the words we speak reflect the presence of Jesus in our lives. Often, our gentle tone and peaceful sincerity attract attention.

That's what God designed us for, to expand his heavenly kingdom into eternity by sparking curiosity in those who don't know him or are struggling to live in a relationship with him. Others are often drawn to Jesus' light within us even when we don't say anything; people see us and notice the radiance of his Spirit when we live the fruit of his Spirit daily.

Jesus of faithfulness, we pray you will imprint your words on our lives so that all who see the way we live will know and read them. We ask that we can be your light for those searching in the darkness so they will be drawn to your eternal kingdom.

Scan To Branch Out

Let's Embrace a Faithful Lifestyle

SCRIPTURE WHISPER

Never let go of loyalty and faithfulness. Tie them around your neck; write them on your heart.

PROVERBS 3:3 GNT

Jesus longs for our loving devotion, for us to pause throughout the day to say, *Lord, I love you*. But how often do we go days without looking up to heaven with gratefulness for all he has done and for all he does that we don't even notice?

Our devotion to Jesus allows us to have confident faith in an unknown future that we can't figure out, faith for what frustrates us, faith for what has us tied up in knots, faith for what wakes us up in the middle of the night, faith for what makes us feel we are losing our minds, faith that doesn't give up on what seems impossible, and faith that ignites God to move mountains in our lives. God promises his immovable power, unconditional love, and faithful devotion to us, which are catalyst to our faith journey.

Jesus of gentleness, thank you for your grace to carry our burdens, to pull us out of the pits that we have dug, and to catch us when we are plummeting in confusion about the unknown. Let us engrave a life of faithfulness on our hearts.

Scan To Branch Out

Let's Choose Jesus to Reconstruct

SCRIPTURE WHISPER

Every house has a builder, but the one who built everything is God.

HEBREWS 3:4 NLT

God created everything from the beginning of time. When he formed each of us, he built the frame of our house but then gave us free will to complete the construction.

So whom did we allow to be the supervisor of the construction of our lives? Did we enable Satan to construct inferior quality, or have we chosen the highest quality that God can provide to build the perfect house for which he drew the plans and arranged our experiences to begin construction? We don't wait on God; he gently and patiently waits on us. All we must do is ask the master builder to get started rebuilding our lives to be used by him. Jesus is delighted to reconstruct the parts of our lives in which Satan interfered. Let's get busy today by firing Satan, giving the reconstruction fully to Jesus, and no longer interfering with his blueprints.

Jesus of self-control, forgive us for the times we've allowed Satan to come in with his secondhand toolbox and shoddy materials. We ask that you remodel our world, our ways, and our devotion, reconstructing our lives into your masterpiece so we can make a difference for you.

Let's Not Trust Ourselves

SCRIPTURE WHISPER

Trust in the LORD with all your heart. Never rely on what you think you know.

PROVERBS 3:5 GNT

We tend to depend on our own understanding instead of making a habit of directing our thoughts toward the insight and wisdom of Jesus. God promises to make our paths straight as we approach life's crossroads. We just need to install his supernatural GPS in our hearts to direct us. Jesus is waiting to guide us at critical decisions or with the simplest choices. We must overlook the detour signs that Satan puts in our way to attempt to take us around the mountain again and again.

Even though we say we turn to God, do we? Is he our automatic default for help, discernment, and direction? Do we place our moments and choices in his care? Is it Jesus whom we immediately call on? He is the one who knows our future, who wants only the best for us, and who makes possible what seems impossible, so let's run to him.

Jesus of love, help us trust you more with the details of our lives and become more committed each day to learning your ways and recognizing your voice more clearly. Ensure that we seek only your insight and understanding at the crossroads in life. Help us trust you more.

Scan To Branch Out

Let's Live with Jesus

SCRIPTURE WHISPER

A person is born physically of human parents, but is born spiritually of the Spirit.

JOHN 3:6 GNT

To transform our lives into spiritual ones is to be reborn by the Holy Spirit. Like the wind, we don't see the Spirit, but we can often feel him moving in our hearts. In the same way that we can see movement that occurs when the invisible wind blows, the Spirit is invisible as God transforms our lives. Although he is invisible, we can see the results, and others will know us by our fruit.

God sent his Son as our sacrifice to make it possible for us to be filled with his Holy Spirit. We must ask and be willing vessels to be filled with his ways, eager for him to transform our lives so it's evident he is living in our hearts, directing our paths in a relationship every day. The benefits are beyond compare when living with Jesus.

Jesus of joy, transform our hearts from the inside out so that others will know us by our fruit. We ask that our lives emulate your character and that others are vibrantly reborn by your Holy Spirit.

Scan To Branch Out

Let's Put Jesus First

SCRIPTURE WHISPER

Christ has shown me that what I once thought was valuable is worthless.

PHILIPPIANS 3:7 CEV

We must open the eyes of our hearts to see more clearly the value and meaning of putting Jesus first in our lives. The things we used to strive for, the goals and dreams we used to have, fade and become insignificant and unimportant when we consider the rewards of living in alignment with Jesus.

The Enemy is devoted to keeping us focused on the value of worldly things instead of the love, joy, peace, patience, kindness, goodness, faithfulness, gentleness, and self-control with which Jesus surrounds us when we value him above all things. Let's consider where we put our emphasis and evaluate the consequences of the choices we make apart from our partnership with the Lord. It's a life journey, like slowly peeling the layers of an onion over the years. We will look back and wonder why we didn't choose to journey in life with Jesus far earlier.

Jesus of peace, when we make you the center of our lives, we realize your blessings are far more valuable than we could ever hope or imagine. Help us prioritize our focus on your ways in everything we think and do and in every word we speak.

Scan To Branch Out

Let's Make Jesus Our Doorkeeper

SCRIPTURE WHISPER

"I know what you do; I know that you have a little power; you have followed my teaching and have been faithful to me. I have opened a door in front of you, which no one can close."
REVELATIONS 3:8 GNT

Jesus navigates our future when we let him, opening doors that no one can close and closing doors that shouldn't be open. It's up to us to invite him to be our doorkeeper.

A globally known Christian playwright and author Richard Montez, founder and director of Cornerstone Theatre, once spoke at my church. He explained how he has walked through doors that seemed closed but then miraculously opened through the grace of God. His life testimony was filled with his faith journey of depending on God to open doors for the purpose of his divine calling. He described an automatic door that remains closed until we start walking toward it, expecting it to open before we crash into it. That's putting true faith into action.

Jesus of patience, we are grateful that you arrange doors to open that no one can shut and you close doors to guide us in a different direction. Help us depend on you to be our doorkeeper.

Let's Wait On Jesus

SCRIPTURE WHISPER

The Lord is not slow about his promise, as some think of slowness, but is patient with you, not wanting any to perish but all to come to repentance.

2 PETER 3:9 NRSVUE

God's timing is perfect, and his delays do not mean he doesn't hear us. He always answers us though not always in the ways we intend, but his ways are the very best ways.

God is managing lives all around the universe. He has a mission to bring others into his eternity. Oftentimes, we are the cause of delays while God is equipping us for what's ahead. When we make life choices apart from him, we can indirectly cause what seem like delays in God's timing. God is masterfully weaving these delays into his unique plan for our lives.

When our patience runs thin, imagine his patience in waiting on us. The ultimate outcome of our prayers looks different when we realize Jesus is working behind the scenes, transforming hearts, and arranging things that will have a kingdom impact.

Jesus of kindness, you design our seasons of waiting to attract more people into your kingdom while equipping us to fulfill our purpose in your creation. As you navigate our lives, help us patiently depend on your perfect timing.

Scan To Branch Out

Let's Enjoy Jesus' Rich Rewards

SCRIPTURE WHISPER

Tell the godly that all will be well for them. They will enjoy the rich reward they have earned!

Isaiah 3:10 NLT

The Bible tells us that the righteous will enjoy the rich rewards they have earned, fruitful blessings from the seeds they planted along the day's journey. Choosing to do the right thing will bring the rewards of favor into our lives and the lives of those around us. Why would we live differently or make choices without seeking God's wisdom and insight?

When we become seasoned and mature and can recognize when Satan is challenging our choices to live Jesus' ways, our days will be productive and meaningful, as God intended. And how do we become seasoned and mature in our faith? By staying focused on the guidelines he offers us in his Word, chatting with Jesus throughout the day through prayer, and putting our moments into his hands.

Jesus of goodness, thank you for providing your road map for life in your Word, explicitly showing us how to do life your way, and helping us seeking your divine GPS so that all will be well with our souls and a delight to our hearts.

Scan To Branch Out

Let's Leave Strategizing to Jesus

SCRIPTURE WHISPER

He has made everything beautiful in its time. He has also set eternity in the hearts of men, yet they cannot fathom the work that God has done from beginning to end.

ECCLESIASTES 3:11 BSB

God has a purpose in every intricate detail of his design, but how often do we wrestle with living in his purpose, something Satan attempts tirelessly to disrupt? It makes us wonder why life is full of ups and downs, good days and bad days. A day that starts with the light of God's favor could suddenly end gloomy with our heart broken.

God has a purpose in mind through life's rhythm, designed uniquely to put eternity in our focus. However, we always seem to long for more. God has created time so that this world will never offer us complete fulfillment. Instead, the world reveals a void in our hearts, something that will only be filled in our heavenly home.

Jesus of faithfulness, we cannot fathom what you have in store for us. Help us not to waste energy on things you have already prepared and instead to leave the strategizing to you.

Scan To Branch Out

Let's Clothe Ourselves with Jesus

SCRIPTURE WHISPER

God's chosen ones, holy and loved, put on heartfelt compassion, kindness, humility, gentleness, and patience.
COLOSSIANS 3:12 HCSB

As we make a daily habit of focusing on one fruit of Jesus' Spirit by reflecting on the color of each day, our lives transform. Let's also put on the traits of compassion, kindness, humility, gentleness, and patience as garments or accessories as we get dressed each day. We must remind ourselves to be clothed in Jesus' anointing of favor as we incorporate his ways into our lifestyle.

Satan's interference will diminish as we dwell in the presence of God. When we walk in the ways of Jesus, there is no room for Satan.

Jesus of gentleness, we are your chosen children, and our Scripture Whisper assures us that you love us dearly. Help us clothe ourselves each morning with a garment of your character so that others will notice the light of your presence shining from within us. Let it act as an invitation for others to inquire about how they also can experience the light, giving them hope in hopeless situations and comfort to their broken hearts.

Scan To Branch Out

Let's Forgive Others

SCRIPTURE WHISPER

Make allowance for each other's faults, and forgive anyone who offends you. Remember, the Lord forgave you, so you must forgive others.

Colossians 3:13 NLT

God says he will be the judge, so we should not be. We are to cast into the care of Jesus the wrongs others have done to us and forgive them. How can we not forgive others when Jesus gave his life to forgive us? Are we innocent of anything that requires forgiveness from God or others? Being the judge of others points a judgmental finger directly back at us because we all need forgiveness.

Unforgiveness is locking ourselves in prison while giving the key to those we refuse to forgive. Let's walk out of the prison, hand over the keys to God, and forgive in all situations, leaving the judgment in the hands of the one who is just in all things.

Jesus of self-control, forgive us for the times when we harbor unforgiveness for others in our hearts, as we are symbolically nailing you to the cross repeatedly if we do not forgive as you forgave us. When we forgive as you do, you can restore relationships far beyond what we could ever hope or imagine; we are grateful for your forgiveness.

Scan To Branch Out

Let's Strengthen Our Confidence

SCRIPTURE WHISPER

We have become partners of Christ, if only we hold our first confidence firm to the end.

HEBREWS 3:14 NRSVUE

Confidence is something that Satan tries to diminish by dangling doubt in our minds when it seems like things are not going our way or as we envisioned. Our confidence is often shaken when it seems the Lord is not answering our prayers.

As God's children, we should walk in assurance that Jesus' legions of angels are working on our behalf to put into place the anointed plan of God throughout our lives in ways we cannot possibly fathom. As we stand strong and courageous, Satan cannot hijack our confidence, even when things seem impossible and when we feel we are down to the very last moment before things will implode. Jesus will save the day, so we can hold on to our unwavering confidence and trust in his promises.

Jesus of love, help us strengthen our confidence in the many promises scattered throughout your Word. Your promises give us assurance that when we call on you in our desperation, you will fight our battles. Victory is won in your powerful name as we confidently ask to abide in your care.

Scan To Branch Out

Let's Think Maturely

SCRIPTURE WHISPER

Let all of us who are mature think this way. And if you think differently about anything, God will reveal this also to you.
PHILIPPIANS 3:15 CSB

To become spiritually mature takes a journey over our lifetime. However, haven't we all met young people whom we call "old souls" because they make sound choices and speak from God's Word with godly wisdom far beyond their age?

We can accelerate our spiritual maturity by focusing on the presence of God surrounding us as we go about our day, chitchatting with Jesus as we would our best friend, and grabbing his Word throughout the day. Even a glance at a verse instead of our phones is an opportunity to draw near to God. As a result of these Jesus-centered moments, our way of life will be filled with an overflowing desire to live in Jesus' footsteps, walking together with him and casting our moments into his care. This creates fertile soil for our spiritual maturity to blossom so that we can live in the niche of God's plan.

Jesus of joy, help us live in excellence in all we do. May we surround ourselves with spiritually minded people who want to excel in their walk with God and who share the same goals and have like-minded hearts and souls. Companions like these strengthen and mature the spirits of us all.

Let's Revive John 3:16

SCRIPTURE WHISPER

This is the way God loved the world: He gave his one and only Son, so that everyone who believes in him will not perish but have eternal life.

JOHN 3:16 NET

The Israelites turned a deaf ear to God just like many today ignore the gospel on posted signs that share John 3:16 in football stadiums, on billboards, and on national television. Let's seize the moment to share the meaning of John 3:16 when we are gifted the opportunity by those holding signs with this verse on them.

Let's pray for a revival of new seedlings of John 3:16 planted so the Holy Spirit can sprout a harvest in hearts across our troubled land, a wave of transformed souls into heaven's eternity.

Jesus of peace, deepen our understanding of the way your unfathomable love affects the way we live. By God choosing to send you, his Son, to earth, he allowed us to become worthy to live in relationship with you, free from eternal destruction, free from all heartache, free from sin, free from the torment of Satan. We can live a life of eternal significance because of your sacrifice. You endured the payment of our sinful ways, forgiving us once and for all, so that we could become heirs of your kingdom and ambassadors of John 3:16 until you come again.

Scan To Branch Out

Let's Cuddle in Jesus' Love

SCRIPTURE WHISPER

"The LORD your God is in your midst; he is a warrior who can deliver. He takes great delight in you; he renews you by his love; he shouts for joy over you."
ZEPHANIAH 3:17 NET

God is devotedly in our midst as our mighty warrior, fighting life's battles for us. We always win when we surrender to his care with unwavering faith. Our Lord is always hovering over us, rejoicing over us, and gently loving us. No matter what we do or say, his unconditional love never fails.

Jesus makes no mention of our past because he has forgiven and forgotten. But we must forgive ourselves, never bringing the past into the present through regret and shame and guilt. That's all from Satan. No matter the darkness, our loving Lord is the same yesterday, today, and into the future. We can always count on his promises and words of blessing. He shouts for joy over his children.

Jesus of patience, please enlighten our hearts and souls amid life's storms with the blanket of your love, which saves and protects us in the weariness of life. We are grateful that you long to live alongside us. Help us be your hands and feet each day, making others aware of your goodness, grace, and mercy.

Scan To Branch Out

Let's Put Words into Action

SCRIPTURE WHISPER

My children, our love should not be just words and talk;
it must be true love, which shows itself in action.

1 John 3:18 GNT

Do we pause to pray when we tell someone we will? Do we live with unwavering faith, free from worry and anxiety? Do we choose each morning to focus our attention on making a habit of living the fruit of Jesus' Spirit, modeling his character with a magnetism that will draw others to his Spirit? Do we put into action what we say we will do, not just speaking empty words?

The Bible describes how wide, long, high, and deep God's love is for his children. We are products of Jesus' unconditional love. Let us return his love by the way we live, being gentle and patient, forgiving as he forgives. Let's choose to put love into action. People will notice, and Jesus will do the rest.

Jesus of kindness, ignite within us a thirst to learn your ways, modeling your character so we can draw others toward your gospel of salvation. As you create opportunities for us to share your truth throughout our day, help us hear your voice leading the way so that we never miss a chance that you arrange for us to draw someone into your kingdom.

Let's Illuminate Light in Darkness

SCRIPTURE WHISPER

This is the verdict: Light has come into the world, but people loved darkness instead of light because their deeds were evil.
JOHN 3:19 NIV

People continually reject the gift of God's grace and mercy to forgive and forget their sins. God has chosen us as his ambassadors to penetrate Jesus' light into their hardened hearts. We can do this by spreading his peace and joy through modeling the fruit of his Spirit.

Have you ever wondered why someone is uncomfortable in your presence? It may be because the light of your life reminds them of what they are not, exposing within them the darkness of their heart, which produces their evil ways. It's not necessarily what we do or say. It's the light of Jesus' presence shining through us that exposes to them the condition of their heart. We are called to plant seeds by the way we live and then water them with our prayers, and God will do the rest, harvesting their souls into the kingdom of truth and into eternal life.

Jesus of goodness, one drop of your light can ignite a wave to flood darkness and reach hopeless souls. Equip us to be all you designed for us to be, living in partnership to make a difference across our land.

Scan To Branch Out

Let's Expect the Impossible

SCRIPTURE WHISPER

[He] who by the power that is working within us is able to do far beyond all that we ask or think.

EPHESIANS 3:20 NET

God can do anything—far more than we could ever imagine or request. When we allow his Spirit to work deeply and gently within us, we share in his world-changing work. Nothing, absolutely nothing, is impossible for God.

We must believe that Satan cannot defeat the power of Jesus when the Evil One attempts to throw in doubts. We must capture those deceitful thoughts and release them into the pit of hell. God looks for impossible situations to showcase that he is our God of promises and answered prayers. Provide Jesus the platform of your life so that his great power may work within you.

Jesus of faithfulness, how can we ever doubt you? You seek opportunities to stretch our faith and equip us for greater things ahead. We only need to believe and boldly expect what is unseen, seeing more clearly through your eyes. The more impossible things look, the more gloriously you will show up just in time to prove that you are God in our lives. We want to live in your world of possibilities, believing that the impossible becomes possible through our faith in you, our miraculous Lord.

Let's Pray to Restore Unity

SCRIPTURE WHISPER

Heaven must take Him in until the time comes for the restoration of all things, which God announced long ago through all His holy prophets.

ACTS 3:21 MSB

Our Scripture Whisper references the coming reign of Jesus, who is coming again to restore all things, including unity. Often in biblical times, people were divided into two groups: Jews and gentiles. To put it another way for today's times: insiders and outsiders. Jesus will return to establish peace where division and hostility rule.

Walls continue to exist, erected to separate people by race, religion, class, culture, and sex. Satan has been erecting these walls since his fall from heaven. God longs to bring us all together into one worshiping family of unity. As Christ followers, we can tear walls down just by the way we live in the likeness of Jesus. However, those who encourage, build, protect, and maintain those walls that divide us are working as enemies of God while Satan gets a foothold. But not for long; Jesus is coming again, and all will be restored and made anew. That's what the Bible says, and it's the truth that we can depend on.

Jesus of gentleness, help us stand strong and work diligently to restore unity as your ambassadors until the day you return to restore our land and establish unity forevermore.

Scan To Branch Out

Let's Live More Compassionately

SCRIPTURE WHISPER

Because of the LORD's great love we are not consumed,
for his compassions never fail.

LAMENTATIONS 3:22 NIV

What is compassion? Compassion is a sympathetic concern for the suffering and misfortunes of others. Compassion motivates us to go out of our way to relieve the physical, mental, or emotional pains of others.

And to think we have God's compassion hovering over us twenty-four seven. That's our Scripture Whisper's promise. This should motivate us to live differently as we model the ways of Jesus and make a habit of imitating his compassionate character, weaving into our lifestyle more Christlikeness when we react to situations in our relationships and encounter others throughout the day. Let's live more compassionately, which is the way of God. That's how we can show our thankfulness for his compassion, which is new for us every morning.

Jesus of self-control, we are grateful for your merciful compassion and overflowing grace, fresh each morning. Please help us live more compassionately, making a difference one life at a time. Compassion brings hope and displays your love. Let us never miss an opportunity to be compassionate as you surround us with people who need your love throughout our day.

Scan To Branch Out

Let's Do It All for Jesus

SCRIPTURE WHISPER

Work willingly at whatever you do, as though you were working for the Lord rather than for people.

COLOSSIANS 3:23 NLT

Living with Jesus, visualizing him walking by our side, is enough. Nothing else really matters. He navigates and maneuvers us in the right direction, moment by moment. So what should we dread when he is right in the middle of our daily life?

As Christ's followers, when everything we do is in alignment with the Lord, we should live a lifestyle of the highest quality. Living worthy of his glory certainly propels us to a different caliber of excellence. People notice our testimony through the way we live our lives. In everything we do, let's do it from the heart of Jesus for the Lord and not for people.

Jesus of love, help us develop a mindset of willingness as we go about our day. May we never do the minimum to get by but always do our best, working from our hearts for you and alongside you, engaging in life together with you, working in partnership for your kingdom growth. Help us never to take shortcuts or compromise but always to act with excellence that reflects your nature and goodness in everything we do.

Scan To Branch Out

Let's Rest Sweetly

SCRIPTURE WHISPER

When you lie down, you will not be afraid; when you lie down, your sleep will be sweet.

PROVERBS 3:24 NIV

What a beautiful verse. We all need a good night's sleep, but that's not what Satan wants as he tries everything in his bag of tricks to keep us restless, tossing and turning, full of anxiety and fretting about tomorrow.

We often don't feel we should bother God with things that aren't significantly life-threatening since we can pray for many other needs. That's a mindset that is straight from Satan. Jesus longs to be in the details of our lives. Nothing is minor or trivial to him. Nothing is too small to take before our Lord. He desires to chat with us about our smallest choices and decisions. He cares about our peaceful sleep, which makes a difference in the day for ourselves and everyone around us, setting the mood, affecting our reactions, and defining our day.

Jesus of joy, we complicate our lives by taking control of every detail. But by surrendering everything to you, we should never have any restless nights or loss of sleep from tossing and turning. We rest in your loving arms, living together in our moments, with restful sleep assured. Jesus, cuddle us gently in your arms as we sleep.

Scan To Branch Out

Let's Wait without the Safety Net

SCRIPTURE WHISPER

The LORD is good to those who wait for him, to the person who searches for him.

LAMENTATIONS 3:25 ISV

God shows compassion as we wait, but often we wait with a safety net of extra prayers in case our initial prayers aren't answered as we envision. He hears and will answer, maybe not in the way we intended or in our timing but in his perfect way.

In situations when it seems that nothing can save the day and it's the eleventh hour and fifty-ninth second, God can make the impossibilities possible by his design. Waiting with unwavering faith makes a difference. It activates the miraculous. Bible stories are God's reminders that he has done it before and will do it again in his miraculous mercy and grace.

Jesus of peace, you didn't design us to live alone, but Satan is crafty at encouraging a sense of separation from you during the wait. You do not call us to do things for which you don't provide, and we are not always the ones causing the wait. Often, you are weaving others into our lives who have a purpose in the eleventh-hour miracle. Help us search for you during the wait and never rely on a safety net but solely on you, Lord.

Scan To Branch Out

Let's Be Confident in Jesus

SCRIPTURE WHISPER

The LORD will be your confidence and will keep your foot from a snare.

PROVERBS 3:26 CSB

What is confidence? It is defined as the complete assurance that one can rely on someone or something with firm trust. When we place our confidence in God, we can firmly trust him to fulfill his many promises throughout the Bible.

As we are faithful to live according to his ways, turn to him for our choices, and remain available to him, then we can be confident he will guard our feet against the snares of Satan. The Evil One will be unable to trip us up when Jesus lives within us. Our confidence strengthens us, and our knowledge deepens when we daily learn from God's Word, nurturing an intimate relationship in partnership with our Lord.

Jesus of patience, whom we can turn to for confidence when things seem to unravel, help us depend on you to be faithful in everything that comes our way. We need you. Help us always be confidently available for anything you call us to do.

Let's Brag about Jesus

SCRIPTURE WHISPER

Can we boast, then, that we have done anything to be accepted by God? No, because our acquittal is not based on obeying the law. It is based on faith.

ROMANS 3:27 NLT

The nature of God is to restore our lives so we can help repair the lives of those who are going astray. Jesus is God's gift of restoration, and we should willingly invite him to start remodeling.

The life we create for ourselves is full of flaws, so we have no reason to boast about our imperfections. But when we accept Jesus as our master craftsman, the one who restores our life to fulfill all he designed, then we have someone to brag about, and that's Jesus! When we hand our lives to Jesus, he will transform the condition of our hearts so that we no longer depend on works or boasting but we rest confident in a life of contentment and peace. Jesus arranges our moments when we let him be God in our lives.

Jesus of kindness, forgive us when we take back control of our lives when things get weary and the wait gets long. Forgive us also when we jump back in the way of your purpose and stop living as you designed.

Let's See Others Like Jesus Does

SCRIPTURE WHISPER

Faith in Christ Jesus is what makes each of you equal with each other, whether you are a Jew or a Greek, a slave or a free person, a man or a woman.

GALATIANS 3:28 CEV

It matters not if we are up or down, rich or poor, employees or employers. Jesus saves all who call on him to be their Savior. He longs for us to live in harmony with one another. When God's children are hypocrites in the way they treat others, then God is the one whom others perceive in the wrong image. We tarnish his reputation.

How often do we say one thing yet do another or hold a standard for others only to break it ourselves? How we treat others comes from the condition of our hearts. Our character and integrity are our testimony as Christ's followers, representing him to the lost and unbelieving all around us, as he loves others through us. He grants us the ability to hear others as he hears them and see others through his eyes.

Jesus of goodness, forgive us for the times when we have caused division by how we look at others. Help us not to see others differently but to see them all as your children.

Scan To Branch Out

Let's Listen More Quietly

SCRIPTURE WHISPER

If you belong to Christ, then you are Abraham's descendants, heirs according to the promise.

GALATIANS 3:29 NET

A promise is a declaration or assurance that one will do a particular thing or that something will happen. It has been said that within the sixty-six books of the Bible, there are over eight thousand promises.

The Bible does not consist of the ideas of men. It is the inspired words of God to those whom he chose to provide a road map for life, directing our pathway toward fulfilling his great plan. It assures us that the best way to navigate life is in partnership with Jesus. As believers, our blessings are in his promises every day, but we must seek them. Someone once said that the closer we get to God, the louder we can hear his whispers. Let's listen more quietly.

Jesus of faithfulness, help us clear the trivial distractions from our agendas so that we can seek your many promises each day, becoming closer to you so that your whispers become louder. We pray for a shout into our hearts so that we have clarity about our purpose and can draw others to your presence.

Scan To Branch Out

Let's Become Less Important

SCRIPTURE WHISPER

Jesus must become more important,
while I become less important.
JOHN 3:30 CEV

Our Scripture Whisper describes Jesus living through our lives in various ways: Jesus must become greater; I must become less. Our self-importance lessens when Jesus becomes more evident in our lives by the way we live in his character and seek to fulfill his intentions. Do we still jump into God's way, or is he the filter of our choices? When we become focused on others, we are modeling the ways of Jesus by considering others first.

Just like a caterpillar gradually morphs into a beautiful butterfly, God transforms our hearts once we become born again, and we gradually decrease our desires for the ways of the world by making Jesus of greatest importance in our lives.

Jesus of gentleness, we are flawed examples of you when we proclaim to be your children yet still make choices to engage in worldly things more than things of kingdom value. Help us decrease the importance of the world's ways with an increased focus on you so that you can accomplish the work you designed for each of us to fulfill. We ask to become unimportant so that you can work through us.

Scan To Branch Out

Let's Live the Light of Jesus

SCRIPTURE WHISPER

God's Son comes from heaven and is above all others. Everyone who comes from the earth belongs to the earth and speaks about earthly things. The one who comes from heaven is above all others.

JOHN 3:31 CEV

Only God offers us complete forgiveness through his unconditional love. Those who reject what Christ did have nowhere else to turn. All other proposed routes of salvation are based on fallible, human, earthly knowledge with no truth. The Bible is clear; there are no other ways to God but through an acceptance of Jesus and the rebirth of our hearts.

Tragically, too many people are opposed to this gift of eternal salvation. Satan is frantically at work to keep them confused and hard-hearted against hearing the gospel. So, as ambassadors of our Lord, let's wear the gospel by living in the ways of Jesus. The peace and joy shining within us from the light of his brilliant presence can melt the hardness of hearts. Jesus calls us to be his penetrating light that draws others to him each day.

Jesus of self-control, help us intentionally put on your presence every morning so the light of your character living through us ignites a movement across this land.

Scan To Branch Out

April

Let's Be a Blessing

SCRIPTURE WHISPER

What causes fights and quarrels among you? Don't they come from your desires that battle within you?
JAMES 4:1 NIV

Often when we fight and quarrel, it's not because of the other person with whom we are disagreeing; it's our inner battle. We are fighting with ourselves as our souls are not satisfied with who we are or what's become of our behavior. Our spirits are in turmoil, searching to find our identity and purpose. The whirlwind of confusion swirls around when we haven't learned how to live in our lane.

These internal battles cause divisions in relationships, disputes, and arguments that stem from a much deeper root—often far more profound than we acknowledge—which erupts into dysfunctional behavior in relationships. Many struggle to release the memories of painful experiences from childhood that can manifest as explosive tempers and unreasonable behavior. But with God, we can learn to become better, not bitter, allowing God's blessings to shower upon us so we can be a blessing to others. Let's put the pain of the past in the past and become blessed to be a blessing.

Jesus of love, you promised to fight our battles with legions of angels to gain victory over Satan's desire for our souls. Let us live in that confident expectation.

Scan To Branch Out

Let's Allow for Others' Faults

SCRIPTURE WHISPER

Always be humble and gentle. Be patient with each other, making allowance for each other's faults because of your love.
EPHESIANS 4:2 NLT

Our Scripture Whisper urges us to live a life that is worthy of our calling in the unique way God created us. We should weave into our lifestyle the character of Jesus, the fruit of his Spirit. When we do, we become focused on others, forsaking our self-righteousness. Our spirit becomes gentler, and we maintain self-control because Jesus is now in control. Like Jesus, we react with more patience, share unselfish love, and clothe ourselves in humility.

Too often, people associate humility with weakness, but it takes strength to be humble. Pride and arrogance are cries of low self-esteem, when we pretend to be strong on the outside to camouflage inner weakness, deceiving ourselves.

Jesus of joy, help us love others with your servant's heart. Putting others first is the example this world needs to see from your children, ambassadors of your kingdom. Help us keep our hearts united by living in the example and atmosphere of your Spirit.

Scan To Branch Out

Let's Unite

SCRIPTURE WHISPER

Make every effort to keep yourselves united in the Spirit, binding yourselves together with peace.

EPHESIANS 4:3 NLT

How can we regain the unity of God's Spirit in a world filled with such divisive and evil tactics, attempting to shut down our voices and Jesus' voice? Unity must be intentional. It is not a seamless process. The entire body of Christ must be willing to speak up instead of living in the silence of complacency. Complacency legitimizes the opposition's message and can hinder people's ability to hear the truth of the gospel.

A team is made of individual players with different roles, but teammates must work together for the same purpose, aligning their unique skills as one body working toward the same goal. So when we relate to people through the heart of God, we become a team. His Spirit will override human differences and unite us through the bond of his peace, gentleness, and tender nature. Let's live in harmony and unity.

Jesus of peace, you created us individually and uniquely but for one united purpose: to live in a daily relationship with you. Just by the way we live our lives, we must encourage others to know that you are the one true and eternal Lord.

Scan To Branch Out

Let's Overcome the World

SCRIPTURE WHISPER

You, little children, are from God and have overcome them, because greater is He who is in you than he who is in the world.

1 JOHN 4:4 BSB

Do we live as though we've received the gift that comes from the suffering and agonizing death of Jesus? Do we embrace the power that is transferred to those of us who accept him into our hearts? We also have a bonus gift, the Holy Spirit, to fight Satan's intrusions. We only need to stay out of the way and let God be the master over the Enemy's strongholds.

Consider the analogy of ocean divers. The tremendous pressure in the ocean's depths will crush a diver who does not have adequate protection, but when a diver descends in a pressurized suit, the internal pressure is maintained to protect against the pressure from the outside. Likewise, there will be extreme pressure for believers, especially as we take on new strongholds that Satan has captured. However, the Holy Spirit's protection inside us is stronger than the pressure on the outside. The pressure from the evil forces is countered by the pressurized covering of Jesus.

Jesus of patience, you have overcome the strongholds of Satan, who is constantly trying to take back territory in our lives. Help us not let him back in.

Let's Live Gently

SCRIPTURE WHISPER

Let your gentle spirit [your graciousness, unselfishness, mercy, tolerance, and patience] be known to all people. The Lord is near.

PHILIPPIANS 4:5 AMP

A person who demonstrates gentleness is a person of quality who acts toward others in a tender way. When we think of a gentle nature, we think of Jesus. He is gentle in his choice of words, his tone, and the look in his eyes. Our Lord is gentle in his smile and his touch. He tenderly takes on our cares and offers to have a relationship with his children, a life together in partnership.

Our Scripture Whisper describes ways we can live with a gentle nature. In all our ways, we should be considerate, reasonable, forbearing in spirit, gracious, humble, modest, kind, unselfish, full of mercy, tolerant, and patient. Let's strive to be known as gentle spirits by all people whom we encounter.

Jesus of kindness, we are so grateful that you give us such grace even when we are not gentle in spirit. We ask forgiveness and pray for help to weave into our lifestyle your character of gentleness so others will take notice of your nature instead of the ways of this world.

Scan To Branch Out

Let's Extend Grace

SCRIPTURE WHISPER

He gives more grace. Therefore it says, "God opposes the proud but gives grace to the humble."

JAMES 4:6 ESV

Grace is such a beautiful name. We should all live as though our name is Grace and in alignment with the Bible's description of grace by spreading goodwill to all. Grace is elegance and courtesy and an extension of the goodness of Jesus even to the proud in spirit. Someone who is gracious is respectful and thoughtful, always putting others first and extending mercy beyond human understanding. They also have both strength and humility. Grace favors those who don't deserve it, always drawing out the best in others.

Our Lord extends grace to us every day in ways we don't even realize. Let's be more mindful of God's grace and, in turn, extend more grace, letting it overflow into the lives of others.

Jesus of goodness, thank you for your grace, which is an expression of your incomprehensible love for each of us. In our frailty and wayward ways, you extended grace to us although we were so undeserving. Because of your sacrifice, you can see us sinless, washed clean, and white as snow, free from our wrongdoings and selfish choices. Help us extend the same grace to others.

Scan To Branch Out

Let's Live in God's Peace

SCRIPTURE WHISPER

You will experience God's peace, which exceeds anything we can understand. His peace will guard your hearts and minds as you live in Christ Jesus.

PHILIPPIANS 4:7 NLT

When we live in the ways of Jesus, God's peace exceeds any understanding. When we feel smothered in the pit of despair, the Bible tells us to choose joy, which slams the door on Satan when he tries to rob us of our peace. So why do we often feel anxious and nervous in a vortex of worry when Jesus makes it plain and straightforward that we should pause and cast our cares on him?

The more we familiarize ourselves with God's Word, the better we can distinguish between God's voice and Satan's lies. God's tender whispers become so loud and familiar that they drown out Satan's schemes and lures. As we daily rely on Jesus as our partner in life, he will guard our hearts and minds.

Jesus of faithfulness, your assurance that you will bestow peace on us when we choose to be joyful in this troubled world is a gift we often ignore. You are in the battle fighting against any confusion overtaking our minds, which is a crafty tool of Satan. Help us choose joy when faced with frustration and worry so your peace floods our hearts.

Scan To Branch Out

Let's Know God's Love

SCRIPTURE WHISPER

Whoever does not love does not know God,
because God is love.

1 JOHN 4:8 NIV

Love has many meanings, but the essence of God's love is
that it is unconditional. No matter what we do, what we say,
or the choices we make, whether within God's pleasure or in
the ways of the world, God's love never changes.

As humans, it's a challenge for us to love unconditionally.
We often love based on circumstances, someone's behavior,
or what others said or didn't say. That's not unconditional
love. We often love based on how we've been loved or the way
our families loved. Did we grow up surrounded by touchy-
feely ways of expressing love, or was it more guarded and less
expressive? Do we set up barriers or constraints on how we
allow others to love us? What a marvel to realize the ways
we are unlovable, yet God loves us anyway. Let's seek ways to
love with fewer conditions, like Jesus.

Jesus of gentleness, you sacrificed yourself so that we can
live in a daily, loving relationship with you. We pray that
your spirit of love gives us a deeper understanding of how to
love those who are hard to love. Loving through your heart
changes the condition of our hearts and the way
we love.

Let's Understand God's Sacrifice

SCRIPTURE WHISPER

By this God's love was revealed in us, that God has sent his one and only Son into the world that we might live through him.

1 John 4:9 web

For those of us who are parents, it is unfathomable to imagine deliberately and intentionally offering our child for ridicule, persecution, beatings, and torture on the cross by those with such hatred, knowing the devastating loss and separation we would endure. Yet this is what God did because he loves us so unselfishly and unconditionally. That kind of love is incomprehensible to our human minds.

Imagine how it grieves our heavenly Father when we don't involve him in our walk and when we are in too much of a rush to turn to him. Let's be mindful that our God longs for a daily relationship with us and willingly sacrificed his own Son so we could live in partnership together.

Jesus of self-control, you showed us your love by coming into this sinful world so that we might live in a relationship with you on this earth and share eternal life with you in heaven. Help us live worthy of the pain and suffering of your sacrifice so that others will be drawn to the incomprehensible love you shower upon us.

Scan To Branch Out

Let's Refine Our Gifts

SCRIPTURE WHISPER

Each of you should use whatever gift you have received to serve others, as faithful stewards of God's grace in its various forms.

1 Peter 4:10 niv

God has graced us all with various gifts, and our life journey continually molds us in unique ways that God intended from before our birth. His purpose includes the refinement of our gifts and talents to be used for his plan. So may we never allow shame or guilt or regret from our past, from Satan's bag of tools, to inhibit us from using our gifts to serve others and to bring glory to God.

There's nothing better at the close of the day than to put our heads on the pillow knowing the Lord has used us to make a difference in someone's life.

Jesus of love, help us realize that you call us to live in the gifting for which you created us so that we may help fulfill your plans. Our gifts may influence and affect others in ways we may never know until we get to heaven. Help us never miss an opportunity to express our gifts. Thank you for making them part of your design so that we will be better equipped to live out the purpose for our existence.

Scan To Branch Out

Let's Be Content

SCRIPTURE WHISPER

I'm not saying this because I'm in any need. I've learned to be content in whatever situation I'm in.

PHILIPPIANS 4:11 GW

Being content is a difficult thing. In our human frailty, there's always some worldly desires that keep us from being content in whatever state we are in. God created longings in our hearts, but have we allowed Satan to hijack those desires into worldly ways? Do our hearts desire the accumulation of things, and do we long for stuff that has no eternal value?

God longs to fulfill our desires when they sync up with his intricately designed plan, but when our desires don't align with God's desires, we often struggle to make a difference in people's lives and continue searching for contentment in things that don't matter. One of the greatest blessings God has ever gifted to us is the ability to be content. By aligning with the author and provider of a contented heart and soul, let's remain content in a daily relationship with Jesus.

Jesus of joy, help us be content instead of allowing Satan to disturb our souls with uneasiness and confusion from the world. Help us seek ways to be content in all things and in all circumstances by aligning our heart's desires with yours.

Scan To Branch Out

Let's Ring Up Jesus

SCRIPTURE WHISPER

The word of God is alive and active. Sharper than any double-edged sword, it penetrates even to dividing soul and spirit, joints and marrow; it judges the thoughts and attitudes of the heart.

HEBREWS 4:12 NIV

We often take for granted that we are privileged and blessed to have many translations of God's Word at our fingertips. Tragically, many people worldwide live in fear of being found with a Bible. Many remote villages or underground churches share a Bible by passing around one page at a time, cherishing each word and daily longing to have Bibles of their own.

The Bible is the only book that speaks back; God talks to us through his Word. Sadly, we often don't take the time to personally converse with God through his Word. When we have questions, we can find the answers in the Bible. When we are fretful and worried, God's Word will give us peace. When we are brokenhearted, God's Word will embrace us in his tenderness.

Jesus of peace, forgive us when we fail to pick up our Bible and make a call to you to enhance our intimacy with you. We pray for you to guide us moment by moment, step by step, choice by choice toward the plan you created us to fulfill.

Scan To Branch Out

Let's Live in Jesus' Strength

SCRIPTURE WHISPER

I can do all things through Christ who strengthens me.
PHILIPPIANS 4:13 NKJV

This verse is often misunderstood. It's not a blanket endorsement that God will support anything we do. It's the assurance that we can do whatever God calls us to do, not whatever we decide to do. Things we do on our own are influenced by Satan, and if God is not involved, we should not want them to happen anyway. Anything outside God's divinely designed plan he will not bless, nor will it flourish. Watching to see if our plans flourish is a simple guideline to determine if our heart's desires are aligned with God's.

Our Scripture Whisper is a powerful way to live, seeking his plan for our lives and boldly expecting him to empower us and provide for us so we can do what he calls us to do. Just as God parted the Red Sea to free the Israelites from slavery in Egypt (Exodus 14), he also enables us to do what seems impossible, to glorify his name, and to draw others into his heavenly kingdom.

Jesus of patience, we are grateful for your strength to fulfill the purpose you specifically impart to us. Help us be more aware that we are not self-sufficient and only sufficient in you, Lord, who strengthens us.

Scan To Branch Out

Let's Plant Seeds of Hope

SCRIPTURE WHISPER

The farmer plants seed by taking God's word to others.

MARK 4:14 NLT

As children of God, we are all farmers, and he wants us to plant seeds daily. God has prepared fertile soil as he arranges those who need the seeds of his words in their hearts to cross our paths so we can plant them. And how do we plant? By the way we live our lives. Living the fruit of Jesus' Spirit, the character of his ways, will plant seeds that only God knows people need. Our Christlike actions can open doors for people who long to hear the truth of Scripture.

We may not even notice the seeds we plant along our daily journey, but we can rest assured that as we sow in obedience, God will water and harvest another soul into his kingdom of eternity. And a crowd in heaven will greet us and will say, "God used you to plant a seed in my heart so I could be here."

Jesus of kindness, thank you for giving us opportunities to share your Word of hope, planting seeds of truth in the lives of hopeless people who walk in confusion and darkness. Please draw others to your Spirit within us as our lifestyle mirrors your ways.

Scan To Branch Out

Let's Make Our Progress Evident

SCRIPTURE WHISPER

Ponder these things; be absorbed in them, so that your progress may be evident to all.
1 TIMOTHY 4:15 BLB

God created us with unique gifts for a specific purpose. Life often keeps those gifts dormant through struggles, hardships, frustrations, and despair, but they're still there. Sometimes God slowly reveals our giftings at the times when he can use them exactly how he intended at our creation.

How often do we pause and ask ourselves what excites our hearts? What gives us delight? What draws us to a particular uncovering of our gifts and talents as designed by God for his purpose? When we can identify something specific that we gravitate to and can do naturally, we're slowly uncovering our gifts and allowing Jesus to weave them into the fabric of our life journey for our good and his glory.

Jesus of goodness, help us use our gifts and talents to serve you. May we walk in partnership with you to make a difference in others' lives every day and live out our purpose so that others may see the progress of you living within us.

Scan To Branch Out

Let's Watch How We Live

SCRIPTURE WHISPER

Keep a close watch on how you live and on your teaching. Stay true to what is right for the sake of your own salvation and the salvation of those who hear you.

1 Timothy 4:16 NLT

People are watching. As Jesus followers, we live on a stage with bright lights on us as the evil ones eagerly attempt to shut us down and cancel our voice, looking for any flaws they can exploit to tarnish the name of Jesus.

We are a walking Bible. Just imagine that others see the Word of God living through our character, in our tone and word choices, and through our actions and reactions. That's daunting to think about, but living the fruit of Jesus' Spirit refines our lifestyle each day in the likeness of his ways. It's a choice, one moment at a time, throughout every day, to be the example of Jesus.

Jesus of faithfulness, help us live according to your teaching, staying true to what is right for the sake of your reputation. We are your ambassadors to this fallen world and want to be your voice to share the good news of salvation by how we live.

Scan To Branch Out

Let's Live Unafraid

SCRIPTURE WHISPER

As we live in God, our love grows more perfect. So we will not be afraid on the day of judgment, but we can face him with confidence because we live like Jesus here in this world.
1 John 4:17 nlt

We are all responsible for our own actions, purposes, goals, motives, use or misuse of our time, opportunities, gifts, talents, and abilities.

Because of Jesus' sacrifice and death on the cross and our belief in him as the only way to salvation, we can stand in confidence that love drives out fear. Our capacity for love is possible only because of the one who first loved us. He invites us to share his love. Let's grow in unity and ignite a Spirit-filled movement, changing the world one life at a time, drawing others by the love of Jesus living through us each day.

Jesus of gentleness, ignite a fire within us so that we can grow in ways that fulfill the purpose you designed for us. Help us make a difference in others' lives. Lord, create a movement that brings your voice back to our fallen world.

Let's Walk the Righteous Road

SCRIPTURE WHISPER

The road the righteous travel is like the sunrise,
getting brighter and brighter until daylight has come.
PROVERBS 4:18 GNT

The condition of our heart reveals how far we've journeyed down the path of righteousness. Why is our heart so important? Because it is the foundation for how we live our life. We should constantly keep our attention on our hearts.

We should be mindful of what we store in our hearts. Our hearts dictate the ways we think, the words we speak, the direction of our journey, and our choices. These all stem from things we allow to penetrate our hearts. We can't unsee things or unhear words spoken. Satan can use these things to damage the condition of our hearts, but we can choose to reject Satan's attempts that affect our testimony of our life in Jesus. As we walk the path of righteousness, the light of Jesus shines through us brighter and brighter.

Jesus of self-control, please give us a keener awareness of the images our eyes see and the words our ears hear so we can make better choices. Help us walk in righteousness so we can prevent the things of the wicked from damaging the condition of our hearts.

Scan To Branch Out

Let's Be Fruitful

SCRIPTURE WHISPER

"All too quickly the message is crowded out by the worries of this life, the lure of wealth, and the desire for other things, so no fruit is produced."
MARK 4:19 NLT

Our purpose is to be fruitful. How do we do that? By living the fruit of Jesus' Spirit and planting seeds throughout our day into the hearts of those whom God arranges for us to encounter, souls that the Holy Spirit will harvest into his kingdom. That's the reason for our lives.

Yet in our daily walk, distractions abound. Worries about medical decisions, the pursuit of a bigger home, and the desire for a comfortable life can all keep us from our God-ordained purpose when we prioritize them over the gospel and become less fruitful.

That, in turn, spills into the lives of those with whom we share relationships, and that's when God's Word gets choked. Many times, our split-second choices define our identity, our influence, and our fruitfulness, so let's focus on mind on Jesus as we make every decision.

Jesus of love, help us become fruitful and not allow the world to choke the harvests you intend our lives to cultivate.

Let's Believe God's Promises

SCRIPTURE WHISPER

[Abraham] did not doubt or waver in unbelief concerning the promise of God, but he grew strong and empowered by faith, giving glory to God.

ROMANS 4:20 AMP

Life has a way of interfering with the promises of God. Satan lurks on the sidelines, ready to capture our thoughts before God's promises seep into our minds and hearts. It's our responsibility to keep away Satan, who attempts to sneak in, so that the promises of God become the compass that directs our ways. Life is tough, complicated, and challenging. However, when we immediately react to any conflict by reaching for a promise of God, promises that are scattered over eight thousand times throughout the Bible, the storm is calmed, and peace overtakes our souls.

But how do we get into the habit of recalling God's promises? We must know of his promises by planting them in our hearts daily when we open his Word. What a blessing in every circumstance to have promises of hope from the one who never fails to do what he says.

Jesus of joy, help us make your promises and our faith the mortar that seals shut the door to Satan.

Scan To Branch Out

Let's Live in Truth

SCRIPTURE WHISPER

You certainly heard about him, and as his followers you were taught the truth that is in Jesus.

EPHESIANS 4:21 GNT

How do we know the truth? The truth is Jesus. His character is truth and goodness. The truth is not as abstract as the world presents. It is found in a personal relationship with Jesus. The more we read the Word of God, the more we know him and the truth that sets us free from the entanglement of the world's false teaching and misunderstanding. It is these confusing patterns that result in the chaotic frenzy that permeates our country today.

We fight against evil. Satan brainwashes with deception and lies, but by reading Scripture and relying on Jesus, we can sort out falsehood from truth. The world presents many ways to falter and fail. So we must seek truth in all matters, speak the truth in our communications, and put truth into action.

Jesus of peace, thank you for providing your Word and an understanding of truth in all matters, including inspiration and encouragement from your Holy Spirit to combat the untruths of today. Help us live based on your character, rooted in the foundation of your truth.

Let's Diminish Old Ways

SCRIPTURE WHISPER

Get rid of your old self, which made you live as you used to—the old self that was being destroyed by its deceitful desires.
EPHESIANS 4:22 GNT

The author of deceit and evil desires is Satan, and he is lurking, continually seeking ways to creep into our lives through any crack in our character, bringing to our hearts shame and guilt for the times we allowed an opening for evil to enter. As children of God, we are to put off the former ways of life, the ways of the world, and the ways that do not align with Jesus. We are to remove from ourselves all corruption that the world applauds as we walk in the renewal of a new life in Christ.

When we falter, people are watching and ready to pounce on us with accusations of hypocrisy and critical words as we profess Jesus as our Savior. Jesus suffered on the cross for those times when we fail to live according to God's will. But God's eyes see us as clean. Self-condemnation after being washed clean by Jesus' blood is a sin. God suffered and died for that too.

Jesus of patience, help us when we feel utter discouragement and vulnerable to Satan's attack because of our actions. Help us automatically put those moments into your care.

Scan To Branch Out

Let's Guard Our Hearts

SCRIPTURE WHISPER

Guard your heart above all else,
for it determines the course of your life.
PROVERBS 4:23 NLT

How do we guard our hearts? By taking captive what our eyes see, what our ears hear, and what we allow our minds to think. This is a moment-by-moment choice to manage what we accept into our hearts. That's the barometer of how we live. Our thoughts control our perception of ourselves and others. We can choose to be branded as Christ followers or to open a door to the ways of Satan and the world.

Experiences from our past that keep ringing in our hearts can promote our happy place of long ago or a terrifying memory that continues to haunt our souls. Maybe it's a movie, a song, or a comment on the playground that takes us to a place of joy or fear. A moment can forever shape our future when we allow our hurtful past to live in our present.

Jesus of kindness, you have provided a way for us to stop unhealthy thoughts and behaviors by gaining control over the condition of our hearts. Help us model your character in our lives and guard our hearts.

Let's Listen with Care

SCRIPTURE WHISPER

"Consider carefully what you hear," he continued.
"With the measure you use, it will be measured to you—
and even more."
MARK 4:24 NIV

We cannot avoid the words we hear, but we can make an immediate choice that negative words will not find a home in our hearts. We can dispute words that reach our ears before they seep into our thoughts.

While we don't have control over the words others say, we do have control over the environments in which we place ourselves. It's our choice to surround ourselves with those like-minded in Christ or those who spew out negative, harsh words that include a vocabulary we absolutely do not condone. People around us influence our lives through the words they speak.

Let's become more mindful of the world's impact on our lives. One phrase can inspire and encourage us or send us into a deep depression for a lifetime. Let's be choosy and surround ourselves with those who speak the words of Jesus. And for those words out of our control in a work environment, God created earplugs.

Jesus of goodness, help us immediately filter out those words that do not align with your character or your ways. Help us dispel negative talk and walk away from gossip without lingering.

Let's Look Straight Ahead

SCRIPTURE WHISPER

Let your eyes look directly forward,
and your gaze be straight before you.

PROVERBS 4:25 ESV

We need to look straight ahead because there is such a
dark covering surrounding us. We must imagine our eyes
like flashlights, beaming forward. The beam of a flashlight
doesn't curve, and it never veers to the left or the right. We
must be intentional to focus ahead like that flashlight beam,
not allowing a curve to bring in the darkness.

People will notice as we devote our lives to moral
courage and integrity. Living the fruit of Jesus' Spirit is the
way to keep our focus straight. We must not allow the ways
of the world to disrupt or compromise our Christlikeness
as we stand strong and firm in the truth that our way of life
models Jesus.

Jesus of faithfulness, help us keep our eyes focused ahead
and keep you in the forefront of our minds. Forgive us when
our eyes veer off course. Help us be aware of those moments
when our peripheral vision brings in darkness so that we
can immediately pause and return our focus to you.

Scan To Branch Out

Let's Ponder More

SCRIPTURE WHISPER

Ponder the path of your feet;
then all your ways will be sure.
PROVERBS 4:26 ESV

Jesus encourages us to ponder as we live. We often use the word *pause* in its place, but let's embrace the word *ponder*. *To ponder* means that we think about something carefully, especially before making a decision or reaching a conclusion.

If we pondered more, Satan would lose his advantage. Taking a moment to ponder and engage Jesus in our decisions leaves no room for Satan to interfere. When we maintain a straightforward partnership with Jesus, life stays on course. The creator of the universe has already thought out our next step. But we must ponder to ensure that we include Jesus in all our moments. This will slam shut any opened door through which Satan can detour us from the Lord's appointed pathway.

Jesus of gentleness, we often rush into things without giving any thought to including you in our plans. As a result, our footsteps take us around the mountain again and again even though you already prepared a clear path through it if only we allow you to lead the way. Lord, remind us always to ponder carefully before taking the next step.

Let's Reap a Harvest

SCRIPTURE WHISPER

"He goes to sleep and gets up, night and day, and the seed sprouts and grows, though he does not know how."
MARK 4:27 NET

As we go about our journey, Jesus arranges divine moments for us to plant seeds in others' hearts, seeds that can sprout and grow night and day. When we become devoted seed planters for Jesus, he waters the seeds we plant in hearts. Although we don't understand how—and we may never know until we get to heaven—our life's journey will be part of someone else's journey to salvation through Christ when we faithfully share the good news.

A harvest starts with one seed planted, one moment at a time, in God's garden of our lives. Despite the darkness permeating our world, as we spread seeds of blessings everywhere, God is growing a harvest of once lost and hopeless souls from the seeds we plant.

Jesus of self-control, help us never miss a moment that you have arranged for us to plant a seed in someone's hopeless heart, giving them hope for a future with you and eternal life in heaven. Please help us be seed planters everywhere we go by living the fruit of your Spirit.

Scan To Branch Out

Let's Remain Faithful in Trials

SCRIPTURE WHISPER

"To do whatever Your hand and Your purpose had determined beforehand to happen."
ACTS 4:28 BLB

As Jesus' followers, we are to remain confident that God has a purpose for our own trials and that he equips us to fulfill his implicit plan. Using someone who is ill-equipped is like putting someone who hasn't attended flight school in the cockpit of a large international flight or choosing someone who never went to medical school to perform a life-saving brain surgery. God doesn't cause trials, but he allows them to prepare us for tasks far beyond our imagination. Just as God predetermined Jesus' crucifixion to rescue us from eternal separation and allow us to have a relationship with our Savior, so he has carefully planned our lives so that we can influence and encourage others to seek our Lord and join us in eternity.

Wickedness is on a rampage throughout our world, but God will accomplish his purposes for those who love him and are called to his purpose. God can take the worst in humans and accomplish his very best. He calls us to be his ambassadors. Let's never let him down.

Jesus of love, help us remain faithful in our trials, knowing you are right alongside us as you equip us for your predestined greatness ahead.

Scan To Branch Out

Let's Avoid Profanity

SCRIPTURE WHISPER

Let no unwholesome words ever pass your lips, but let all your words be good for benefiting others according to the need of the moment, so that they may be a means of blessing to the hearers.

Ephesians 4:29 wnt

Our word choices are critical. They can encourage someone or tear them down, affecting their future and their legacy. It's disturbing how people throw profanity around, using God's name in ways that open the door to Satan. It's heart-crushing how casually, frequently, and haphazardly people pepper their conversations with vulgarity. This has become an acceptable way of life.

We even hear believers inviting hell into the conversation, with phrases like "what the hell," "a hell of a time," or "a hell of a guy." Why do we so casually invite hell into the situation? The evil forces seek any opportunity to swoop in and create turmoil, frustration, and separation from the ways of God. Too often, we let words roll off our tongues with no thought of their impact. Let's not take for granted our word choices. And let's not stay in conversation with those who choose to speak worthless words and profanity to communicate.

Jesus of joy, we pray that no unwholesome words proceed from our mouths but that the words of our lips be gracious to you.

Scan To Branch Out

Let's Seek to Please Jesus

SCRIPTURE WHISPER

Don't give God's Holy Spirit any reason to be upset with you. He has put his seal on you for the day you will be set free [from the world of sin].
EPHESIANS 4:30 GW

We should not bring sorrow to God's Holy Spirit by how we live but seek ways to please him. God identified us as his own, sealed us like a wax imprint on an important document, and branded us as belonging to him. He has guaranteed that we will be saved on the day of redemption, the final deliverance from the consequences of our sins and wayward lifestyle.

The incomprehensible price God paid for us was the precious blood of his own Son, Jesus Christ, and the moment we believe in him, we are part of his family. We are his children, and we will join him at our heavenly destination. What kind of sacrificial love is that? God desires to live in a relationship with us all.

Jesus of peace, it's the plan of Satan to throw questions and doubts into our minds to make us feel unworthy to be in your presence. Thank you for assuring us that once we invite you into our hearts and live a life pleasing in your sight, our home will be in heaven.

Scan To Branch Out

May

Let's Choose the Yoke of Jesus

SCRIPTURE WHISPER

It was for freedom that Christ set us free;
therefore keep standing firm
and do not be subject again to a yoke of slavery.
GALATIANS 5:1 NASB

Why do we live as if we're bound up in fear of the future, not knowing which way to turn in the turmoil within our personal lives? We feel knots in our stomachs, confusion in our hearts, and frustration in our relationships, and they are all part of the evil plan of Satan to keep us in bondage.

When we stick our necks in Satan's yoke, then we disregard Jesus' suffering and agonizing death that set us free from bondage and gave us the freedom to live in a personal relationship with him. Jesus offers us his yoke, which is easy, is light, and frees us from Satan's bondage. Jesus gives us a choice to be yoked with him, our world's Savior, or with the Evil One, who will live an eternity in hell.

How we live our lives is determined by the yoke we choose: freedom or bondage.

Jesus of patience, we get caught up in worldly ways instead of turning to you, the provider of peace through the storms. Help us thirst to live in alignment with you.

Scan To Branch Out

Let's Love Unconditionally

SCRIPTURE WHISPER

Walk in love, as Christ also loved us and gave himself for us, a sacrificial and fragrant offering to God.

EPHESIANS 5:2 CSB

Think of those we love beyond compare. When we think of them, we often remember the things they have done for us in love that they didn't have to do.

Jesus walked this earth while extending love toward everyone he encountered. He loved us so much that he died in our place, becoming an offering as payment for our sins. Romans 5:8 tells us he sacrificed himself while we were still sinners. We did nothing to deserve his unconditional love. Others see love in our smiles, hear love in our voices, and see the burning sense of love in our eyes as we emulate Jesus' nature by giving ourselves to others for the love of God. Let's love others as Jesus loves us through our mess-ups and failures, wrong choices and foolish decisions. He loves us through it all unconditionally. Our Lord's love never changes.

Jesus of kindness, help us love more like you love. We know that Satan tries to change how we love by injecting conditions on our love. Some people in our lives seem hard to love, but no one is unlovable in your eyes. Help us, Lord, to love through your heart.

Let's Persevere

SCRIPTURE WHISPER

Not only that, but we also glory in tribulations,
knowing that tribulation produces perseverance.
ROMANS 5:3 NKJV

It's challenging to glory in our trials and tribulations, but
Paul tells us that perseverance produces character, and
character produces hope (v. 4). God doesn't cause problems,
but he uses them to sharpen our skills to persevere in the
faith-stretch seasons. Once we pass that test and purify our
faith, he takes us into a new season to sharpen us even more.

When we stop wishing to rapidly get past the trouble
and finally realize that, along the journey, we will learn
lessons that will better equip us for what's ahead. Then we
can approach challenging days more prepared for what
God has planned. What we don't realize during difficult
situations is that when we choose to be in control and do
things on our own, often we can prolong our trials with
shortsighted foolishness. When we partner with Jesus, who
has it all planned out, and choose joy and glory in trials and
tribulations, he navigates us on the most direct route.

Jesus of goodness, help us not to desire shortcuts to get
through difficult situations but to trust that you will direct
us through the minefields of Satan's attacks.
Refine and equip us for the days ahead.

Let's Build Character

SCRIPTURE WHISPER

Endurance produces proven character, and proven character produces hope.

ROMANS 5:4 HCSB

Our character and unique personality are made up of our integrity and values. Our character builds throughout our journey as others come in and out of our lives, we react to challenging situations, and we uphold the quality and values of the character we desire to portray.

As followers of Christ, our character reflects the reputation of Jesus. Who are the ones we choose to include in our world? Are they in alignment with the character of Jesus? Do we choose to be influenced by those with good character standards? And what impact is our influence having on those we encounter?

It just takes one tiny drop of oil to cloud fresh, purified water. The same applies to our character. When we allow the impure words and choices of others to influence our behavior, our character is at risk of being tarnished. On the other hand, associating with people of faith and integrity strengthens our character. When people think of us, how do they perceive our character? It's up to us to live like Jesus.

Jesus of faithfulness, help us build our character by making a habit of living the fruit of your Spirit as we focus on a different one each day.

Scan To Branch Out

Let's Pray, Not Wish

SCRIPTURE WHISPER

Hope does not disappoint, because the love of God has been poured out in our hearts by the Holy Spirit who was given to us.

ROMANS 5:5 NKJV

The worldview of always expecting positive outcomes is different from an unwavering belief that life will turn out the best way in God's plan. The outcomes may not be "positive" or what we envision because our finite minds cannot comprehend the supernatural way in which God makes the impossible possible.

Too often, Christian's pray safety-net prayers in case something they want doesn't happen. Prayer becomes more like wishing. That's not Jesus' kind of hope, which is full assurance that he will do what he promised in his perfect way for our good and his glory. So when our prayers turn to disappointment, it's a sign that we rely more on wishes according to worldly expectations rather than on the bold expectation that God's plan will manifest better than we can hope or imagine.

Jesus of gentleness, we are so grateful that you help us realize when we've faltered back into the world's ways and our trust in you has wavered. Help us rest in the assurance that you desire the very best for those who love you and will take what Satan meant for harm and turn it into greatness.

Scan To Branch Out

Let's Thirst for Jesus' Ways

SCRIPTURE WHISPER

Blessed are they that hunger and thirst after righteousness: for they shall be filled.

MATTHEW 5:6 ASV

The world offers to fulfill our desires in inferior ways that keep us from thirsting after Jesus. Of course, many of those worldly hungers come with consequences that aren't worth it.

The joy and delight that come from living in right standing with God far exceed any benefit worldly desires can offer. When God's goodness nourishes us and we actively seek ways to please him, we become satisfied. Contentment and satisfaction fill us with a sense of peace and joy beyond our imagination. Jesus offers us a life of spiritual prosperity when we fill our days in partnership with him, living with him in peace above the world's woes, thirsting to be equipped and used by Jesus more every day.

Jesus of self-control, we ask for a renewed hunger and thirst for you and an insatiable desire to avoid the consequences of living by worldly standards. Instead we seek to follow the pattern of your character, living the fruit of your Spirit with intentionality and fervent passion.

Scan To Branch Out

Let's Be Patient

SCRIPTURE WHISPER

My friends, be patient until the Lord returns. Think of farmers who wait patiently for the autumn and spring rains to make their valuable crops grow.

JAMES 5:7 CEV

We all tend to become easily impatient in this culture of instant gratification. Our Scripture Whisper reminds us that when we wait for God's timing, our patience cultivates valuable results. Too often we jump in his way and thwart his plan with our impatience. We must focus on Jesus working behind the scenes when we see no growth even though the rains come, for God is getting us ready for his harvest in his perfect timing. When we attempt to accelerate the process, our crops lose their value. Patience produces a crop of excellence when we invite Jesus to be our harvester.

Jesus of love, we want to live in your vibrant character of patience, calm, and fearlessness in the chaos of this world. Please help us shine brightly and ignite a desire in our souls to spread the fruit of your character of patience. And help us, Lord Jesus, to walk in faith for things that we cannot see. May we patiently wait in trust as you work behind the scenes to save souls and bring us all into your kingdom of everlasting peace, free from this world of turmoil.

Scan To Branch Out

Let's Be Pure in Heart

SCRIPTURE WHISPER

"Blessed are those whose thoughts are pure.
They will see God."
MATTHEW 5:8 GW

God blesses those whose hearts are pure, but what is a pure heart? Purity of heart is to be authentic, to have complete honesty before God, and to engage respectfully in transparent conversations with Jesus, pouring our hearts out to the one who cares and knows every detail of our lives, even our future.

When we go to our Lord with our vulnerabilities, exposing the deepest, darkest parts of our hearts and souls, hiding nothing, he pours out his cleansing Spirit to free us. That freedom enables us to be pure and faithful in our daily lives, with transparency that draws others to his light that shines from within us. Let's live in the purity of his authenticity everywhere we go.

Jesus of joy, we pray as we come to you today that we may share with you the things deep within our hearts that we have hidden away and not exposed. You are tender and gentle and have suffered and died to forgive us of those hidden sins, anger, regrets, and shame. Help us, Lord, live a life of authenticity, drawing others to you. We are nothing without you but everything with you.

Scan To Branch Out

Let's Be Peacemakers

SCRIPTURE WHISPER

"Blessed are the peacemakers,
for they will be called children of God."
MATTHEW 5:9 NIV

God blesses those who work for peace, especially when the world's peace is disrupted on all fronts. Panic, stress, and chaos loom all around, but when the atmosphere of peace is present, there's a brilliant light that cannot be ignored.

When someone barges in front of you in line or says a hurtful comment, it can be easy to say an unkind word to them or fume about them in your mind. But the peacemaker overlooks offenses because they never know what might be going on behind the scenes in someone's life to prompt their actions or unkind behavior. A peacemaker is forgiving and seeks ways to spread seeds of encouragement, which can spark a renewed peace within troubled souls. As peacemakers, we can make a tremendous difference in others' lives when we make a habit of living in the fruit of Jesus' peace.

Jesus of peace, it's easy to allow our negative reactions to flare when we fail to pause and alter our responses in alignment with your character. We come to you today and ask you to please help us make a difference by being peacemakers to those around us.

Scan To Branch Out

Let's Do What's Right

SCRIPTURE WHISPER

God blesses those people who are treated badly for doing right. They belong to the kingdom of heaven.
MATTHEW 5:10 CEV

We live in a temporary world. We are just passing through here on this earth, moving toward only one of two destinations: heaven or hell. The Bible is very clear about that. Our doing right does not get us to heaven. It's God's grace and our belief that Jesus is the Son of God, who suffered inhumanely as payment for our sins. He died and was raised from the dead to set us free from hell and open an entrance into his heavenly home, a place without Satan. Isn't the kingdom of heaven worth doing the right things in all our ways during this season on earth?

We must refuse to allow Satan to affect us when challenges come our way. The Bible says to roll our cares over to the shoulders of Jesus and expect him to gain victory. Even if we are mistreated for following Jesus, we can know that God will bless us. Let's remain steady and go with Jesus' flow, the only constant in our lives who never changes and who promises never to fail us.

Jesus of patience, you know the condition of our hearts. Give us a thirst to do what's right and pleasing in your eyes.

Let's Be Encouragers

SCRIPTURE WHISPER

Encourage each other and build each other up, just as you are already doing.

1 Thessalonians 5:11 nlt

As Christ's followers, we should be God's ambassadors of encouragement. We can offer hopeful encouragement to the hopeless as times grow dimmer and the day of Christ's return draws nearer.

We can be encouragers in an abundance of ways. When we see a talent or gift in someone who has been struggling with their identity, our encouragement can give them confidence to live in their gifting and focus on their talent, finding their niche, possibly starting a new career, and, more importantly, furthering the kingdom of God. When we compliment someone in passing, our words could be what ignites hope in their day of hopelessness.

When we need encouragement, God invites us to turn to him by reading his Word and chatting with him in prayer. He knows our hearts and always will wrap his tender Spirit around us and lead us to open Scripture precisely to the words we need at that moment to lift our spirits and encourage us during prayer.

Jesus of kindness, you encourage us when life gets the best of us. Help us, in turn, to encourage others, as many don't know how to turn to you to receive your loving care.

Scan To Branch Out

Let's Live in Favor

SCRIPTURE WHISPER

You bless righteous people, O Lord. Like a large shield, you surround them with your favor.

Psalm 5:12 gw

We should take our Scripture Whisper to heart and walk expecting God's favor. God promises to shield with his kindness those of us who live in his character. But we aren't perfect. Satan continually challenges our righteous living because he certainly doesn't want God's promises to shield us. However, each time we choose to live Jesus' ways instead of Satan's evil ways, we strengthen that shield of protection around us. Over time, that shield grows a thickness that defeats Satan's attack.

So each day that we make a habit of living the fruit of Jesus' Spirit, Satan's grip diminishes, our protective shield becomes more powerful, and victory in Jesus is won in those vulnerable areas of our lives. Satan stands down when he sees God's children in the atmosphere of Jesus' favor, so let's choose to walk in a blanket of his favor.

Jesus of goodness, give us strength to walk in righteousness even when Satan attacks. Thank you for shielding us with your favor when we choose to live as the mirror of your character.

Let's Pray and Be Cheerful

SCRIPTURE WHISPER

Is any among you suffering? let him pray. Is any cheerful?
let him sing praise.

JAMES 5:13 ASV

When we are in trouble, suffering hardship, sick, afflicted,
downhearted, sad, brokenhearted, or lonely, we should pray.
Jesus is continuously extending his hand to help us, save
us, and provide a clear direction in a time of need. When
we are feeling happy with goodness surrounding us and are
flourishing and full of joy, we should sing praises and rejoice.

Our Scripture Whisper sends a clear message: the best
way to shut down Satan's evil attempts to invade our peace is
to pray, sing, praise, and rejoice.

Jesus of faithfulness, we are so fortunate to have your Word
to give us clarity, direction, and guidance along our life
journey. You make it quite simple. However, we don't often
go to your manual, the road map in your Word, preserved
thousands of years ago for us today so that we can know
how to navigate trials in these troubled days. Please help us
pause and engage with you when we find ourselves forlorn
and in need of direction for our weary souls. Help us rejoice
in you, the only one who turns our hearts to gladness.

Let's Display the Gospel

SCRIPTURE WHISPER

"You are the light of the world. A town built on a hill cannot be hidden."

MATTHEW 5:14 NIV

Jesus tells us to be the light of his presence and character, sharing hope to diminish the darkness in our fallen world. As we engage with his Word and devote ourselves to prayer, with a thirst to learn more of his ways, his light within us brightens, and he can use us more effectively.

We don't have to stand on a stage and preach the gospel. It's how we live our lives that draws others to the hope in Jesus when their hearts feel hopeless. Smiling tenderly or fulfilling a need with a gentle gesture can lighten someone's day with hope. Let's not hide our light but rather thirst to live in the way of Jesus to brighten this world.

Jesus of gentleness, forgive us when we miss opportunities to be your light in someone's life by the way we live. Please give us an insatiable thirst to brighten our inner light each day so that you can use us to lighten up the world. Together we can ignite a movement to make a difference for you, Lord, expanding your kingdom so that others can join us in your heavenly home.

Let's Not Live Like Fools

SCRIPTURE WHISPER

Be careful how you live. Don't live like fools, but like those who are wise.

EPHESIANS 5:15 NLT

As Jesus followers, we should be intentional about how others perceive us. The ways we frame our words and our tone, our reactions and responses to others, show that we live with a purpose. We should be careful not to surround ourselves with the ways of the world, instead refusing to tolerate and enable evil, living wisely and sensibly with a filter of discernment. When we profess to be a child of God yet live like fools, making rash decisions and not reflecting the image of Christ, we can negatively affect our Lord's reputation and deter others from following him.

It's the motive of Satan to veer us off course so others perceive our testimony as hypocritical. Those who profess Jesus yet live in ways that do not reflect his character often do more damage to the body of Christ than those who do not believe at all. Let's be aware of how others perceive us. We can draw people into Jesus' light by how we live or send them falling deeper into darkness, turning their backs on the hope found only in Jesus.

Jesus of self-control, through your wisdom, help us discern how others perceive our lifestyle and create an atmosphere that draws others to you.

Let's Accelerate Opportunities

SCRIPTURE WHISPER

Make the most of every opportunity in these evil days.
EPHESIANS 5:16 NLT

These words were written thousands of years ago and preserved for such a time as this. In our world, evil prevails in ways we never could have imagined. And throughout history, it always seemed that the end of time was near. The Bible says when certain events take place in one generation, you can expect the Lord's coming to be near.

So we must embrace every opportunity to reach those without hope. Many have no hope because they don't know about the hope found in Jesus, the one who knows the future and wants the best for his children. God uses us to draw others into an understanding of living in a daily personal relationship with him. Amid dark and evil days, our light in Jesus shines more brightly.

Jesus of love, when the world is dark, light shines more brightly, and it only takes one light to start a movement and ignite change. Jesus, help us create an awareness of you, our only hope, our only salvation. As we go about our day, may we become intentional about planting seeds by the way we live, choosing to make a habit of living the fruit of your Spirit every day.

Scan To Branch Out

Let's Let God Work

SCRIPTURE WHISPER

Jesus responded to them, "My Father is still working, and I am working also."

JOHN 5:17 CSB

Jesus walked this earth for thirty-three years and acted in perfect harmony with God our Father. John 5:19 tells us that "the Son does exactly what the Father does" (GW). Their relationship is a model of the relationship God longs to have with each of us as his children. He sent his only Son as a sacrifice for our sins so that we can live in a daily, intimate relationship together.

So whatever Jesus is doing, his Father is doing. The Godhead is united in perfect love, transparency, and intimacy, and God weaved that design within us as Christ's followers. Jesus' suffering and sacrifice on the cross transferred the same relationship to us and aligned us to walk hand in hand as Jesus works through us to accomplish his will. We are blessed to live in Jesus' anointing as he walks by our side, laboring on our behalf when we let him. So we need to let God work in every moment of every day, every footstep, every decision, in all our choices as we live to imitate Jesus.

Jesus of joy, help us stay out of the way and let you be Lord in our lives.

Let's Be Thankful Always

SCRIPTURE WHISPER

Whatever happens, keep thanking God because of Jesus Christ. This is what God wants you to do.

1 Thessalonians 5:18 CEV

How can we be joyful with all that's happening around us? There's sadness, hurt, fear, and hopelessness in many we encounter daily, but the Bible tells us to be joyful, always praying, and thankful in all circumstances. The only way we can constantly give thanks and be joyful is by embracing the promise that God is working out something in our lives for our good and his glory.

He who calls us is faithful. God has never spoken into someone's heart a vision that he does not finish when we allow him to work through us. And if he starts something in our lives, we can be assured that he will provide the means to accomplish his work as he transforms and equips us from the inside out—our spirit, soul, and body—as he promised in the Bible. When we act joyfully amid stormy circumstances, Satan is defeated. Victory is won when we are thankful and joyous in all circumstances.

Jesus of peace, help us be prayerful in all things and joyful always. May we be pleasing to you so others are drawn into an atmosphere of hope in you, Lord.

Scan To Branch Out

Let's Find Songs in Our Hearts

SCRIPTURE WHISPER

Sing songs from your heart to Christ. Sing praises over everything, any excuse for a song to God the Father in the name of our Master, Jesus Christ.

EPHESIANS 5:19 MSG

Music changes the atmosphere and brings joy into our souls. It's interesting how a tune from the past can flood our minds with memories, taking us far away into a happy place. Worship music sings to the depth of our troubled souls, broken hearts, and exhausted spirits, taking us into another world with just a song.

We all need a way of escape and often sadly retreat to a silent world. Emptiness fills the air when no more music plays in our heart and when we fail to remember the gift of music. We can find peace in the melody of a song, God's gift of joy.

Jesus of patience, thank you for the gift of music, which communicates to our spirits when we are downhearted. Lord, use us for the melodies that you uniquely inspire to bring cleansing to souls and renewal within hearts. Help us value your gift of music as we sing joyful songs of praise to you. Music reaches the throne of heaven when we sing prayers of rejoicing.

Scan To Branch Out

Let's Plead to the Lost

SCRIPTURE WHISPER

We are Christ's ambassadors; God is making his appeal through us. We speak for Christ when we plead, "Come back to God!"

2 Corinthians 5:20 NLT

God has chosen each of us to be an ambassador for a task that no one else has been created or equipped to accomplish, yet many fail to accept the honor. We can be ambassadors in various walks of life, both in ministry and the secular world. God wants his followers everywhere, and all he asks of us is that we remain empty vessels for him to work through. He will do it all, directing and advocating for us every step of the way. We just need to let him.

We may be chosen as ambassadors to our children, extended family, friends, and coworkers to reach their hearts and souls so they can find Jesus and be with us in heaven. Sometimes we plead among crowds of millions on a big stage or from the quiet of our home. God can use willing hearts and surrendered spirits.

Jesus of kindness, people are hurting, many are lost, and this world is in disarray. We all need you, and you equip us to reach others in need. Help us never miss an opportunity to be your ambassadors.

Scan To Branch Out

Let's Examine All Things

SCRIPTURE WHISPER

Examine all things; hold fast to what is good.
1 Thessalonians 5:21 net

We live in a world of deception. There are many wolves in sheep's clothing, and we must seek discernment in every aspect of our lives. People even speak Scripture out of context and twist it with meaning other than what the Lord inspired. How do we discern deception? We go to the Lord, spend quiet time with him, learn of his ways through his Word, and have a continual conversation in prayer.

Peace is our barometer. When our hearts are disturbed, we must take notice, pause, and seek God's whisper in our spirit, his voice of wisdom and clarity, and the atmosphere of his peace.

Jesus of goodness, we come to you today and ask for heightened discernment. May we become more intentional in seeking your wisdom to recognize the deception all around us. There's darkness everywhere, but your light prevails as we become more aware of the sound of your whisper in our spirit. Help us distinguish between your ways and the evil ways of the world and lead others to your light.

Let's Live in Jesus' Spirit

SCRIPTURE WHISPER

The fruit of the Spirit is love, joy, peace, patience, kindness, goodness, faithfulness, gentleness, and self-control. Against such things there is no law.

GALATIANS 5:22–23 NET

Jesus' presence within us provides us with the character of his love—the foundation of living in unselfish concern for others—joy when others experience favor, inner peace when the atmosphere is in turmoil, and patience in waiting for God's plan to unfold. His presence allows us to display kindness when others treat us unfairly, share goodness in bad situations, be faithful to the truth of God, remain gentle when harsh words fill the air, and exhibit self-control when we feel like losing it. That's living like Jesus, and he will use us to reach the hard-hearted.

The fruit of Jesus' Spirit is our goal as we make a habit of living a little more like Jesus every day. Use idle moments to practice the fruit of Jesus' Spirit each day, live more like the character of Jesus, and change our world.

Jesus of faithfulness, help us be more intentional about living in your ways so the fruit of the Spirit becomes a habit that deters Satan.

Scan To Branch Out

Let's Respect Jesus' Sacrifice

SCRIPTURE WHISPER

I pray that God, who gives peace, will make you completely holy. And may your spirit, soul, and body be kept healthy and faultless until our Lord Jesus Christ returns.

1 THESSALONIANS 5:23 CEV

Our Scripture Whisper tells us to remain holy, separated from evil, and cautious of Satan's traps, which can trip us up and affect God's testimony living through us each day. By remaining holy, we are set apart for God's purpose and uniquely designed plan for us. We are to remain in a spirit that lives in the character of Jesus until his return so that others will be drawn to him and join us in heaven.

This does not mean we never mess up, as only Jesus was perfect. He suffered in death to forgive and forget our sinful ways, past, present, and future, rendering us blameless. It's the condition of our hearts that Jesus longs to see, a thirst within us to live in the ways of his character.

Jesus of gentleness, your suffering to forgive our sins renders us blameless in your eyes. Help us respect your once-and-for-all suffering by forgiving ourselves. Otherwise, it's as if we nail you to the cross repeatedly. Let us live in the forgiveness of your grace even when Satan keeps reminding us of our past shame and regret.

Scan To Branch Out

Let's Wait Faithfully

SCRIPTURE WHISPER

He who calls you is faithful; he will surely do it.

1 Thessalonians 5:24 esv

Waiting for a vision to become a reality is challenging. In these times of expectation, God stretches our faith to see if we will obey his calling. When our faith is tested, often persecution is present, ridicule is loud, we're perceived as crazy, the ideas God has placed in our hearts seem impossible, and we're hanging on by our fingertips in obedience to Jesus' whisper in our hearts. It's tough.

None of us wants to go through trials or remain stuck in the in-between, the period from first feeling the excitement of the vision to seeing it fulfilled. That's an uncomfortable place to be. Often we feel something like a tug-of-war between Satan, who doesn't want the vision to happen, and Jesus, who assures us it will happen. The in-between is often heart-wrenching because we live on the edge, wondering how provisions will be made, how we can go on one more day, whether our Lord will send someone to help bring his vision to fruition. Today's Scripture Whisper is a reminder of the promise from God that he will remain faithful. Not maybe but surely he will.

Jesus of self-control, help us stay faithful to your vision, knowing your plan will unfold as we stay obedient to your whisper in our hearts.

Scan To Branch Out

Let's Follow the Spirit

SCRIPTURE WHISPER

Since we are living by the Spirit, let us follow the Spirit's leading in every part of our lives.
GALATIANS 5:25 NLT

When we invite Jesus to live in our hearts, it's a journey to train ourselves to hear the leading of his Spirit in every part of our lives. It takes an intentional effort to throw out the unproductive chatter of the world and cling to the whisper of the Holy Spirit's leading.

As we mature in our time devoted to God's Word and in prayer, the tone of his voice becomes familiar and drowns out the camouflaged, deceptive efforts of Satan. It's as if the evil distractions become a frequency that cannot penetrate through the voice of God.

Jesus of love, many are hopeless and lost and don't even know about you or that you are the only way to hope and eternal life in heaven. Help us live by the Spirit with every step we take so we can illuminate you as the only path to a place with no more pain, sickness, or despair. You have prepared and equipped us to be used for kingdom growth. Help us never miss an opportunity you divinely arrange along our daily journey.

Let's Pray with Bold Expectancy

SCRIPTURE WHISPER

Everyone was amazed and gave praise to God.
They were filled with awe and said,
"We have seen remarkable things today."
LUKE 5:26 NIV

Let's approach prayer with bold expectancy, praising the
awesomeness of God's goodness and grace for things in
our hearts that align with his plan for our lives. There's no
room for wishful prayers, those with a safety net in case
God answers differently. Instead, we should charge forward
with confidence that if his answer is different from what we
envision or expect, it will be better than we hope or imagine.

Once we put our petition before him, we can fill
our prayers with thankfulness and anticipate with bold
expectation that his plan will unfold from our prayers. God
gave us free will, so we can expect delays in seeing his plan
unfold when we allow Satan's distractions to veer us off
course. That is, until we surrender to living in alignment with
Jesus and get back on track for his perfectly designed plan.

Jesus of joy, help us mirror a racehorse, coming out of the
gates with eyes focused on the light of your presence. As you
lead the way, help us see remarkable things today as we live
in alignment with your plan.

Let's Weigh Our Humility

SCRIPTURE WHISPER

You have been weighed in the balances and found wanting.
DANIEL 5:27 ESV

This Scripture Whisper refers to King Belshazzar, who had not yet humbled his heart by praising God for all the Lord had done for him. Instead, he worshiped idols and turned his back on God.

As the story continues, a strange writing appeared on the wall, and Daniel interpreted the words to King Belshazzar, explaining that this would be the last day of the king's life. The expression "the writing on the wall" became famous because of this story, and it has come to mean that one can expect a miserable fate by choosing the prideful ways of Satan over Jesus' redeeming salvation.

Jesus of peace, we pray you will find a humble heart within us, a reflection of your character. Help us see the writing on the wall and understand the consequences of a prideful spirit. When opportunities tempt us to be prideful, help us cast those intrusions into your care as you invite us to, closing the door to pride. A humble heart is a sign of strength; pride is a sign of insecurity buried deep within our souls. Help us be an example for those living in the spirit of pride by modeling the humble character of your Spirit.

Let's Live in Readiness

SCRIPTURE WHISPER

Their arrows are sharp, all their bows are strung; their horses' hooves seem like flint, their chariot wheels like a whirlwind.

ISAIAH 5:28 NIV

Let's always be ready, sharpened, on guard, and equipped with the armor of God in these evil days unfolding throughout our world. We are to influence others by expressing the importance of readiness to those with lost souls and hopeless hearts. As Jesus' ambassadors, we are to draw others to him so they can join us in heaven's eternity, a place of peace where Satan can no longer abide.

Let's be ready to share God's love to the brokenhearted, always sharpened with the Scripture that fits the individual needs of someone's hurting soul. May we create a whirlwind of his gentleness and tenderness, drawing in those who are confused and downhearted and transforming the chaos into the peace of God.

Jesus of patience, help us live a life of readiness, always aware of your divine moments. Give us courage to show joy amid the storms of life, attract others to our open door of your love, and always be prepared to share the gospel. Please keep us strong, courageous, and moving forward toward your path of light in this world of darkness.

Scan To Branch Out

Let's Be Heaven's Ambassadors

SCRIPTURE WHISPER

"They will rise again. Those who have done good will rise to experience eternal life, and those who have continued in evil will rise to experience judgment."

JOHN 5:29 NLT

There is a time coming when everyone who has lived with the heart of Jesus will walk out into an eternal resurrection in heaven. Those who have lived according to evil will be thrown into the lake of fire, into an eternal condemnation and judgment. Eternal life is available only through Jesus, and there are no exceptions. Whether people experience eternal life or condemnation depends entirely on their response to Jesus in this life.

If we live in relationship with Jesus, we will be known by our fruit and will do good things, reflecting his character because of our love for him, and we will be destined for eternal life. Those who do not follow Jesus will do wicked things, allowing Satan to rule their ways, and they will live in eternal condemnation unless they believe and repent. Let's be ambassadors of influence into heaven.

Jesus of kindness, we surrender our lives to you so we can influence others to yearn for you as their Lord. May we show the way to peace and joy amid the storms raging in these troubled days.

Scan To Branch Out

Let's Leave Judgment to God

SCRIPTURE WHISPER

"I can do nothing on my own. I judge as God tells me.
Therefore, my judgment is just, because I carry out the will
of the one who sent me, not my own will."
JOHN 5:30 NLT

We are often quick to judge others and conjure assumptions
about them with no knowledge of their past journey or
current reality. Our Scripture Whisper tells us that Jesus
allowed his Father to carry out judgment. We should do
the same as we have the same Father. Jesus told us that he
does everything in conjunction with his Father, who sees all.
When we surrender our all to our Father, he promises that
greater works in us are to come.

As God's children, it is foolish to do a single thing on
our own. We should learn the art of pausing to take all
things to God for clarity and direction and let him decide.
We don't know others' past, the heartaches of their lifelong
journey, or the wounds that are deep within them, but God
does. Let's leave judgment to him.

Jesus of goodness, give us hearts to do nothing on our own,
not allowing Satan to interfere. Guide us to relinquish our
thoughts, our words, our actions, our reactions, and our
judgment to you.

Let's Be Jesus' Healing Vessel

SCRIPTURE WHISPER

"It is not the healthy who need a doctor, but the sick."
LUKE 5:31 NIV

Too often, we get comfortable until someone walks into our lives who is sick in spirit, hardened of heart, and utterly without hope. They have words and comments that don't meet our criteria of a Jesus follower. We become uncomfortable and often judgmental, and we ignore their wounds because we're too complacent to go deep with them. But what would Jesus do? We should seek to minister to those who are hurting and lost just as Jesus did.

The deepest parts of one's heart and soul rise into their thoughts and determine their behavior, based either on God's truth or the lies of Satan. We must be mindful of those who live in a sea of hopelessness instead of reflecting the fruit of Jesus' Spirit. Extending a branch to hope in imitation of Jesus leads us into the divine appointments he arranges for each of us every day.

Jesus of faithfulness, heal the sick in spirit through our lives. May we administer the anointing of your love, grace, and forgiveness by the way we live.

Scan To Branch Out

June

Let's Restore with Gentleness

SCRIPTURE WHISPER

Brothers, if anyone is caught in any transgression, you who are spiritual should restore him in a spirit of gentleness. Keep watch on yourself, lest you too be tempted.

GALATIANS 6:1 ESV

Sin is real, rampant, and deadly, and we are to draw others out of the darkness and into God's light of eternity in heaven. Sadly, we've become complacent due to the fear of being branded as judgmental and self-righteous, so we fail to reach those trapped in the vortex of sin, which leads to their spiritual death.

When we see someone who is suffering in a sea of hardship, we may take the attitude that they deserve the harvest they've sown and should have made better choices. However, we should show empathy as we acknowledge the goodness, kindness, forgiveness, and gentleness of God toward us and extend to others that branch to hope, compassion, and tenderness.

Jesus of gentleness, help our hearts to be grieved by the gravity of sin's effects and to be stirred into action to help gently restore those whom it has trapped. You suffered in agony so that we could stand before you sinless and live with you for eternity in heaven. Ignite our hearts to share your living gospel. Let us never miss an opportunity.

Scan To Branch Out

Let's Live Gospel Truth

SCRIPTURE WHISPER

God says, "At just the right time, I heard you. On the day of salvation, I helped you." Indeed, the "right time" is now. Today is the day of salvation.

2 CORINTHIANS 6:2 NLT

Our lifestyle should represent the light of Jesus, the evidence of his sacrifice, and the transformation of our hearts so others will know us through the fruit of his Spirit. One way to demonstrate God's transforming work in our lives is prayer. The power of prayer with bold expectancy gets attention because it shows others that we trust God to answer us.

We must also emphasize and model the power of Jesus' character so his light illuminates and diminishes the darkness that prevails across our land. It is God's plan that we ignite a movement by encouraging others to share the vital importance of salvation in these last days. Let us be mindful and devoted. He calls us to reach the lost by the way we live in his peace and joy amid the chaos.

Jesus of self-control, help us walk in your favor, which is the evidence of our salvation for others to grasp hold of in troubling days. Let us do all you created and designed for us to fulfill. Thank you for equipping us to draw others into your kingdom from the divine moments you arrange throughout our day.

Scan To Branch Out

Let's See through Jesus' Eyes

SCRIPTURE WHISPER

They scoffed, "He's just a carpenter, the son of Mary and the brother of James, Joseph, Judas, and Simon. And his sisters live right here among us." They were deeply offended and refused to believe in him.

MARK 6:3 NLT

Too often, people see aspects of our past and define us based on who we were, what we did, how we spoke, and how we reacted, which may be far from who we are today. We are all guilty of seeing people as they once were and assuming things about them. Satan wants us to see imperfections in others and ourselves and to be blinded to the perfection Jesus sees in his children. Rather than condemning us for our past, the Lord uses our past to change us into the person he created us to be.

We have free will and fail daily, which Satan exploits. Still, the offenses of our wayward choices were washed white as snow at the cross. Jesus tenderly guides us back onto the path of his plan, seeing us through his lens of perfection.

Jesus of love, help us put on holy spectacles and see others as you do by giving grace to those who are in the process of transformation. Help us influence them by our lifestyle and see them through your eyes as they are today, not as they were yesterday.

Scan To Branch Out

Let's Share the Reasons for Jesus

SCRIPTURE WHISPER

It is impossible to bring back to repentance those who were once enlightened—those who have experienced the good things of heaven and shared in the Holy Spirit.

HEBREWS 6:4 NLT

We all have questions about those who profess to believe in Jesus but don't display any fruit. If we don't see fruit in our lives, we need to go to the Father and examine the sincerity of our hearts. When one's heart is truly transformed by the overpowering, unconditional love of Jesus, one's desires change, as evidenced by the way they live, rejecting worldly ways and negative vocabulary. At salvation, the condition of one's heart is transformed, and it desires to please God from pure love, not from works or phony facades.

We are to be empty vessels for Jesus to draw lost souls into a clearer understanding of what living apart from him truly means. Satan's evil ways only lead to eternal destruction. Instead, Jesus calls us to attract people toward his immovable love.

Jesus of joy, we ask for discernment to be on guard for wolves in sheep's clothing. Make us aware of how they attempt to involve themselves in our lives, pretending to be of you while manipulating us into aligning with a worldly culture. Protect us, Lord, and help us be your light.

Let's Find Quiet

SCRIPTURE WHISPER

Love the LORD your God with all your heart, with all your soul, and with all your strength.

DEUTERONOMY 6:5 GW

Moses called the Israelites to take notice of the greatest and most important commandments. When he declared the words from our Scripture Whisper to the Israelites, he expressed the vital importance of understanding that their focus should remain on the love of the Lord so they could survive in the wilderness as they headed toward the promised land.

Today, it seems we are wandering around in the wilderness of confusion and despair, much like the Israelites. Even more so, we should remain focused and dependent on our Lord, who will lead our way through troubled times. We must seek an atmosphere of quiet to express our love to God with all our heart and strength. Our faithful expression of love by the way we live is pleasing to Jesus, and following the direction for which he has designed us thrills his heart.

Jesus of peace, we are grateful that you never fail to shower on us your unfathomable love. Please help us return this blessing of your tender love by seeking your continuous presence so we can express to you our love and share it with others by the way we interact with them.

Let's Not Be People Pleasers

SCRIPTURE WHISPER

[Obey] not like those who do their work only when someone is watching—as people-pleasers—but as slaves of Christ doing the will of God from the heart.

EPHESIANS 6:6 NET

Too often, we get caught up in people pleasing, a form of idolatry. Our focus should be on pleasing God, not people. Of course, we want to be favorably accepted in the eyes of others, but their approval is often fleeting. As we emulate the character of Jesus, we are pleasing in his sight. In God alone can we find our secure identity and purpose.

Let's pause and evaluate with transparency the purity of our hearts and why we do what we do. Is it to feel good about ourselves, to impress someone else, or to check it off our do-good list? Do we seek to do as little as possible, putting on a show to appear to be doing more than we are? And what is our character when we feel no one is watching, even though Jesus is? It is the attitude of our heart that determines our character.

Jesus of patience, help us refine our motives by focusing on living in your ways, pleasing you with our whole hearts, purely, with no condition or expectation in return.

Scan To Branch Out

Let's Sow and Reap

SCRIPTURE WHISPER

Don't be deceived. God is not mocked, for whatever a man sows, that he will also reap.

GALATIANS 6:7 WEB

The more time we season our hearts for the service of others through our love and devotion to Jesus, the more our life will gain meaning. The seeds planted will harvest blessings for both the receiver and us as the giver. Whether it be good or bad, whether generously or sparingly, our sowing will come back to us. It's vain to think the outcome of bad choices will result in something good, and this thinking mocks God, the knower of all things.

When we allow our passions and appetites to follow corrupt desires or we are temporarily gratified and indulge in worldly ways for satisfaction, convenience, or pleasure, that behavior leads to destruction and affects everyone along the way. But those of us who follow the guidance of Jesus' Spirit, live under the influence of God, and devote our resources to planting seeds for the glory of God will reap mightily from our gifting and talents.

Jesus of kindness, we pray to become more aware of how we sow and to tailor our sowing based on the example of Jesus and in the ways God intended for us to reap a harvest for his kingdom.

Let's Be Assured That He Knows

SCRIPTURE WHISPER

Do not be like them, for your Father knows what you need before you ask him.

MATTHEW 6:8 ESV

When we are aligned in a personal relationship with Jesus and our desires align with his desires, we can count on him to be devoted to our needs because he knows them before we even ask. It's a dialogue between us that he longs for. The purpose of his agonizing suffering and death on the cross was to live in a relationship with us each day. He wants to keep the communication channel open as if we were spending the day with our best friend. He longs to be our very best friend, one whom we turn to in every circumstance throughout our day.

As we open our Bible, God wants to be our counselor, and he longs for us to depend on him as our navigator and our master scheduler. For us to live in a relationship with almighty God is his ultimate desire and our greatest blessing. We get to live alongside the one who knows the future and wants the best for his kids on earth while we await our destiny in heaven.

Jesus of goodness, you know our needs before we ask, and for that gift, we are grateful.

Let's Not Grow Weary

SCRIPTURE WHISPER

Let us not grow weary in well-doing, for in due time we will reap a harvest if we do not give up.

GALATIANS 6:9 BSB

It's easy for Christ followers to become discouraged, weary, and worn. Life can beat us down, and we can face resistance and opposition even when we do good. It often feels like our diligent effort is spinning a wheel for nothing. Growing weary of doing good is a concern in a believer's life.

Though it might seem like our good works are done in vain, they aren't. Jesus is behind the scenes orchestrating and arranging things for our good and his glory. But we often jump in his way by becoming weary and stopping the motion. We live in a culture of instant results with expectations of immediate satisfaction all at our fingertips. But the reality is that a planted seed doesn't grow overnight. That's when our faith gets stretched and we learn to let God be God in his perfect timing. God has designed life this way. By waiting for his proper time, we will reap a harvest.

Jesus of faithfulness, we are grateful for clear direction inspired by you throughout your Word, which gives us a precise road map to follow your carefully designed path. In your strength, we should never grow weary.

Scan To Branch Out

Let's Build Our Strength in Jesus

SCRIPTURE WHISPER

Build up your strength in union with the Lord and by means of his mighty power.

Ephesians 6:10 GNT

When we feel weak, we are strong in Jesus if we dress in a covering of his anointing daily. Spiritual warfare surrounds us, creating discord and conflict and division in even the closest relationships, but Jesus died so the forces of heavenly angels can fight the battles for us when we let them. Victory is guaranteed, so we are never to feel weak, unworthy, or ill-equipped. It's not us. It's Jesus living within us in unity.

Our job is to be empty, willing vessels and to clothe ourselves in righteousness, doing our part to refer to God's life manual, his Word, and to remain in constant communication with God in prayer. He will direct our every moment when we ask him.

Jesus of gentleness, as your children, we are no longer weak as our strength is in you. We ask that we never fail to clothe ourselves in your ways of right living, emulating the fruit of your Spirit. Please help us be known by your goodness and grace and immeasurable strength living through us.

Scan To Branch Out

Let's Keep Loving Others

SCRIPTURE WHISPER

Our great desire is that you will keep on loving others as long as life lasts, in order to make certain that what you hope for will come true.

HEBREWS 6:11 NLT

God's purpose is to transform his children into the likeness of Jesus so God can use us for his design here on earth, which is for us to love others as he loves us. Our usefulness matters and increases as we navigate through the trials in this earthly journey. As we grow in spiritual maturity, God can use us to attract others to Jesus as the only way to eternity and to help others develop a personal relationship with him. The way we love others can show them his unconditional love.

While we are becoming useful for God's work through us, he is behind the scenes preparing for things he has in store for us in this life and the life to come. Our earthly journey requires faithfulness and patience while waiting for his perfect plan to unfold in his perfect timing. That's when our faith is stretched and our love becomes purer. He's got our back and will never leave our side or forsake us as we keep on loving others.

Jesus of self-control, you tell us to love others as a demonstration of your love, pure and unconditional. Help us love like you.

Scan To Branch Out

Let's Value the Gift of Prayer

SCRIPTURE WHISPER

At that time Jesus went up a hill to pray and spent the whole night there praying to God.

LUKE 6:12 GNT

Prayer is the most vital gift, a cherished blessing, that enables us to talk to the creator of the universe at any hour, like Jesus did. God our Father devotes his undivided attention to each of his children when we approach him in prayer to converse about the things on our hearts: our regrets, our shame, our despair, our joys, and times when our hearts feel grateful for his many blessings. We can visit with God anytime.

Jesus, God's Son, felt a need to go off alone and share in quiet communion with his Father, apart from the hustle of life. We should do likewise and intentionally schedule quiet, meaningful times to visit with the Master. In the meantime, amid the noise and busyness of life, we can talk with God all day long. He will devote his attention to anyone who calls him up for a chat. He always cherishes hearing from his children even if only in our thoughts or for a few quick words.

Jesus of love, help us not take for granted this enormous gift of twenty-four seven communication with you.

Let's Close Temptation's Door

SCRIPTURE WHISPER

"Don't let us yield to temptation,
but rescue us from the evil one."
MATTHEW 6:13 NLT

God is not the one who tempts us. It's Satan. That's his evil mission. Jesus suffered in agony to wipe away our sins. The least we can do is to be aware when the temptations lurk. We know our hot buttons, and Satan knows our open doors and vulnerable areas that offer him the opportunity to tempt us too. Do we turn to God, who is right by our side, and slam shut the door that Satan is trying to enter? It's our choice.

When we make a conscious effort to live the fruit of Jesus' Spirit, we set up a barrier against Satan's interferences. When we reflect Jesus' character and cling to God's presence, Satan cannot find an entrance to tempt us. Let's remain on alert for the areas of temptation. When we continually communicate with Jesus in prayer, chatting with him on our spiritual cell phone—our Bible—we exude an enhanced vibrancy from being in the presence of Jesus.

Jesus of joy, thank you for the victory in our moments of temptation when we turn our vulnerable places to you.

Scan To Branch Out

Let's Forgive to Be Forgiven

SCRIPTURE WHISPER

If you forgive others for the wrongs they do to you,
your Father in heaven will forgive you.
MATTHEW 6:14 CEV

Forgiveness is the key to life. Jesus Christ, our Savior, has thoroughly forgiven us. How can we not forgive others when we have been forgiven and washed clean of our past, present, and future sins in the eyes of God? God no longer sees the times when we followed Satan instead of allowing God to lead our lives.

A crafty tool of Satan is to instill a spirit of unforgiveness deep within our soul, creating division in our relationships. It's our choice to stay in bondage from someone else's behavior or to be set free by forgiving through the love of Jesus. Unforgiveness is like locking ourselves up in jail while those whom we have not forgiven hold the key. When we find ourselves with an unforgiving heart, we must love and forgive others through Jesus' heart. That's the only way our hearts can be softened and forgive in many heart-wrenching circumstances.

Jesus of peace, search us and reveal any unforgiveness within our hearts. Please help us forgive through your unconditional love, which releases the stronghold and bondage of an unforgiving spirit. Help us discover freedom and peace in forgiveness.

Scan To Branch Out

Let's Learn to Wait Patiently

SCRIPTURE WHISPER

Having patiently endured, he obtained the promise.

HEBREWS 6:15 WEB

Our faith journey is about waiting. But often, we blame God for the wait and question his timing when he is waiting on us or others to shift into alignment with the plan he has for us. God gave us free will, and Satan is working every moment to bend our choices toward his evil ways.

Often, we question what would have happened if we had done this or not done that. We can't unring the bell or create a do-over, but we can learn from the choices that were not of God. We can prevent many if-only moments in our lives by making choices in alignment with God. So pointing the finger at God because his timing seems too long is pointing the finger in the wrong direction. We should point in our own direction and at those around us who are preventing God's plan from unfolding. If we wait on God's timing, Scripture assures us that we will obtain God's promised blessings.

Jesus of patience, help us temper our patience, knowing you are just waiting for us all to shift into alignment so that you can move mountains as we boldly and expectantly pray.

Scan To Branch Out

Let's Make Our Faith Our Shield

SCRIPTURE WHISPER

Let your faith be like a shield, and you will be able to stop all the flaming arrows of the evil one.

EPHESIANS 6:16 CEV

What is faith? It's knowing that God is telling the truth and will fulfill what he promised, being obedient to him, and trusting him in every situation we encounter. No matter the temptation Satan throws at us, we can overcome it by activating our faith, trusting that God's promises will become a reality in his perfect way and perfect timing, believing in God's Word, and acting on our belief.

The arrows Satan attempts to throw at the target to try to interrupt God's plan cannot reach the bull's-eye if we have the shield of faith, God's Word, to throw off the flaming arrows. We gain victory in Jesus.

Jesus of kindness, you give us many promises throughout your Word. Help us become intentional about engraving your Scripture on our hearts to be our shield of faith as we boldly and expectantly come to you in prayer. When Satan attempts to interrupt your perfect plan, please equip us for combat. Help us recall your words so that we can divert the flaming arrows and gain victory in your glory.

Scan To Branch Out

Let's Use the Armor of God

SCRIPTURE WHISPER

Take the helmet of salvation, and the sword of the Spirit, which is the Word of God.

EPHESIANS 6:17 AMP

A helmet protects our mind, our central control center. Our spiritual helmet protects our thoughts and patterns of thinking. We must intentionally be saturated in God's Word so that our thoughts are protected. We must choose to think of God's wisdom to shield ourselves from acting on human foolishness stemming from corrupt knowledge.

The sword of the Spirit, the Word of God, is the only offensive weapon in our arsenal, effective because it cuts through Satan's lies. Speaking the Word of God can remind us of the truth and power of God, who defeats the evil forces. As children and ambassadors of Christ, we must learn to use the Bible as our weapon against Satan just as Jesus did when Satan tempted him in the wilderness. Jesus said, "It is written: Man must not live on bread alone but on every word that comes from the mouth of God" (Matthew 4:4 CSB).

Jesus of goodness, because of the sword of your Spirit, your Word, we have a defense readily available to combat the snares of the evil forces. Help us do our part to gain victory in your power, being worthy and equipped to encourage and influence others into your kingdom.

Scan To Branch Out

Let's Pray Persistently

SCRIPTURE WHISPER

Pray in the Spirit at all times and on every occasion. Stay alert and be persistent in your prayers for all believers everywhere.

Ephesians 6:18 NLT

Praying in the Spirit invites God to align our prayers with his heart. Talking with the Lord transforms our desires to be without selfishness or hypocrisy but with passionate enthusiasm. Under the influence of the Holy Spirit, we can be woven into God's majestic plan. We pray in all sorts of ways: in our thoughts, verbally in a group or public arena, or aloud in private. We pray for petitions and in praise of his mercy and grace. Prayer should be continual, chatting with Jesus throughout our day, just as we would our best friend, as he surely should be.

Let's pray for those who don't pray at all or who pray only 911 prayers in times of desperate need and distress. Prayer is a privilege that came with a heavy price: Jesus' death for our sins so that we can live in a relationship with him. We should pray as often as we have an opportunity, even under our breath. He hears that too.

Jesus of faithfulness, help us surrender our moments in prayer with your Holy Spirit, aligning our desires with yours and attracting others into your presence by our devotion to prayer.

Let's Accumulate Eternal Treasure

SCRIPTURE WHISPER

"Do not accumulate for yourselves treasures on earth, where moth and devouring insect destroy and where thieves break in and steal."

MATTHEW 6:19 NET

We have all accumulated lots of stuff over our lifetime. In comparison, how many lives have we influenced into the kingdom of God? Our treasures of stuff here on earth can be destroyed and will fade away. We can't take a U-Haul to heaven! But sharing the gospel by the way we live, planting seeds of hope for the hopeless, will accumulate treasures in heaven, and we will be greeted by a host of believers who will say that God used us to show them that Jesus saves.

It takes energy and resources to reach the lost with the gospel of Jesus. The return on the investment of saved lives is far more valuable than our earthly treasures. Let's evaluate the fruit we have accumulated. Do we have more stuff than lives influenced toward Jesus? Let's pray that Jesus directs our path when we feel the urge to accumulate more stuff rather than investing in something far more valuable, the kingdom of God.

Jesus of gentleness, help us do our part and listen to your voice as it guides us to accumulate heavenly treasure instead of stuff.

Let's Be Ambassadors for Jesus

SCRIPTURE WHISPER

I am in chains now, still preaching this message as God's ambassador. So pray that I will keep on speaking boldly for him, as I should.

EPHESIANS 6:20 NLT

No matter how bound we are to things of this world, we are to be ambassadors for Jesus. God works through us and calls us to embrace the opportunities he creates to showcase his miraculous power, attracting others into his kingdom. We should be a magnet for others by how we live in the lifestyle of Jesus, in his tenderness and goodness.

We should be intentionally committed to the task of being an ambassador of Jesus' voice by being his gentle Spirit in harsh situations, speaking peace when there is turmoil, and declaring self-control when we are tempted to indulge ourselves. Let's never fail to do all the things he arranges before us.

Jesus of self-control, our unique mission on earth is by your design. You created and set us apart individually to be your ambassadors as you weave our lives together in the divine moments you arrange. Please help us take this responsibility more seriously, seeking never to miss an opportunity to be your example or to draw others into a personal relationship with you, Lord.

Let's Evaluate Our Treasures

SCRIPTURE WHISPER

Where your treasure is, there your heart [your wishes, your desires; that on which your life centers] will be also.
MATTHEW 6:21 AMP

Where are our treasures? If God is the treasure of our souls, hearts, and affections, then our desires will be placed on things above. An earthly minded man proves his treasure is temporary; a heavenly minded man shows that he finds his treasure is in God alone. Jesus blesses us to be a blessing, and we have the option to use our blessings and provisions to promote worldly things or to expand the kingdom of God.

God intends for us to enjoy life on earth. Still, there's a priority and a balance that God's children should embrace to align our hearts and partner with Jesus. Let's pause and evaluate how we might channel our treasures toward the things that matter. Lives are far more valuable than material accumulation, offering much more satisfaction at the end of every day.

Jesus of love, please help us pause and evaluate what matters. Lost souls matter more than things of temporal value. May we strive to store up a heavenly wealth of saved lives to join us in heaven. Please help us center our wishes and desires and the condition of our hearts toward your treasures.

Scan To Branch Out

Let's Let God Be God

SCRIPTURE WHISPER

"What blessings await you when people hate you and exclude you and mock you and curse you as evil because you follow the Son of Man."
LUKE 6:22 NLT

While on the cross for each of us, Jesus endured the sufferings described in our Scripture Whisper. Jesus took on our sins so we could be in the presence of God and enter a personal relationship with him. This is the reason God sacrificed his only Son.

Have you ever noticed that certain people don't warm up to us, shy away, or distance themselves before they really know us? Often, our lives serve as reminders to others of what they are not and what they missed out on becoming. But we should not become discouraged. The truth is that not everyone will accept Christ, even when we model Jesus in our lives. We are called to live in the character of Jesus and then pray that their hearts will be transformed. God can change the way people see us. He can do all things. Nothing is impossible with our Lord.

Jesus of joy, help us stand strong, never waver, and never miss an opportunity to let you be God in our lives.

Scan To Branch Out

Let's Be the Lamp of Jesus

SCRIPTURE WHISPER

The Law of the Lord is a lamp, and its teachings shine brightly. Correction and self-control will lead you through life.
PROVERBS 6:23 CEV

The Word of God is full of instructions to correct us, to keep us from harm, to refine us, and to equip us for what he has designed for each of us that no one else can fulfill. A lamp cannot shine until a light bulb is placed in its socket. In the same way, we cannot demonstrate the characteristics of Jesus until we fill ourselves with his teachings from God's Word and learn what it is to be like Jesus.

Even with a light bulb, a lamp emits no light until we plug it into electricity. Likewise, the Holy Spirit ignites the teachings we receive from God's Word as we seek to hear his voice of direction and guidance along his divinely orchestrated pathway. Even so, a lamp with a light bulb plugged into electricity still does not shine unless we turn it on. Similarly, the Holy Spirit lives within us and through us, enabling us to put into action the teachings we read in God's words.

Jesus of peace, remind us to turn on our lamps each morning, illuminating a path to your light living through us.

Let's Embrace Our Blessings

SCRIPTURE WHISPER

"The LORD bless you and keep you."
NUMBERS 6:24 ESV

There's value in passing along a quick "God bless you" as we journey through the day. It's an opportunity to share God's blessings of grace, showered in great measure upon those he divinely arranges for us to encounter. God loves to bless his people and has promised his peace, guidance, and protection over all who are his. He calls us as his ambassadors to bring him our prayers on behalf of his people; we get to be God's conduits of blessings.

We are to be an example and evidence of God's amazing grace manifested throughout our lives. As we extend prayers of blessings and grace on those we encounter, we pass along God's blessing. God loves to bless his people, but he also wants his people to call on him to ask for his blessings and share them with others. Let's be more intentional in passing along God's blessings as he prompts us daily.

Jesus of patience, help us be mindful of your whisper into the depths of our souls by prompting us to share your goodness in the way we mirror your example, blessing others to also be a blessing.

Scan To Branch Out

Let's Share Jesus' Smile

SCRIPTURE WHISPER

"May the LORD smile on you and be gracious to you."
NUMBERS 6:25 NLT

These are beautiful words to cling to today. What does it mean to be gracious? It is having divine grace. And what is grace? The free and unmerited favor of God. And what is favor? An act of kindness beyond what is deserved. It's up to us not to allow a cloud of separation to diminish Jesus' radiant smile on us. However, Satan works his trickery to create a barrier to God's goodness and graciousness by interfering in our lives, seeping in evil thoughts of unworthiness when our guard is down, and attempting to deflect the ways of our Lord.

When obtaining a PhD, one diligently devotes years to research and study, absorbing the subject to become more proficient in a particular field. Likewise, when we saturate ourselves in the Word of God, we learn his ways and become more proficient in discerning his voice. Then we become keenly aware of the camouflage of Satan as we recognize more clearly the voice of God.

Jesus of kindness, help us be pleasing to you in all our ways so your face shines upon us and your tender, gentle smile beaming through us draws others into your presence and toward a life everlasting with you in heaven.

Let's Cast Our Cares on Jesus

SCRIPTURE WHISPER

"Look at the birds in the sky: They do not sow, or reap, or gather into barns, yet your heavenly Father feeds them. Aren't you more valuable than they are?"

MATTHEW 6:26 NET

Our Scripture Whisper today reminds us that we should never worry about any details when we invite Jesus to navigate the moments of our lives. Since he cares about feeding the smallest bird, how much more is he concerned about providing our every need? We are his chosen ambassadors, vessels for him to make a difference through our lives. May we share the gospel by the way we live, magnetically drawing others to his kingdom to join us in his heavenly home.

Let's intentionally commit any sign of worry to the care of Jesus since God asks us to cast our cares on him. He cares for us, and that includes all our worries too. He already has every detail of our lives planned. Everything is all part of God's design when we get out of the way and let God be God.

Jesus of goodness, deafen our ears to worrisome thoughts and instead remind us to give our cares to you because you provide for all our needs.

Let's Seek God's Approval

SCRIPTURE WHISPER

"Don't be so concerned about perishable things like food. Spend your energy seeking the eternal life that the Son of Man can give you. For God the Father has given me the seal of his approval."

JOHN 6:27 NLT

How are we spending our time and our money? Is it on worldly accumulations so we leave behind an overabundant inheritance that may be squandered? Instead we could use our time and resources to share the gospel of Jesus. Are we missing opportunities? Are we blessed with skills and provisions to be a blessing? Are we listening to God's nudge? Are we more engaged in worldly and mindless activities, spending our energy on things that bring no hope to the hopeless?

Jesus blesses us to be a blessing, and we have many choices throughout the day, such as whether to be self-focused or to be focused on making a difference in others' lives. Changing one life at a time can change a legacy as Jesus weaves lives into the tapestry of his plan. Let's live for God's seal of approval.

Jesus of faithfulness, please help us assess how we use our time, energy, and resources. Help us never miss an opportunity you arrange before us each day.

Let's Love When It's Not Easy

SCRIPTURE WHISPER

"Bless those who curse you, pray for those who mistreat you."
LUKE 6:28 NIV

Who can do what our Scripture Whisper for today advises?
No one I know can bless those who curse them and pray
for those who mistreat them without Jesus' unconditional,
immeasurable love.

As Christ's followers, we are distinguished from the
rest of the world because we have different values that are
based on God's standards, the fruit of Jesus' Spirit. We are
to love our enemies, do good to those who hate us, and pray
for those who mistreat us. We are warriors against Satan,
responding with blessings and generosity rather than cursing
and retaliation. We are to love those who don't love us with
a thirst to bring those who are lost and confused to the
knowledge of God's love through Jesus.

Jesus of gentleness, help us not to judge others by their finite
standards of the world but to love them in their frailty as we
see them through your eyes. May we faithfully fulfill all that
you have designed for us and be a delight of your heart.

Scan To Branch Out

Let's Share Our Belief in Jesus

SCRIPTURE WHISPER

Jesus told them, "This is the only work God wants from you: Believe in the one he has sent."

JOHN 6:29 NLT

To prompt Jesus' response in our Scripture Whisper today, someone in the crowd asked him what we must do to do the works God requires. Jesus replied that we should believe in the one sent by our Father, God, creator of heaven and earth. We can believe with our minds, but we must genuinely believe with our lives so that our spirit reflects the purity of our belief. We must show proof of our understanding of Jesus' sacrifice to reveal our overwhelming gratefulness for the gift of salvation—that we can be in the presence of almighty God—and the gift of walking beside Jesus, hand in hand, in a personal relationship together.

The evidence of the depth of our belief and involvement in seeking to be God's daily ambassadors to the hopeless and lost will be the fruit our lives reap. Let's strive each day to more intentionally live in tandem with Jesus.

Jesus of self-control, help us, as your ambassadors, to share that the only way to salvation is found in you.

Scan To Branch Out

Let's Not Worry

SCRIPTURE WHISPER

God gives such beauty to everything that grows in the fields, even though it is here today and thrown into a fire tomorrow. God will surely do even more for you! Why do you have such little faith?

MATTHEW 6:30 CEV

Birds don't worry about where they will get their next meal; our heavenly Father feeds them. So when we hear the beautiful melody of the birds and see them flying through the air, let's remember not to worry. God provides the grass of the fields like a luscious carpet over the earth. Every time we see a new birth of green grass in the spring and inhale the fragrance of fresh-cut lawns, let's remember not to worry. Flowers don't agonize to look pretty, but not even Solomon in all his splendor could match the beauty in the fields of God's creation (v. 29). When we catch the fragrance of flowers and see their lovely colors, let's remember not to worry.

If God provides so lavishly for birds and grass and flowers, why should we ever worry? Won't God do much more for us, his children? Handling the worries of the day is God's job. Our job is to believe that he has everything arranged.

Jesus of love, how can we ever doubt that you will be there for us in every capacity. Strengthen our faith in you.

Scan To Branch Out

July

Let's Not Be Judgmental

SCRIPTURE WHISPER

"Don't judge, so that you won't be judged."
MATTHEW 7:1 WEB

Judgmental people seem to find no problems with their own behavior because when sinners create a standard, they tend to become the standard. Those who hypocritically judge others use their own standard instead of God's standard. Judgmental people fail to realize the boomerang effects of their judgments. They, too, will be judged by their standards, as the same measuring stick they use against others will be used against them. There's truth in the saying "What goes around comes around."

Instead of judging others, Scripture says to let God do the judging. His standards are based on truth with compassion and grace to better equip those who are willing to be taught how to rise from their shortcomings. If we are true to ourselves and honest, we will realize that we fall short every day and have no room to judge others. Satan's lure to judge can destroy relationships and further division in the world. When we admit our sin, we will become more understanding and compassionate toward others and let God do the judging.

Jesus of joy, help us show self-control when we are tempted to judge others or questionable situations, leaving the judging to you.

Scan To Branch Out

Let's Discover the Bible

SCRIPTURE WHISPER

Keep my commands and you will live; guard my teachings as the apple of your eye.

PROVERBS 7:2 NIV

The insight, wisdom, and teachings from God's Word are like discovering a treasure chest of gold nuggets. But how often do we stumble over this gift he provides for us every day? The Bible should become not just a top priority but also part of who we are and what we do. We should carefully keep God's commandments that he provided for our well-being, safety, and protection, just like the rules parents provide for their children.

Our Scripture Whisper asks us to see God's ways through the lens of our hearts, living the fruit of Jesus' character through our lifestyle and guarding his teachings as the apple of our eyes. These nuggets of wisdom should be a reminder to make God's Word part of our everyday lives. Scripture is our divine road map toward the life God created us to live. We should write God's words of instructions on the tablets of our hearts.

Jesus of peace, help us weave your Word into our conversation and put into action your instructions, encouraging others to realize your Word is a cherished treasure to never take for granted, a remedy of hope for the hopeless and brokenhearted.

Let's Be Remolded

SCRIPTURE WHISPER

"Why worry about a speck in your friend's eye when you have a log in your own?"
MATTHEW 7:3 NLT

Imagine straining to see a speck in another's eye while ignoring the log protruding from our own eye! Jesus has a way of getting our attention, doesn't he? He was not saying we shouldn't help others when they fall short and need help—that's what Christian fellowship is, the true meaning of the love of Jesus toward others. What Jesus meant is that we must evaluate our own flaws, living in the character of Jesus, before we correct others.

We must be willing to hop on the potter's wheel to be remolded into the person God created, mended from the brokenness that is the effect of life. This remolding is not easy and comes with pain as we are equipped for all God has in store for us to fulfill in his great plan. But this process prepares us with more understanding, gentle compassion, and kindness, allowing us to extend a branch to hope to others.

Jesus of patience, help us take the time to analyze our willingness to be remolded and equipped to be all you desire us to be as your ambassadors for the lost and hopeless.

Let's Renounce Foolishness

SCRIPTURE WHISPER

The heart of the wise is in the house of mourning, but the heart of fools is in the house of pleasure.

ECCLESIASTES 7:4 NIV

Nobody wants grief, and if given a choice, we often choose foolish things to avoid feeling grieved. When we choose to avoid pain and grief, we're escaping the realities of life. There are things we must face that bring us grief, but the wisdom we gain in those lessons of pain far outweigh the foolishness of resisting these inevitable situations. Instead, facing our grief allows us to obtain the truth and wisdom to equip us through life.

If we foolishly continue to chase after worldly pleasures, our souls will become numb and accustomed to avoiding the reality of life. God intended for us to experience pure pleasures of life, those of value, those that truly matter. Living along the path of God's wisdom is what our souls need to be truly satisfied. We must set our priorities on the foundation of God's many promises. That's putting foolishness in its place, a wise way of living.

Jesus of kindness, we pray for an insatiable appetite for your wisdom to take over any foolishness that lingers in our lives. Please guide us to wisely live the fruit of your Spirit daily.

Scan To Branch Out

Let's Listen to Wisdom

SCRIPTURE WHISPER

It is better to listen to a wise person's rebuke than to listen to the praise of fools.

ECCLESIASTES 7:5 ISV

Why would we want to listen to a rebuke over praise, as our Scripture Whisper describes today? The value of each type of speech is determined by the source, the counsel from a wise person or the folly of a fool. We must listen carefully for the wise voice of truth instead of the melody of a fool.

Scripture tells us that wisdom is found when we not only know what is right but also act on that knowledge. Foolishness, on the other hand, means a lack of understanding and a failure to act on the prompting of God's voice of wisdom. God breathed his words of wisdom in Scripture and preserved them for us today. Just like we eat food to sustain our lives each day, it is our responsibility to partake of the morsels of wisdom we need to navigate life and share with those whom Jesus arranges for us to feed. Foolishness cannot survive in an atmosphere of God's wisdom.

Jesus of goodness, we seek your wisdom each day to set our feet toward the divine appointments you have already arranged for our days ahead.

Let's Be Holy

SCRIPTURE WHISPER

"You are a holy people, who belong to the LORD your God. Of all the people on earth, the LORD your God has chosen you to be his own special treasure."

DEUTERONOMY 7:6 NLT

The Lord is a holy God. Therefore, his people must live a life of holiness. But some of the messages from Christians to the world today are tainted, tarnished, and confusing, which gives the world a distorted view of what true believers are all about. Too many consider holiness as goody-goody, boring, and void of fun, as if walking in a defeated posture, but that's far from the truth.

People look to believers to see who Jesus is. And that's all holiness is, living alongside Jesus, who leads the way. Believers demonstrate love to the unlovable, joy in difficulties, peace in chaos, patience when tempers rise, kindness when treated poorly, goodness when wronged, faithfulness when betrayed, gentleness in response to harsh words, and self-control when tempted to indulge or seek instant gratification. That's living in holiness as God's chosen people.

Jesus of faithfulness, help us become more aware that our lifestyle demonstrates who you are. Help us become more intentional about representing you with the purity of your character, genuinely spreading the fruit of your Spirit everywhere we go.

Scan To Branch Out

Let's Ask with Expectation

SCRIPTURE WHISPER

"Keep on asking, and you will receive what you ask for. Keep on seeking, and you will find. Keep on knocking, and the door will be opened to you."

MATTHEW 7:7 NLT

Children are masters at persistence when asking for gifts before their birthday. It becomes a pattern of expectation in their little minds for years to come.

Why don't we look at the power of prayer that way? We should expect that the door will be opened, often not exactly as we envisioned nor in our timing but according to what's best for the plan God arranged in his infinite knowledge of the future for his children. He knows the future and wants the very best for each of us, and when our prayers align with the desires of God's heart, life falls into place like the perfection of a completed jigsaw puzzle.

Jesus of gentleness, help our asking and seeking and knocking to be with thanksgiving and praises for what you are doing behind the scenes from the moment we voice our prayers. May we be content when we hear your answer, knowing you are arranging the very best for us to fulfill the goodness of your plan.

Scan To Branch Out

Let's Examine Our Integrity

SCRIPTURE WHISPER

Jehovah ministereth judgment to the peoples: judge me,
O Jehovah, according to my righteousness, and to mine
integrity that is in me.
PSALM 7:8 ASV

God knows everything, even our thoughts and emotions.
To be pleasing to him, we should seek the thoughts of Jesus
and share every detail of our emotions with him. David
proclaimed that God not only judges human actions but also
examines our thoughts and emotions. He desires to walk
alongside us and do life together. That's why Jesus died.

Nothing escapes our all-knowing and ever-present God.
The evil and wickedness in our country do not go unnoticed
by our almighty God. He is aware of the evil deeds, and he
will show his wrath according to Scripture. Not all judgment
is reserved for the future. Daily, God carries out judgment
on the wicked. We may not realize it, but we should become
more mindful that God is always taking care of his children
and chosen people in ways that surpass our imagination and
understanding. That's what the Bible says.

Jesus of self-control, help us examine our righteousness
and integrity so we can be in alignment with your ways
and remain expectant for the victory you are
arranging in your mighty name.

Scan To Branch Out

Let's Live in Unwavering Faith

SCRIPTURE WHISPER

Jesus was surprised when he heard this; he turned around and said to the crowd following him, "I tell you, I have never found faith like this, not even in Israel!"

LUKE 7:9 GNT

The Bible records a story of a centurion who had a servant near death, and the centurion's unwavering faith that Jesus could heal his servant from afar amazed Jesus. He felt that this gentile had more faith than anyone he had encountered in Israel. Jesus honored the centurion's faith and healed the servant from a distance, rewarding his faith by doing exactly what he had believed Jesus could do.

The key lesson in our Scripture Whisper about faith today is to believe and never doubt that the supernatural power of Jesus and his many promises throughout his Word will manifest when we are living with the unwavering faith of expectancy, just like the centurion. We should mirror this kind of faith.

Jesus of love, help us shut the door on Satan's attacks to shake our faith. Instead, we pray that we will never fail to believe that the answer to our prayers will be fulfilled according to your desire, Lord, for our best and in your perfect timing to fulfill your kingdom plan.

Let's Not Miss Opportunities

SCRIPTURE WHISPER

In loud voices they were exclaiming, "It is to our God who is seated on the throne, and to the Lamb, that we owe our salvation!"

REVELATIONS 7:10 WNT

We are to proclaim that Jesus created and unconditionally loves his creation, and we should mirror his love for all, loving everyone in unity. The message the world is proclaiming fails to be clear about that truth and the only way to salvation. Our culture is confusing, and Satan is working overtime to exploit the divisive message that Jesus isn't the one to whom we owe our salvation, which will keep many out of the kingdom of God.

Jesus calls us to clearly and boldly deliver the gospel message. God carefully appoints us to declare the way of hope to specific people so that they can stand at the throne of God and live in heaven for eternity. Let's not miss the opportunities he gives us to share the gospel.

Jesus of joy, we pray we do not walk away from opportunities to share the truth of the gospel so that others can join us in heaven. You chose us to be your ambassadors, your hands and feet and voice of salvation.

Scan To Branch Out

Let's Ask with Trust

SCRIPTURE WHISPER

"If you, then, though you are evil, know how to give good gifts to your children, how much more will your Father in heaven give good gifts to those who ask him!"

MATTHEW 7:11 NIV

God never gives harmful gifts in response to our prayers, just like loving parents would never give their children anything that would harm them. Often our prayers request things we aren't aware would be harmful to us, but God knows and protects his precious children. So what we sometimes feel are unanswered prayers are blessings as God answers in ways to protect us from future harm that only he can perceive.

We must trust him even when what we receive seems different from what we ask. For those who trust him, Jesus will take what Satan meant for harm and transform our prayers into greater things than we can imagine for his glory. We as sinful people know how to give good gifts to children, but how much more will our heavenly Father give what is most beneficial to us when we ask?

Jesus of peace, our trust is strengthened when we believe that you know best. May we have unwavering faith that the manifestation of your plan will always be for our good and your glory.

Let's Boomerang Jesus' Love

SCRIPTURE WHISPER

"Do to others whatever you would like them to do to you.
This is the essence of all that is taught in the law and the
prophets."
MATTHEW 7:12 NLT

Jesus teaches the boomerang principle in our Scripture
Whisper. Whatever we want others to do for us, we should do
the same for them. We call this the Golden Rule. It's loving
others the way Jesus loves us. It's clearly stated throughout
the Bible that we should do for the people around us what we
want God to do for us and watch how he delivers.

Let's trust Jesus as he leads and directs us. We can send a
boomerang by showing the love of Jesus every day. Consider
writing a note to a friend, helping a neighbor with a project,
or making a meal for someone who's been struggling. But
look out! That boomerang will chase you down.

Jesus of patience, we pray for more ways to do unto others
as you would do, learning how to love others as you whisper
into our spirits in creative ways that we may not even have
thought about. Listening intently to understand other's
needs is mirroring the ways you take care of us, your
children. Help us boomerang your Spirit by allowing you to
love others through us.

Let's Travel the Narrow Path

SCRIPTURE WHISPER

"Go in through the narrow gate, because the gate to hell is wide and the road that leads to it is easy, and there are many who travel it."

MATTHEW 7:13 GNT

Those who live on the wide path are not aligned with Jesus. Instead they follow rules and regulations to try to make themselves acceptable to God. That's not the way God intended for us to worship, not the reason Jesus suffered on the cross. Jesus died so we can live sinless in God's eyes. Going through the narrow gate is not the easiest path through the challenges of life, but it leads to a life filled with the light of Jesus.

The only legitimate way to a relationship with God is to do life his way, through accepting the forgiveness offered by his Son's ultimate sacrifice on the cross. It is up to us as Jesus followers to show others the way to a life filled with goodness and grace by reflecting a lifestyle that draws others into God's kingdom in heaven. Often people travel through the wide gate because they've never been given clear direction to eternal life.

Jesus of kindness, help us never miss an opportunity to show others the only way to salvation and to be on guard against false teaching camouflaged in the confusing messages of our culture.

Let's Pray to Heal Our Land

SCRIPTURE WHISPER

"If my people, who are called by my name, will humble themselves and pray and seek my face and turn from their wicked ways, then I will hear from heaven, and I will forgive their sin and will heal their land."

2 Chronicles 7:14 NIV

If we've ever needed these words of God's promises in our Scripture Whisper, it is for such a time as this. We must call on our Lord, humble ourselves, pray, seek him with all our heart, and turn from our wicked ways. God promises he will hear us from his throne in heaven and will forgive us and will heal our land.

God promises we can always count on him, even during turbulent times. God rescued his people before, and he will do it again. We must do our part as his children and be an influence on others to turn from wicked ways, seek him, and stand on his promises in unity to heal our land just by the way we live our lives.

Jesus of goodness, we join in a unified prayer that you will hear the humble calls of your obedient children as we believe with bold expectancy that our land will heal as you promised.

Let's Beware of Counterfeits

SCRIPTURE WHISPER

"Beware of the false prophets, [teachers] who come to
you dressed as sheep [appearing gentle and innocent], but
inwardly are ravenous wolves."

MATTHEW 7:15 AMP

It seems our country has an overflow of mixed messages
and counterfeit perceptions about God's intentions for us to
live in harmony with one another. We know we can depend
on Jesus for the peace and hope lacking in hopeless lives
today. It's in heaven where we will live without Satan and free
of all conflict and chaos, illness and offense, suffering and
heartbreak, and evil and despair.

But God uses us to bring peace and harmony to earth by
our awareness of false prophets. We must guard against evil
intentions that breach the unity for which Christ suffered on
the cross. Let's sharpen our discernment and clarify Christ's
message to others. Let's exercise every day the habit of living
the fruit of Jesus' Spirit along with honing a keener insight
into false prophets and wrong teaching.

Jesus of faithfulness, we pray that our devotion to living
in your character becomes our daily habit and catches on
like wildfire. Help us become more aware of counterfeits
corrupting your name.

Scan To Branch Out

Let's Recognize Their Fruit

SCRIPTURE WHISPER

"By their fruit you will recognize them. Do people pick grapes from thornbushes, or figs from thistles?"
MATTHEW 7:16 NIV

Let's dig a little deeper to gain a clearer understanding of the fruit God intends for us to showcase as we discern the true walk of Jesus in others. How will we know true believers when we see them? We will recognize them by their fruit and read from their character and devotion to fulfill God's plan. Jesus uses an illustration that makes perfect sense. If a tree is healthy, it will produce good fruit; if the fruit is bad, it's because the tree itself is corrupt.

Our lesson in identifying true believers is to examine their lifestyle. Is it consistent with the Word of God? Do they demonstrate a genuine love of the Lord and his ways? We should be keenly aware and not be deceived as we watch out for those whose lives don't reflect the fruit of the Spirit. But the only way we can do this is with a thirst to learn and understand and practice the teachings of God so clearly placed in his Word. That's our responsibility.

Jesus of gentleness, we pray for an insatiable longing to sharpen our knowledge and wisdom in your ways and to never miss an opportunity to put them into action.

Scan To Branch Out

Let's Live as God Called

SCRIPTURE WHISPER

As the Lord has assigned to each one, as God has called each person, so must he live. I give this sort of direction in all the churches.

1 Corinthians 7:17 net

Let's embrace where we are in life at this very moment. Let's be content exactly where God has us, allowing God to be God in our lives right where we are. God is working on our behalf when we allow him access and when we surrender to his care. Living the life God created should be our goal. It's a lifelong journey through which so many circumstances and people attempt to shift us off course, but God will correct the course of his children without condemning us. That's why Jesus died: so that we can start a clean, new journey with the Holy Spirit leading the way.

So our part is not to allow old habits to slip back in by doing what others expect, but rather we should take the high ground, walking daily in partnership with Jesus. We should not let others define us. That's God's role.

Jesus of self-control, we pray to be more intentional in living the life that you have assigned us. Each of us is uniquely created and accountable for our choices and conduct. May we be content to walk in your instruction in every way.

Scan To Branch Out

Let's Devote Our Lives to Jesus

SCRIPTURE WHISPER

I know that good does not dwell in me, that is, in my flesh; for the willing is present in me, but the doing of the good is not.
ROMANS 7:18 NASB

Why would Paul say such a thing? He has observed the pattern in himself repeatedly and in others as well. As followers of Christ, we sincerely want to do the right thing. However, all too often, we end up doing wrong. This teaching reveals to us that we are unable to keep the law, that we are truly slaves to sin, and therefore, we must realize our need to be delivered from sin through the sacrifice of Jesus.

When we accept Jesus, we are free from our obligation to follow the law. But the law reveals to us how very sinful we are in the flesh, living on our own, and that no matter our good intentions, we still sin and need deliverance that is available only by surrendering our lives to Jesus and adopting his ways.

Jesus of love, we pray that we become more aware that we need you to fight our battles. When you call on you, Lord, to be a daily presence in our lives, sin has no entryway.

Let's Seek Clear Discernment

SCRIPTURE WHISPER

"Any tree that fails to produce good fruit is cut down and thrown into a fire."
MATTHEW 7:19 GW

Too often we see a person who claims to follow Jesus for some perceived benefit in the marketplace, business world, and even in the church family when they are not true believers. Good works might fool some people and might even fool us from time to time, but they will never fool God.

Lifestyles, actions, and choices that reflect the life of Christ are the good fruit, proof of one's commitment to Jesus. We must beware that good deeds are not absolute evidence that someone has true faith; there are counterfeits all around. But if we know the Word of God and his expectations from true followers, we can more easily recognize those who don't truly follow God by their lack of fruit. May we pray for them to genuinely seek the Lord.

Jesus of joy, we pray for a clearer discernment so we will not be fooled by those who have motives that aren't in alignment with your plan. Help us watch out for those who attempt to penetrate the good, trusting hearts of believers for their personal gain and benefit.

Scan To Branch Out

Let's Secure Our Identity

SCRIPTURE WHISPER

If I do what I do not want, it is no longer I who do it but sin that dwells within me.

ROMANS 7:20 NRSVUE

When we accept Christ into our lives, our identity changes. There should be a distinction between who we once were and who we are now, brand-new in Christ. However, we live in a world contaminated by evil forces, so while we should never excuse our sin, we should also remember that Jesus has also forgiven any sins we've committed after accepting Christ. We don't have to listen to voices of condemnation. Our identity is in Jesus, who defeated Satan's hold on us at the cross. And now we have the same power as Christ to defeat Satan's intrusions by daily engaging Jesus in a personal relationship.

Whom do we allow to define us? Is it voices of the past, our shame and guilt, Satan's deception and lies, or the only one who matters, Jesus? God defines us by who we are in Christ, and Satan has no power other than the power we give him to invade our lives.

Jesus of peace, we know we should ask you more often to fight the intrusions Satan attempts to create before they lead us to sin. May we cast every temptation into your almighty care.

Scan To Branch Out

Let's Attract Others to Jesus

SCRIPTURE WHISPER

"Not everyone who says to Me, 'Lord, Lord,' will enter the kingdom of heaven, but only he who does the will of My Father who is in heaven."

MATTHEW 7:21 AMP

Jesus is loving and gentle and kind, but when it comes to those who use his name for their personal gain and fame, they are not going to enter his presence in heaven unless they repent. They can do more harm to the body of Christ with their hypocrisy than atheists and agnostics. That grieves our Lord and should grieve us all deeply.

Our lives lived in obedience to Jesus is an example for others to follow. We should be on constant alert for those whom Satan is using to cause division, using trickery about the message of God's plan of salvation through the ultimate sacrifice of his Son, Jesus Christ. Their day of judgment will come, but in the meantime, Jesus shows us how to weed out the counterfeit confusion and share the true and pure message of God's unconditional love and mercy.

Jesus of patience, help us become alert and wise to clearly identify your characteristics in others so we are not deceived. Help us recognize those who are diligently living in the fruit of your Spirit and leading others into your kingdom by the way they live.

Let's Help the Confused

SCRIPTURE WHISPER

"Many will say to me on that day, 'Lord, Lord, didn't we prophesy in your name? Didn't we force out demons and do many miracles by the power and authority of your name?'"
MATTHEW 7:22 GW

There is much talk about the day of judgment. It will be a horrific day for some because they will be sent into an everlasting life sequestered forever from the mercy and goodness of God. For those who genuinely accept Jesus as their Savior, as evidenced by their fruit, an eternity of overwhelming joy in heaven awaits.

Our choices and actions reveal the condition of our hearts and the authenticity of our relationship with Jesus. Someone can call Jesus their Lord and even have a ministry that appears to be genuine, but nevertheless, a lack of good fruit will easily expose them. They may pridefully think they fooled others and even themselves, but God knows their true heart, and they will hear on the final judgment day, "I never knew you. Depart from me" (v. 23 WEB). Let's change that final judgment message by the influence of our lifestyle.

Jesus of kindness, we pray for those who have been fooled into believing their works gain them access into heaven. Please work through us to unveil the truth that the only way to eternity is by believing in you.

Scan To Branch Out

Let's Offer Hope

SCRIPTURE WHISPER

I told them, "If you listen to me and do what I tell you, I will be your God, you will be my people, and all will go well for you."
JEREMIAH 7:23 CEV

As children of God, we are brokenhearted by the hopelessness all around. Our Scripture Whisper declares explicit ways that all will go well if we listen to God and do what he tells us. It's our responsibility to proclaim these rich words, a promise God gave for us to extend hope to the hopeless.

Living amid chaotic worldly changes seems unimaginable without the hope of Christ, who will save the day when he returns for those who acknowledge him as their Savior. But that day will not go well for those who refuse to listen to God. It will be too late to escape eternity in hell. Share the truth of salvation so no one is left behind.

Jesus of goodness, help us offer hope to the hopeless by introducing others to the value of obeying your voice and inviting you to be God of their lives so they, too, will be known as your people, walk in your ways, and live a life that goes well.

Scan To Branch Out

Let's Look at the Heart

SCRIPTURE WHISPER

"Do not judge by appearance [superficially and arrogantly], but judge fairly and righteously."
JOHN 7:24 AMP

We know we are to let God do the judging, but more often our minds tend to jump to conclusions, and we are too quick to consider outward appearance. Instead, we should look at the heart. A person's appearance can be deceiving, but the words they speak and the actions they take all come from the heart. Their lifestyle tells it all.

We all know people who are beautiful on the outside but sour and evil-spirited on the inside. As well, some are beautiful on the inside, and that beauty shines through outwardly. They become outwardly beautiful and captivating by the purity of their heart. Authenticity is the key, and it's been camouflaged in many ways through the dramatic changes we see in our world every day. Therefore, we must remain true to Christ and seek the truth in the hearts of others.

Jesus of faithfulness, we pray to display a pure heart sold out to living in your ways, showcasing your love to attract others to the goodness of living in your care.

Scan To Branch Out

Let's Build a Firm Foundation

SCRIPTURE WHISPER

"The rain fell, the flood came, and the winds beat against that house, but it did not collapse because its foundation had been laid on rock."

MATTHEW 7:25 NET

Our Scripture Whisper describes storms, water rising, and winds beating us through the circumstances of life. But when we are grounded on a firm foundation from the teachings of God's Word and a continual conversation with God in prayer, our lives will survive just like that house founded on rock in our verse today.

A builder plans the foundation before building a house. We must also be intentional in constructing our foundation when we surrender to a remodel and reconstruction of our lives in Christ. When we do, we can withstand the storms of our journey and stand strong against the Enemy's attacks to tear us down. We can be assured when God is our solid-rock foundation that nothing can destroy his plan. That's God's promise.

Jesus of gentleness, help us always remain conscious of our foundation that Satan tries to chip away and wear down every chance he gets. But Jesus, you died to give us the power to destroy the work of the Evil One. It's up to us to keep our foundation on solid ground by putting your Word into action.

Scan To Branch Out

Let's Notice Camouflaged Idols

SCRIPTURE WHISPER

Destroy it. If you bring it home with you, both you and your
house will be destroyed. Stay away from those disgusting idols!
DEUTERONOMY 7:26 CEV

We think of idols as golden statues mentioned throughout
the Bible, but in our modern-day world, a variety of idols
have grabbed our focus and attention away from God,
maneuvering into our way of life. Idolatry is when we
put anyone or anything above God: our families, careers,
material desires, hobbies, social media, television, and
entertainment. If it takes precedence over time with God,
moving him out of our day, it has become an idol.

In today's culture, idolatry often manifests itself in
the form of busyness. It's difficult to admit, but most
churchgoers don't open a Bible outside of church services.
Too many simply admit that they have good intentions, but
their lives seem to become too busy. Idols can't save us in
times of trouble, but studying God's Word, spending devoted
time in prayer, and singing glory to God in times of need can
shut down Satan in his tracks.

Jesus of self-control, help us not let anything or anyone ever
come between us and distract us from you. Help us today to
identify our modern-day idols and replace them
with a closer relationship with you.

Scan To Branch Out

Let's Imitate John the Baptist

SCRIPTURE WHISPER

"John is the man to whom the Scriptures refer when they say, 'Look, I am sending my messenger ahead of you, and he will prepare your way before you.'"
LUKE 7:27 NLT

John the Baptist prepared the people for the arrival of Jesus, God's Son, who came to save the world. Likewise, as children of God, we should be about the work of preparing for his return by sharing with others about Jesus and that glorious day before it's too late for them to understand the truth of the gospel.

John took on the challenge to never miss an opportunity to encourage a lost soul at all costs. Out of love for Jesus, in honor of his suffering on the cross to save lost souls from eternal destruction and seclusion from a loving God, we should do the same by following the pattern of John. As people cross our path, let's live true to God's Word, influencing others to seek a life eternally in heaven.

Jesus of love, we pray that we become more intentional about following in John's footsteps and preparing the way for others to join us in eternity.

Scan To Branch Out

Let's Stand Up for Truth

SCRIPTURE WHISPER

"You shall say to them, 'This is the nation that did not obey the voice of the LORD their God or accept correction and warning; truth and faithfulness have perished and have completely vanished from their mouths.'"

JEREMIAH 7:28 AMP

Our Scripture Whisper was written thousands of years ago, yet with the similarities between the nation described and those we see now, you would think it was written today. Our world is falling into the same pattern that prompted Jeremiah to deliver a warning to the people of his time. The United States was founded on truth from the Bible. The cornerstone of our nation's principles was based on God. Tragically, society has been whittling God's voice out of our culture much like Israel did during Jeremiah's time.

As Christ followers, we must not be complacent or allow integrity, truth, and faithfulness to perish and vanish from our mouths. Jeremiah spoke up. Let's do the same and never miss a chance to stand up for the truth of God and never fail to encourage others to keep God's voice vibrantly flowing across our land.

Jesus of joy, we pray that we become more intentional to obey your voice and accept your correction as we live in truth and faithfulness with you leading the way.

Scan To Branch Out

Let's Live Upright

SCRIPTURE WHISPER

"This only have I found: God created mankind upright, but they have gone in search of many schemes."
ECCLESIASTES 7:29 NIV

God made men and women true and upright. We're the ones who've made a mess of things. We have allowed Satan to make a mess of things. Entitlement and generational disparities are rampant. The lack of respect, responsibility, and accountability in this world is a travesty. Where is decency and courteous behavior that conforms to the once-accepted standards of morality and respectability?

We must pray against the evil forces that are overtaking and brainwashing with untruths, twisted views, disrespect, and impurity of minds. Jesus transferred to us on the cross the power to shut down the demonic forces infiltrating our world. In unity, let's rediscover the upright ways Jesus created in us all and rebuke the many schemes that attempt to tarnish the goodness of our world. Let's stand together and regain the integrity of right living, spreading seeds of love, joy, peace, patience, kindness, goodness, faithfulness, gentleness, and self-control, and igniting a brilliant light through his glory and grace across our land.

Jesus of peace, it takes one light to dispel darkness. Help us be your light for the world.

Let's Never Reject God's Purpose

SCRIPTURE WHISPER

The Pharisees and the lawyers rejected the purpose of God for themselves, not having been baptized by him.

LUKE 7:30 ESV

How many hardened hearts have turned to stone as they reject God's purpose and attempt to remove Jesus from their lives? God has a unique purpose for each of us from the beginning of his creation, and that also includes those with stone-cold hearts who have turned their backs on God. It's never too late until the day of Christ's return.

Rejecting God and making choices apart from him alter the dynamics of the world. As a result, many lives are tumbled around in disarray and shambles since they refuse to surrender to God's plan. But we can be assured God's purpose will unfold. When we put our moments into the hands of God and engage in life's decisions and choices through his omnipotent wisdom and knowledge, the life he created for us will manifest into the greatness he intended from the start of creation.

Jesus of patience, we join and pray for hearts to be softened by your power, like a surge of lightning from the throne of God, transforming others into a model of your tender heart.

Let's Simplify

SCRIPTURE WHISPER

Those who use the things in this world should do so but not depend on them. It is clear that this world in its present form is passing away.

1 Corinthians 7:31 GW

It's time to simplify and make life less complicated, asking Jesus for discernment about the things we depend on and eliminating unnecessary things in our lives. Keeping it simple can be a new way of life for all of us in this complicated world of chaos and busyness. But how refreshing it is to just pause and take a breath of simplicity, even in ordinary things, in our daily routines, and throughout the moments of our days.

The phrase "just passing through" offers a less stressful viewpoint, a more temporary perspective. Knowing we are just passing through on this earth to our eternal home, life seems less complicated, breezing rather than toiling. Nothing is permanent except eternity in heaven for those who choose to live with Jesus in their hearts.

Jesus of kindness, we pray for a passing-through mentality, wherein we use our energy and resources toward things that bring value to your kingdom and your calling. As we make life simpler, may we never miss an opportunity you arrange in our lives to do all you created us to fulfill.

August

Let's Stop Condemning Ourselves

SCRIPTURE WHISPER

Those who are believers in Christ Jesus can no longer be condemned.

ROMANS 8:1 GW

Condemnation was crushed at the cross. For believers, God no longer remembers the things for which we deserve eternal punishment. So why do we continue condemning ourselves for what Jesus agonized and suffered to wipe away?

It's one of Satan's favorite entrances into our lives. He maneuvers into our thoughts and highlights the guilt and shame of our past, keeping us from freeing ourselves from condemnation. Let's extend ourselves the same grace that Jesus offered to us at the cross and end this condemnation. Through God's grace, he has given us the choice to walk in obedience, setting us right with him, each other, and ourselves. We must decide moment by moment to offer Jesus our hands, our feet, our hearts, our eyes, and to invite him to live in and through us along life's journey.

Jesus of goodness, we join in praying that we become intentional about leaving the past in the past, not condemning ourselves, and living to honor your sacrifice to set us free. Help us share this redeeming gospel of your goodness and grace.

Scan To Branch Out

Let's Live Set Free

SCRIPTURE WHISPER

Because you belong to him, the power of the life-giving Spirit has freed you from the power of sin that leads to death.
ROMANS 8:2 NLT

God did something the law could never do. He sent his own Son to bear our sins and transform us into his likeness. A mind focused on the flesh is destined for death and declares war against God, refusing his path and plan. But a mind focused on Jesus will find everlasting peace.

God breathes into our spirits a continual flow of his complete peace, but it's up to us to keep that pipeline open. We must recognize that Satan attempts to put a kink in the flow by disrupting our peace every chance he gets. When we surrender our worldly flesh into Jesus' care by making a habit of living the fruit of his Spirit, the Holy Spirit keeps flowing through our lives, which increases his peace in us as we grow in our devotion to him.

Jesus of faithfulness, help us become more aware of any kinks that inhibit the flow of your breath within us and that allow Satan to influence our actions. Lord, set us free by the power of your life-giving Spirit.

Let's Be Amazed at Creation

SCRIPTURE WHISPER

I observe your heavens, the work of your fingers,
the moon and the stars, which you set in place.
PSALM 8:3 CSB

How privileged we are to be God's children and to witness
the majesty of his creation, the brilliance of colors in the
canvas of his sky, the unique melodies of each bird, and
the individual fragrances assigned to each flower. How
God's heart is saddened by those who refuse to accept the
blessing of Jesus. If only they lived life in and through the
Lord, entrusting the trials of life to the only one who is
all-knowing, who placed each star in the sky and still cares
about the details of our lives, and who can make miracles out
of our messes.

It should grieve our hearts as well when we see the
struggles others are enduring alone when Jesus has his
outstretched arms ready to lead them out of their storm and
into his peaceful and joyous care. But many don't know that
about Jesus. Evil forces have corrupted their perception of
him, but we can share the pure message of Jesus.

Jesus of gentleness, help us reflect and share your
magnificent creation. May we be your voice for lost souls
who are unaware of the wonders of accepting you
into their hearts.

Scan To Branch Out

Let's Be Jesus' Wind of Hope

SCRIPTURE WHISPER

"Jeremiah, say to the people, 'This is what the LORD says: When people fall down, don't they get up again? When they discover they're on the wrong road, don't they turn back?'"
JEREMIAH 8:4 NLT

We live in different seasons throughout our lifetime, and we are in a season of destruction if we don't heed the voice of God through Jeremiah's instructions and repent and turn to Jesus.

Many don't comprehend the severity of ignoring God and his warnings throughout his Word. As Christ followers, we are the light to illuminate the way to peace and restoration found only in Jesus. Our world is in disarray because we have been silent and complacent, allowing the evil forces to take over. Enough is enough, and we must not sugarcoat things any longer. God uses each of us to reach the hearts of the lost and be the light of his presence by the way we live in his character.

Jesus of self-control, we ask that the winds of your hope will blow throughout our land and shower your anointing upon those who need the hope found in your salvation.

Scan To Branch Out

Let's Live for Eternity

SCRIPTURE WHISPER

The place where they serve is a sketch and shadow of the heavenly sanctuary, just as Moses was warned by God as he was about to complete the tabernacle. For he says, "See that you make everything according to the design shown to you on the mountain."

HEBREWS 8:5 NET

This Scripture Whisper reminds us that God is in the details, so we should invite him each morning to handle every aspect of our moments. By obeying him, we represent a shadow of his design that we can anticipate in heaven.

This verse also reminds us that our journey on earth is preparing us for what God has planned for us in heaven, a new life without Satan. We will not be strumming harps in the clouds. We will be using our gifts and talents and lifelong training from our experiences while here on earth. Our earthly journey may have us involved in things that will not exist in heaven, but God knows what he is doing to prepare us, equip us, and weave our earthly work into our heavenly purpose in eternity.

Jesus of love, still our hearts and stir our souls for the things that matter for eternal value and help us be more focused on preparing for our heavenly life.

Scan To Branch Out

Let's Bask in Jesus' Love

SCRIPTURE WHISPER

Set me as a seal upon your heart, as a seal upon your arm, for love is strong as death, jealousy is fierce as the grave. Its flashes are flashes of fire, the very flame of the LORD.

SONG OF SOLOMON 8:6 ESV

Our Scripture Whisper describes the bonds of love that our Lord has for his children as a seal upon his heart, as a force that is stronger than death. And he has an intense love for each of us that's vibrantly unchangeable; his love never fails. Reflecting on such a deep love reconfirms there is nothing we can ever do to affect God's love for us.

When we have a day of gray clouds covering us, that's Satan's attempt to overshadow our sense of God's immeasurable love. He is a God who not only forgives but also forgets our past sins and wrong choices, and he will design them into a beautiful tapestry when we allow him to be the weaver of our moments. We are sealed by the love of Jesus, so when we feel downhearted, let's bask in his love.

Jesus of joy, help us never forget the depth of your incomprehensible love for us. Help us love others more by the example of your love.

Scan To Branch Out

Let's Live in Jesus' Aura

SCRIPTURE WHISPER

The LORD told him: "Listen to all that the people are saying to you; it is not you they have rejected, but they have rejected me as their king."

1 SAMUEL 8:7 NIV

How often do we battle against others who use us, abuse us, spread untruths about us, conjure up ways to tear us down, or attack us in ways out of our control or understanding? It's Satan inside them. They've allowed the Enemy to work within them to attempt to destroy the work of the Lord in our lives.

Have you noticed those who scramble not to be in our presence, quick to position themselves at a distance? It's the aura of our Jesus-focused spirit that reminds them of what they are missing, what they are not, and what we are. Some people create division and chaos to distract themselves from the reality of Satan's turmoil fighting within them to keep them in their comfort zone. By living how God calls us to live, we can show them his love and peace and power, which far exceed anything Satan offers.

Jesus of peace, help us better understand that people who have rejected you may also reject us because our lives are aligned with you and your ways. Help us love them through you.

Scan To Branch Out

Let's Rely On Jesus' Strength

SCRIPTURE WHISPER

That's why those who are still under the control of their sinful nature can never please God.

ROMANS 8:8 NLT

Living in the flesh and by the world's standards causes people to focus on self rather than on the ways of God. Anyone completely absorbed in self ignores God and how he longs to live alongside us. He longs to take our worries and woes upon his shoulders, guiding our every next step along a pathway of joy and peace that surpasses our human understanding. How can we possibly ignore the unconditional love of God by choosing the ways of the world?

Jesus provides a life free from the bondage of Satan and his tactics that chain us down. It's a life of freedom and peace and joy found only in faith and trust in our Lord. When we are faced with challenges, troubles, and despair, let's examine the root cause. Is it a result of the choices we made that we should have discussed with Jesus? Let's join in seeking the joy of the Lord as our strength, and let's share it with everyone.

Jesus of patience, help us seek ways to please you more, and when temptations threaten to separate us from you, may we call on your strength.

Scan To Branch Out

Let's Proclaim Jesus' Majesty

SCRIPTURE WHISPER

LORD, our Lord, how majestic is your name in all the earth!
PSALMS 8:9 NIV

How much do we focus on the darkness permeating our world instead of the magnificence of all God has created for us? How often do we pause and just glory in the intricate details God provides for us each moment of every day? How much do we echo God's name through our days and in our conversations with others? We should strive to overcome our imperfections by modeling the character of Jesus more each day.

As they say, we are often the only Bible people read, and when our actions differ from the ways of God, we create confusion in others and affect how people understand the gospel of God's saving grace through Christ Jesus. So how can we ensure we keep the anointing of his character fresh and vibrant? Our Scripture Whisper reminds us that we should reflect on the never-ending goodness of God by continually saying, "Lord, how majestic is your name in all the earth!"

Jesus of kindness, send a continual, overflowing spring of your glory from our spirits so that we may proclaim your magnificence by the way we live in the fruit of your Spirit.

Scan To Branch Out

Let's Make Plans with Jesus

SCRIPTURE WHISPER

Make your plans! But they will never succeed. Talk all you want to! But it is all useless, because God is with us.
ISAIAH 8:10 GNT

If we devise plans alone or listen to others without the counsel of the only one who knows the future, we won't be on the most strategic course for God's plan to unfold.

What a gift we all take for granted. We have access to the infinite wisdom of God when we pause to determine God's will before we make a decision. And when we become better at recognizing the Holy Spirit's whispers into our thoughts, we are better equipped to live along God's intended pathway. Our lives and the lives of those around us will thereafter be headed in a different trajectory because God will be with us. We must be diligent in seeking his voice over the camouflaged voice of Satan by spending time in God's Word and learning his ways and the tone of his voice, just like our family and close friends recognize our voices because they become familiar with them over time.

Jesus of goodness, help us pause before making decisions and thirst to recognize your voice in prayer by studying your Word.

Scan To Branch Out

Let's Exemplify Jesus' Spirit

SCRIPTURE WHISPER

God raised Jesus to life! God's Spirit now lives in you,
and he will raise you to life by his Spirit.
ROMANS 8:11 CEV

There are two choices in life: a life lived with Jesus, inviting
his Spirit to live through us, or a life lived according to the
flesh, headed toward eternal destruction. For those who
refuse to know the Lord, there's a world of condemnation
ahead for them, an eternity of suffering with the one they
chose, Satan.

Those not part of the family of God make choices apart
from the love of Jesus. Instead of love, their choice will be
hatred. Instead of joy, anger; instead of peace, outbursts;
instead of patience, irritability; instead of kindness, apathy;
instead of goodness, discord; instead of faithfulness,
betrayal; instead of gentleness, chaos; instead of self-control,
they will choose indulgence. Let's be an example of the right
choice, the choice to live with Jesus, so that more lives are
transformed and more people get to experience the peace
and joy of the Spirit living inside them.

Jesus of faithfulness, help us become more aware and
committed to doing our part in defusing the turmoil
throughout our land by sharing the fruit of your
Spirit with at least one person every day.

Let's Become Set Apart

SCRIPTURE WHISPER

"Do not call conspiracy all that this people calls conspiracy, and do not fear what it fears or be in dread."
ISAIAH 8:12 NRSVUE

We are to be set apart from the ways of the world and those who are always afraid somebody is plotting against them. We have no reason to fear what they fear and should never take on their worries when we live in alignment with the ways of God. If we are going to worry, then let's be concerned that we are living in the favor of our Lord, in the ways he expects us to live as his ambassadors, encouraging the lost into his kingdom.

The state of the world always gives us reason to worry, but God promises that we will never be forsaken. Jesus is working behind the scenes for the benefit of those who have invited him into their hearts and seek to live in his ways every day. Life is full of choices. Let's influence others to live in the love of Jesus and end their worry about the state of things that are out of their control. Let's be set apart and not worry.

Jesus of gentleness, help us make a habit of turning over to your care any reason we may have to worry.

Scan To Branch Out

Let's Show Respect

SCRIPTURE WHISPER

You must recognize the authority of the Lord of Heaven's Armies. He is the one you must respect; he is the one you must fear.

Isaiah 8:13 net

Our holy, all-powerful God is the only one we should fearfully respect. *Respect* means a feeling of deep admiration for someone or something because of their abilities, qualities, or achievements. *Fear*, as it is used in the Bible, is unlike the way we define *fear* today but is rather a term used for reverence and awe.

The act of respecting others is lost today. Few people show respect for others as God created them. Not many young people demonstrate respect for their parents and grandparents or wiser folks in their lives. Many don't respect our forefathers who fought for our religious freedom, our churches, or the Christian faith. And there's almost no respect for God our Father, his Son our Savior, and the Holy Spirit our Counselor. How dare we fail to show God respect by the way we live and the way we treat others? Out of respect for God, let's forgive others when they fail us just like our Lord has forgiven us.

Jesus of self-control, help us always live in respect of your unconditional love that you continuously shower upon us.

Let's Cut Away Thorns

SCRIPTURE WHISPER

"The ones that fell among the thorn bushes are the people who listen, but as they go on their way they are choked by the worries, wealth, and pleasures of life, and their fruit doesn't mature."

LUKE 8:14 ISV

It's sad how many have not heard of the gospel of Jesus and the hope for eternal life. How it should grieve us that some have heard the gospel of salvation and profess that they are Christians while continuing in the ways of the world. They often do more harm to those who haven't accepted Jesus, living the message of hypocrisy that turns unbelievers further away.

Some of us who hear the Word are on fire for the Lord, but as time passes and the daily challenges and anxieties become our focus, along with the pursuit of wealth and life's addicting delights, the ways of the world overtake the harvest of our message. Even if seeds spread, the fruit never fully matures because the thorns choke out the plants' vitality. Worrying about tomorrow, making money, and having fun become rooted in our souls unless we keep our eyes on Jesus.

Jesus of love, we pray for those who know the truth but who do not reflect it in their way of living. Help us plant seeds in good soil, bearing fruit in lost souls.

Let's Seek Joy

SCRIPTURE WHISPER

I commend the enjoyment of life, because there is nothing
better for a person under the sun than to eat and drink and
be glad. Then joy will accompany them in their toil all the
days of the life God has given them under the sun.

ECCLESIASTES 8:15 NIV

In today's world, with turmoil and chaos and confusion
every way we turn, pursuing joy sometimes seems
purposeless. It seems like a yo-yo life: we pursue joy only to
be blindsided by despair before then pursuing joy once again
just to be blindsided again. After a while, it gets wearisome,
and our vitality is diminished.

That's the vicious circle we live when we depend on
others instead of Jesus for our joy. People let us down and
bring disappointment. No one is perfect as we all have
flaws from past hurts and experiences, but pinning our
expectations on others is not what we should do. When
we rely on Jesus, our source of strength, then our joy does
not depend on others or circumstances, and we can better
maintain a spirit of joy through the storms of life.

Jesus of joy, we pray for a deeper dependence on you as our
confidant and best friend to turn to when we need your joy.
You will never let us down.

Scan To Branch Out

Let's Display Tough Love

SCRIPTURE WHISPER

You must be truthful with each other, and in court you must give fair decisions that lead to peace.

ZECHARIAH 8:16 CEV

We live in a society that tends to walk on eggshells. We refrain from speaking the truth because we do not want to create tension in this chaotic culture. It's become too typical for people to react with outbursts, anger, and rage when they hear the truth, which is often something they don't want to hear. Too many have taken the easy road, the posture of complacency, and avoided the tough-love road, which often leads to confrontation when the truth is told. It's easier to stay quiet with our thoughts.

But when we share a true relationship with someone, we must be willing to speak truth with love even when it's hard, which may open up wounds or situations in life that are often ignored or buried. But left alone, these wounds can inhibit an environment for God's plan to unfold. We all have past hurts that affect our behavior and influence people's perceptions about who we are. But we must step away from what is comfortable and say and do things in truth while being receptive when others speak truth to us.

Jesus of peace, we pray that we live in truth and love as you intended.

Scan To Branch Out

Let's Make Jesus Our CEO

SCRIPTURE WHISPER

I realized that no one can discover everything God is doing under the sun. Not even the wisest people discover everything, no matter what they claim.

ECCLESIASTES 8:17 NLT

We may not always understand what God is up to or make sense of his intentions, but God knows what he's doing. When we grasp that and use it to strengthen our dependence on him, it's sweet.

Many claim to know God, but they live according to the world's ways. That's difficult for those with a more mature faith because they know that those who depend on Jesus for their decisions can avoid many negative consequences. Instead, they rest assured that Jesus will navigate things in a way that fulfills God's ultimate plan, which brings peace and joy instead of chaos and turmoil. There is no business model or reality check needed when we allow God to be in control. He makes the impossible possible for those who allow him to be God, even when things make no sense by the standards of this world. Nothing is impossible in the hands of Jesus.

Jesus of patience, be the CEO of our lives. That's not what Satan wants, so we ask for a barrier of protection as we devote our moments to your care.

Scan To Branch Out

Let's Focus on Days Ahead

SCRIPTURE WHISPER

I consider that the sufferings of this present time are not worth comparing with the glory about to be revealed to us.
ROMANS 8:18 NRSVUE

There's no comparison between the present hard times and the glory God has waiting for us ahead. As Christ followers, we should focus on those glorious times ahead instead of moaning about difficult circumstances and the state of the world today. We should allow our joyful anticipation of greater days to deepen.

By focusing exclusively on troubled days, we may be tempted to lose heart. Paul reminds us in this Scripture Whisper that the sufferings of this present time are not even worth comparing with a glory that is going to be revealed to us. For believers, the glory ahead is so much greater than our current challenges, suffering, and heart-wrenching moments. When we are in our heavenly home, we will wonder, *What was suffering?*

Jesus of kindness, help us focus our attention on the good things in our lives and diminish our focus on the negative. May we no longer focus on the intrusions of the Evil One but solely on the glory you provide and the greatness of the days ahead.

Let's Watch for Divine Moments

SCRIPTURE WHISPER

All creation is waiting eagerly for that future day when God will reveal who his children really are.

ROMANS 8:19 NLT

Many we wouldn't expect will be sitting at the Father's table when we get to heaven. Also, many we expect to be there will not be there because their outward behaviors didn't align with the condition of their hearts. They fooled us all and even themselves, resulting in a life spent eternally in darkness.

Jesus is our only hope for an eternity in heaven. As our world is playing out biblical prophecy, we must diligently show the love of Jesus, extend a branch to hope for the hopeless, and invite the lost to sit with us at our Father's table. Let's ask Jesus to be in the details of our lives as we watch devotedly for the divine moments he sprinkles throughout our day and pray that we never miss an opportunity he has arranged ahead.

Jesus of goodness, we pray that we never miss a chance to encourage others to join us in heaven. Until we get to heaven, we may never realize the results of the moments that you sprinkle into our hearts that draw others into your kingdom.

Scan To Branch Out

Let's Extend Jesus' Invitation

SCRIPTURE WHISPER

You are to answer them, "Listen to what the LORD is teaching you! Don't listen to mediums—what they tell you cannot keep trouble away."
ISAIAH 8:20 GNT

There are so many mixed messages these days that are not based on the truth. They declare that Jesus is not the only way to salvation. Many are lost and looking everywhere for hope, through horoscopes, fortune tellers, and evil spirituality concepts, when the only true source of hope is in God's inspired Word. It is preserved for us today in many Bible translations designed to reach each of our hearts.

Those who explore these alternative, wayward ways travel down a frustrating dead-end road every time. They are on a vigorous search, trying one thing after another. When nothing works out, they get angry, frantically turning this way and that, up, down, and sideways, arriving empty and remaining in a life of darkness. Yet we, as Jesus' followers, can represent the truth through the way we live. By adopting his lifestyle and making a habit of the fruit of his Spirit, we can encourage and influence those on endless searches that a relationship with Jesus is the hope for which they are desperately searching.

Jesus of faithfulness, live through us so the lost are moved to invite you into their hearts.

Let's Make Jesus Our Treasure

SCRIPTURE WHISPER

"I bequeath wealth to those who love me,
and I will fill their treasuries."
PROVERBS 8:21 ISV

Our minds tend to turn to financial provisions when we think of treasures. However, true riches are found in the peace, joy, and fulfillment by living alongside Jesus. Today, our Scripture Whisper reminds us of the abundant treasures he pours into us, fulfilling the niche that he has specifically carved out for each of us.

Too many live in other people's lanes, trying to live in a niche not their own. How many in their later years are still searching, chasing someone else's dreams instead of their own? Often it takes a lifelong journey to prepare and equip us to be all God intended when he created us in our mother's womb, developing our unique personality, unlike anyone else's, to live out the specific niche he had in mind. The influence of others throughout our life journey is part of who we are today. Just an essence of an encounter with others develops our personal identity as Jesus weaves our lives together.

Jesus of gentleness, we pray that we make you our treasure by making a habit of living the fruit of your Spirit each day, becoming the unique person that you created us to be by your intricate design.

Let's Cross to the Unfamiliar

SCRIPTURE WHISPER

One day Jesus said to his disciples, "Let's cross to the other side of the lake." So they got into a boat and started out.
LUKE 8:22 NLT

This verse speaks of living as Jesus directs, crossing over to the other side that is unfamiliar, unknown, and uncertain, but with Jesus in the boat, we can be assured that we remain under his protection. Life is full of terrible storms. Everything seems to be capsizing all around, and we feel we are drowning. Yet when Jesus speaks into our storms, the waves will be silenced. Stormy waters will become like glass.

It takes many trials and tribulations, heartaches and suffering, often for a lifetime, to feel that assurance deep within our souls to go to the other side when Jesus asks. But we can always count on his promise that he will never leave us nor forsake us, even on the other side. Jesus will provide for what he has called us to accomplish for him. That's what the Bible says.

Jesus of self-control, we pray that we approach our troubles knowing that you are in the boat with us when we invite you aboard. May we rest in your presence with assurance that all is well.

Let's Live above the World

SCRIPTURE WHISPER

He said to them, "You are from below, I am from above;
you are from this world, I am not from this world."
JOHN 8:23 NRSVUE

As we go about our days, it's becoming more apparent
who is of this world and who is living above the chaos
and confusion of life. What is the message that sounds the
loudest? Our message of Jesus is being overshadowed by
the clanging sounds of the Evil One gaining more territory.
We must end our silence and be more direct. The days are
drawing near when there will be no more time for the lost.
If they refuse to believe that Jesus is the only way to eternal
salvation, they're soon to run out of time.

And there's no time for complacency or depending
on someone else to do what Jesus has arranged for us to
accomplish in someone's heart. Let's step out of our place
of comfort, live above this world, and make a difference in
someone's life today.

Jesus of love, we pray for those who are missing you in
their lives. May you speak their language through us and
encourage them to rise above this world and hope in you for
a life of eternal salvation.

Let's Wait in Expectant Hope

SCRIPTURE WHISPER

In hope we were saved. Now hope that is seen is not hope, for who hopes for what one already sees?

ROMANS 8:24 NRSVUE

Our Scripture Whisper makes it clear and so simple: hope does not involve what we already have or see, for who goes around hoping for what they already have? If we wait expectantly for things we have never seen, then our hope is with true perseverance and eager anticipation. That's faith.

When we get overwhelmed and feel weak, not knowing how to pray, the Holy Spirit steps in and articulates prayers for us in a language we do not understand, prayers that reach the throne of God in a powerful appeal. We must remain confident with unwavering faith that God can design everything to work toward the unimaginable when we love him and accept his invitation to live according to his plan.

Jesus of joy, when we get tired in the waiting, the Holy Spirit does our praying for us, making prayer out of our wordless sighs, our aching groans, and broken hearts. You know us far better than we know ourselves, and that's why we can rest in the assurance that you will transform every detail in our lives into something good according to your purpose as we hope with unwavering faith in you.

Scan To Branch Out

Let's Walk Daily with Jesus

SCRIPTURE WHISPER

He said to them, "Where is your faith?" But they were fearful and amazed, saying to one another, "Who then is this, that He commands even the winds and the water, and they obey Him?"
LUKE 8:25 NASB

The disciples questioned who Jesus was even though they saw firsthand his miraculous power. Even his brothers, who grew up with Jesus, doubted he was the Son of God. And, in Nazareth, the city in which Jesus grew up, the people did not have any faith or belief in him. How that must have grieved God's heart! His plan was to free mankind from sinful ways and engage in a personal relationship with them as if walking together in the garden of Eden each day.

Jesus' purpose is to rid our hearts of worldly distractions and for us to follow him each moment of every day, living in his strength, goodness, and gentleness while handling challenges together. How it delights the heart of God when one of his children feels the joy of walking through life together with him.

Jesus of peace, a sweet, tender way for us to approach every day is to walk in relationship with you. You are all-knowing and all-loving, and we ask you anoint to us and equip us for the day ahead.

Let's Study Jesus' Voice

SCRIPTURE WHISPER

He sent him home, saying, "Don't even go into the village."
MARK 8:26 CSB

There's a process in life, and it's a mystery to us. Rest assured;
God knows exactly what he is doing. That's why we must
be diligent in learning how to hear his voice of direction
from his Word so he can guide our steps. In our Scripture
Whisper, Jesus instructed the newly healed blind man not to
enter the village. Too many times we have missed the voice
of God whispering, *Don't enter,* to protect us from what he
knows is destruction or a dead-end road.

Keenly listening in a world of noisy clanging is
challenging. That's why we must be students of God's
vocabulary, which is often hidden in nature and in ways
we can recognize only by being attuned to his way of
communicating with us. But we must be aware that Satan
camouflages his voice to confuse and distract us. That's
another reason to study the Word of God: to clearly know
the true voice of the Lord.

Jesus of patience, we pray that we will develop a thirst to
identify your voice distinctly, following as you direct with
no confusion, distractions, or delays.

Scan To Branch Out

Let's Jabber to Jesus

SCRIPTURE WHISPER

The Father who knows all hearts knows what the Spirit is saying, for the Spirit pleads for us believers in harmony with God's own will.

Romans 8:27 NLT

Have you ever felt so overwhelmed that you just didn't know how to verbalize a prayer? We've all been there as we face life's challenges. But our Scripture Whisper gives us comfort that Jesus knows our heart's cry even when we can't make a sound.

The Holy Spirit interprets our heart cries and translates them into a language that reaches the throne of God and penetrates his heart of compassion. When we are in a place that seems too deep for words, the Holy Spirit will take over as our master translator. Our heavenly Father searches and knows our hearts and is intimately connected with the Holy Spirit within us.

Still, God is pleased when we formulate our prayers into words and talk to him as we would our best friend. We should never be concerned that we are praying incorrectly. God knows our hearts and is delighted when we have the freedom to talk with him as a little child jabbers to their daddy.

Jesus of kindness, you understand the language of our hearts and prayers. Thank you, Holy Spirit, for being our intercessor when we are too broken to know how to pray.

Let's Depend On Jesus' Promises

SCRIPTURE WHISPER

We know that God causes all things to work together for good to those who love God, to those who are called according to His purpose.

ROMANS 8:28 NASB

When times are rough, the meaning of our Scripture Whisper has been proven to give strength and hope that God will take what Satan meant for harm and turn it into his glory for those who love him and are called according to his purpose.

We all have a purpose for which God has uniquely created us as part of his plan. So why shouldn't we expect him to correct our course when we falter and allow Satan to interrupt? It would be against God's promises if he didn't orchestrate everything to work toward good when we love him and accept his invitation to live according to his plan. That takes a load off our shoulders and should prevent us from beating ourselves up for wrong choices and the mess-ups we get ourselves into. We can cast those cares into Jesus' arms because he promises unimaginable good even from our wrong choices.

Jesus of goodness, help us anticipate the goodness of tomorrow, cherishing today in honor of your promise in Romans 8:28 and your desire to do "immeasurably more than all we ask or imagine" (Ephesians 3:20 NIV).

Scan To Branch Out

Let's Be Pleasing to Jesus

SCRIPTURE WHISPER

"He who sent Me is with Me. The Father has not left Me alone, for I always do those things that please Him."
JOHN 8:29 NKJV

These words from Jesus speak of his intimate relationship with his Father. Jesus provided a way through his suffering to wipe away our sins. Now God can be in an intimate relationship with us, too, as our Father. He will never abandon us as we seek to please him with our love and faith in his Son.

The plan for salvation is rooted in God's indescribable and unfathomable love for those who open their hearts to receive him. He loves us more deeply than we can comprehend. He sent his only Son to suffer inhumanely so we could call on our Father to live in our hearts.

Jesus of faithfulness, help us be pleasing to you and feel your love flowing through our lives so we can direct hopeless, broken, and confused hearts into your care. You are moving throughout our land although it's hard for many to see. In faith we know from our Scripture Whisper today that you will not leave us alone when we call on you and seek you to answer our heartfelt prayers.

Scan To Branch Out

Let's Draw Others to Heaven

SCRIPTURE WHISPER

As Jesus spoke these things, many believed in Him.
JOHN 8:30 MSB

When Jesus walked the earth, people heard his wisdom and saw firsthand his miraculous power. While many believed, many others did not. Even his brothers doubted (7:5). Through answered prayers, there's evidence of Jesus living in and through our lives that is as compelling today as it was for those who sat in the crowd listening to his teaching many years ago. When we let Jesus into our lives and walk through life together with him, it's undeniable that he is as real today as he was in ancient days.

Today we get to be teachers of the crowd through our lifestyle, mirroring his character and showcasing the fruit of his Spirit as he navigates our journey. So the least we can do is give him a little more time each day to equip us to be all he intends for us to be, expanding the opportunity for others to receive him in their hearts and join us in eternity.

Jesus of gentleness, live more fully through us and use us to attract others to be heaven bound.

Let's Remember God Is for Us

SCRIPTURE WHISPER

What then are we to say about these things?
If God is for us, who is against us?
Romans 8:31 NRSVUE

Where there's fear, there is no faith; they cannot coexist.
If God is for us, then why, oh why should we ever fear the
things of this earth? What can mere man do to us? God
promises to be on our side when we invite him into our lives,
believe he will do all he promised, and allow him to live in
an intimate relationship with us.

What else do we need to be free from the bondage of
fear? With God for us, no one can be against us. That's our
assurance that he will fight our battles when we ask him to.
In Jesus' hands, nothing is impossible. But it's up to us to
depend on Jesus with unwavering faith and invite him into
our lives to calm our stormy seas.

Jesus of self-control, help us always be aware that you are by
our side. May we never fail to engage you in our moments.
As your ambassadors, may we share your comforting hope
for those who seem to live in confusion by offering the
goodness of your love. May faith in you overtake the fear
that many in this world are feeling today.

Scan To Branch Out

September

Let's Thank Jesus

SCRIPTURE WHISPER

I will give thanks to the LORD with all my heart,
I will declare all your wonderful deeds.
PSALM 9:1 ISV

Even in the chaotic, ever-changing world, we should thank the Lord with all our heart and shout about the amazing things God is doing every day. As God's children, we know the end of the story, and he allows us to share it with everyone in the world.

Jesus won the victory at the cross, and he rose out of death into life and will come again to take us to his heavenly home. This is the message we need to share every day. God will rescue us from the turmoil of life into his world with no more sickness or pain or brokenness because Satan will not be there. What a glorious new life it will be for those who are transformed by the gospel of Jesus. Let's reach out to the lost and hopeless and invite them to know of the Lord's wonderful deeds.

Jesus of love, we ask you to use us to share the salvation found only in you and to encourage lost souls to be found. May we always give thanks for your wonderful deeds that make a difference in our lives every day.

Let's Shine Jesus' Light

SCRIPTURE WHISPER

The people who walk in darkness will see a great light. For those who live in a land of deep darkness, a light will shine.
ISAIAH 9:2 NLT

It seems as if Isaiah wrote our Scripture Whisper specifically for our current times. Just imagine all that God maneuvered for thousands of years to protect and preserve these words so we can read them today. We, as God's children, can shine with the true light of Jesus and his message in the darkness permeating the world. God calls us to invite Jesus to live through us, arranging divine moments between us and those who need the hope of encouragement and inspiration in their sea of despair.

God does not create problems, but he does use them to draw the lost to his kingdom and to invite all to live in the aura of his love. This world is full of conflicting and confusing messages that create darkness for those who don't understand the truth. Let's share the light of hope in Jesus.

Jesus of joy, many are walking in darkness and need to see your light in us. Help us take a bold stand for the gospel of salvation.

Let's Follow the Fire

SCRIPTURE WHISPER

Understand today that the LORD your God who goes before you is a devouring fire; he will defeat and subdue them before you. You will dispossess and destroy them quickly just as he has told you.

DEUTERONOMY 9:3 NET

We have heavy hearts when dissension enters families and long-term friendships. Satan is creating discord and is on a rampage to disrupt relationships in any way he can. We're battling spiritual forces, and it hurts.

Fortunately, our Scripture Whisper tells us that victory is won because Jesus goes before us. We must let him lead the way in these challenging situations. As a devouring fire, he will light the way, and truth be told, God shines brighter as the world gets darker. As Christ followers, it's not for us to fight our battles on our own. We must call on the Lord to heal the situations and mend hearts, for he is always working behind the scenes for his children.

Jesus of peace, everything can turn to good for those who love you and are called for your purpose. Help us radiate your light so darkness is disposed and destroyed. Thank you for your promise to go before us.

Let's Not Leave the Lost Behind

SCRIPTURE WHISPER

"I must work the works of Him who sent Me while it is day;
the night is coming when no one can work."
JOHN 9:4 NKJV

The time when the light of Jesus living through us on this
earth will be no more is growing near. We will be called
up to heaven, and those who are left behind will no longer
have the chance to hear his gospel through us. We must be
obedient to the Holy Spirit urging us to be his voice of hope,
even when it seems out of our comfort zone.

There was nothing comfortable about the inhumane
death Jesus endured so that we can be with him in heaven
for eternity. It is our purpose to be all Jesus created us to be
so we can inspire and encourage others to believe in Jesus
and adopt his lifestyle. Then they, too, can know his love and
join us in heaven.

Jesus of patience, help us be more devoted to our purpose,
seeking opportunities that you arrange for us to share
who you are. Broken hearts are all around, and people are
confused, scared, and looking for the light of hope. Lord,
help us introduce them to you, their only hope.

Let's Keep Jesus' Flame Burning

SCRIPTURE WHISPER

"As long as I'm in the world, I'm the light of the world."
JOHN 9:5 ISV

We need to energetically work while the sun shines. Someday the time to reach lost souls will be over. Today Jesus is not in this world in the flesh. He's at the throne of God, but he is vibrantly shining through each of us who have surrendered our lives to his ways and who live in his guiding footsteps.

That light of Jesus was illuminated within us when we invited him into our hearts. Through various turns in the journey of life, that light became brighter, yet at other times, it has been dulled because we allowed Satan to turn down the flame by interrupting God's plan, sending us on a detour from the journey Jesus prepared for our lives. Sadly, many never return. But we choose whether Satan or Jesus steers our journey. Jesus can lead us through the maze of life, equipping us to be all he created us to be so our light shines just a little brighter each day.

Jesus of kindness, we pray that we continually keep your light on so it diminishes the darkness, allowing others to see that you are in the world and the light of the world.

Scan To Branch Out

Let's Sow Generously

SCRIPTURE WHISPER

This I say: He who sows sparingly will also reap sparingly, and he who sows bountifully will also reap bountifully.

2 Corinthians 9:6 NKJV

We plant seeds in many ways: through our gifts and tithes in support of God's kingdom growth and through our time, efforts, and service to him. By devoting time in his Word, in prayer, and in worship, we plant seeds into the garden God continually grows within us. When we cultivate the garden within ourselves, we are better equipped to plant seeds in others through the knowledge, wisdom, and anointing of God's voice of direction.

When we generously plant seeds by embracing the numerous opportunities God arranges, we can be assured that Jesus will harvest blessings into our own lives and in those around us. God is pleased when our giving hearts plant seeds so that the harvest is plentiful for his glory. He blesses us to be a continual blessing to others.

Jesus of goodness, help us develop an insatiable thirst to plant seeds each day. It's an exhilarating blessing when we end our day knowing you are pleased. We long for the blessing of hearing, "Well done, faithful servant," from your fatherly voice.

Scan To Branch Out

Let's Remember God's Peace

SCRIPTURE WHISPER

His power will never end; peace will last forever. He will rule David's kingdom and make it grow strong. He will always rule with honesty and justice. The LORD All-Powerful will make certain that all of this is done.

ISAIAH 9:7 CEV

God promises to bring peace, but how does that factor into the chaos and unrest throughout the world today? We are to carry his peace in our hearts, much like a cloud of peace that follows us in our spirit despite the turmoil surrounding us. It's God's promise to restore and ensure justice. We can depend on that. He promised not to fail us.

Our heavenly Father longs to have a daily relationship born out of our own free will, but Satan is still free to disrupt our lives. Ultimately, when Jesus comes again, Satan will be defeated completely and will burn in eternity forevermore while we live in heaven without evil. There will be no more sickness and heartache nor the evil schemes that plague our land today. There will be no more entrance for Satan's sinful nature to overtake lives.

Jesus of faithfulness, may we walk in your presence, focusing on the words in our Scripture Whisper that tell us that you are all-powerful and will make certain that all you promised will be done.

Let's Depend On God's Generosity

SCRIPTURE WHISPER

God will generously provide all you need. Then you will always have everything you need and plenty left over to share with others.

2 CORINTHIANS 9:8 NLT

God promises that he will generously provide for our needs, and we will have plenty to share with others. It's in our time of greatest need when we must seek God's provision the most. The world calls us foolish, irresponsible, and delusional to depend on God's generosity when things seem hopeless. It's a battle as Satan sends his expert demons to keep us from stretching our faith.

Feeling abandoned in despair because of Satan's clamoring voice, it's so tempting to jump in the way and try to help God, to pull the parachute cord before we crash, failing to believe he will catch us before we fall. The Evil One does everything to instill fear as we fall, but we must intentionally keep our faith from wavering with the assurance that Jesus is waiting at the bottom to catch us with his opened arms. He will save us from despair, so we will have a testimony of his miraculous saving power through our unabandoned faith.

Jesus of gentleness, stretch our faith so we can be prepared for your great and mighty generosity if we should ever fall.

Scan To Branch Out

Let's Remain in Jesus' Shelter

SCRIPTURE WHISPER

The Lord is a shelter for the oppressed,
a refuge in times of trouble.

Psalm 9:9 nlt

Oppression is defined as the state of being controlled by others. Whom do we allow to affect or control who we are, what we do, or the decisions we make? Who is framing our personal, God-ordained future? If it's those with a lifestyle that mirrors the fruit of Jesus' Spirit, then we can rejoice with gratitude that we are aligned together. But if the evidence of their fruit is rotten, then they are affecting who we are in ways that are not of the Lord. They may be keeping us from the blessings that come from being who God created us to be and from uniquely fulfilling his great magnificent plan for the world.

Our almighty God promises to shelter us safely within a sanctuary of his presence where Satan cannot forever remain. All God asks is that we call on him. If we believe in the promises of God and that his Word has survived the test of time for us today, then we must cling to its every word in these troubling days.

Jesus of self-control, we ask to remain in your shelter, trusting with unwavering faith that you will do what you promised when we place everything in your masterful hands.

Let's Be the Lasso of Jesus

SCRIPTURE WHISPER

The one who provides seed for the sower and bread for food
will also provide and multiply your seed and increase the
harvest of your righteousness.

2 CORINTHIANS 9:10 CSB

God is both the source of what is planted and the source of
what is harvested. When we acknowledge his great gift, we
can expect a transformation in ways that seem impossible
in the eyes of the world. Nothing is impossible when we
depend on Jesus for all things.

We often encounter people whom we feel could never be
transformed or would never surrender into the loving arms
of Jesus, but when the source who created the heavens and
the earth gets involved, lives change. When God provides
seeds for us, his sowers, he promises he will also multiply
our seeds and increase the harvest of our righteousness.
Then our source of all things will transform even the most
hopeless.

Jesus of love, we pray that we remain focused on you.
You are the source of divine appointments that bring the
supernatural into our lives and into the lives of those you
choose to lasso into your kingdom, into your loving arms,
and into your way of life. We pray we never miss
an opportunity you arranged before us.

Scan To Branch Out

Let's Overflow with Blessings

SCRIPTURE WHISPER

Here is something else I have learned: The fastest runners and the greatest heroes don't always win races and battles. Wisdom, intelligence, and skill don't always make you healthy, rich, or popular. We each have our own share of misfortune.

ECCLESIASTES 9:11 CEV

There's no luck in the lives of believers. There are only blessings in the hands of God. Even though, as our Scripture Whisper says, we each have our own share of misfortune, these are not from God. But he promises he will use them for his glory.

Those who depend on luck, their own plans, or their abilities will be disappointed. Life on earth is short, and nothing is guaranteed. But God's Word tells us that God "will clear the road for you to follow" if you depend on God to lead you (Proverbs 3:6). There's no happenstance or luck when we surrender our all into the care of our Creator and Lord. We must share this assurance when so many struggle with their perception of bad luck from their choice to live apart from God.

Jesus of joy, we pray for those who live for luck instead of blessings and for the opportunity to share the difference between depending on God and depending on random happenings. May we have a chance to share the hope of your overflowing blessings.

Let's Seek Jesus' Wisdom

SCRIPTURE WHISPER

If you become wise, you will be the one to benefit.
If you scorn wisdom, you will be the one to suffer.
PROVERBS 9:12 NLT

The journey of life creates opportunities to reach either
a deeper degree of wisdom or a pit of foolish setbacks.
It depends on the choices we make: to move forward or
go backward, to become better or bitter because of the
challenges that we face. Those mature in wisdom have
established a daily, personal relationship with Jesus and are
committed to living his way. They react immediately with his
wisdom when their spirits are tempted to veer off track.

Then there are the mockers and fools who reject God's
teaching and consistently do what is wrong despite the
consequences. And then there are the complacent who
straddle the fence, one day going this way, another that way.
Without God's wisdom, people live in a vortex of confusion
and foolish ways, always fret about their lack of stability, and
never understand why their life remains in a state of chaos
even though wisdom is available to all who turn to God.

Jesus of peace, we pray for deeper insight into your wisdom
and to be an example for those who don't know you.

Let's Live Who Jesus Is

SCRIPTURE WHISPER

"Go and learn what this means: 'I desire mercy, not sacrifice.'
For I have not come to call the righteous, but sinners, to
repentance."
MATTHEW 9:13 MSB

Our Scripture Whisper consists of words spoken by Jesus
when he walked this earth. Jesus came for those in distress
and in need of the hope of his salvation. Many of us were
brought up in churches that taught us about religion instead
of having a personal, intimate relationship with Jesus and
allowing his Holy Spirit to guide and direct our lives.

A religious spirit is a tough groove to retrench because
a religious way of life structured on rules and regulations
takes time to strip away. It requires peeling the religious
habits formulated through our childhood and adult life until
we are introduced to the personal side of our Lord. Jesus
is not a tyrant waiting to scold us and put us in spiritual
time-out when we don't follow his rules. He's our best friend,
our counselor, the comforter to widows, and the daddy to
orphans.

Jesus of patience, we pray that we will engage you as a
partner in life and that we reflect that friendship along our
daily journey, influencing others to walk hand in
hand with you in their daily walk too.

Scan To Branch Out

Let's Flourish

SCRIPTURE WHISPER

How much more certainly shall the blood of Christ, who strengthened by the eternal Spirit offered Himself to God, free from blemish, purify your consciences from lifeless works for you to serve the ever-living God?

HEBREWS 9:14 WNT

Jesus Christ offers complete purity for those who accept him into their hearts, transforming their lives from worldly, sinful ways to a personal relationship with our Lord. Jesus' life was without blemish, and our rebirth through him provides a permanent transformation. But Satan, the accuser of all wrongs committed in the past, is very good at messing with our conscience, bringing into our minds a spirit of unworthiness.

Have you forgiven yourself as Jesus has? Are you allowing Satan to continually remind you of the things from your past that Jesus has forgiven and forgotten? Satan uses his tools of regret, guilt, and shame to play the recording of your past. It keeps you from moving forward into God's goodness ahead and allows others to hijack God's plan. This disrupts blessings in store for us.

Jesus of kindness, we pray to be able to shift from allowing the accusers to inhibit our lives to flourishing and living the plan you created for us.

Scan To Branch Out

Let's Trust God's Mercy

SCRIPTURE WHISPER

He says to Moses, "I will have mercy on whomever I have mercy, and I will have compassion on whomever I have compassion."

ROMANS 9:15 AMP

God's mercy has nothing to do with our will or the things we pursue. It is completely up to God. In our human minds, we question the fairness of God's mercy. We often compare our plight with the plights of people who aren't sold out to Jesus yet seem to receive mercy in areas where we could use a strong dose of mercy ourselves.

But there is no injustice with God. He has an intricate plan. God grants his mercy for his kingdom plan not for our individual gain. He will accomplish his purposes with his chosen children or without us. But if we refuse to follow him, our blessings will be diverted. When our hearts become aligned with Jesus, we begin to understand freedom and the true joy of living full of Jesus' mercy and compassion, which protects us and navigates us around the land mines to bring us in sync with his plan.

Jesus of goodness, we surrender any areas of our lives that we've allowed to interfere in your plan. Help others understand the freedom found in living your way.

Let's Value the Rainbow Promise

SCRIPTURE WHISPER

"Whenever the rainbow appears in the clouds, I will see it and remember the everlasting covenant between God and all living creatures of every kind on the earth."

GENESIS 9:16 NIV

We can count on God's promises. No matter how dark the clouds and whirling winds through the storms of life, we can be assured there will always be a rainbow of promise awaiting when we depend on our Lord to lead us. The rainbow is God's smile, and when we feel the smile of God upon us, Satan's interference is shattered as Jesus' favor surrounds us.

God provided the ultimate gift to us through the sacrifice of his Son, breaking the stronghold of sin for those who accept Jesus as the Son of God. All we must do is call on the name of Jesus, and Satan's stronghold is loosened.

Jesus of faithfulness, we pray that we never take for granted the rainbows of your promises that you have arranged to help us heal from the hurt and heartaches we all go through. You bring meaning to our suffering, and we can rest in the assurance that you are coming to carry us as believers toward an eternal rainbow, where there will be no more stormy days in our lives.

Scan To Branch Out

Let's Display Jesus' Power

SCRIPTURE WHISPER

The Scripture tells Pharaoh, I raised you up for this reason so that I may display my power in you and that my name may be proclaimed in the whole earth.

ROMANS 9:17 CSB

We have the same power that raised Christ from death on the cross so that we can be his voice to declare the gospel of Jesus by the way we live. Through the declaration of this Scripture Whisper today, we have Jesus' authority as ambassadors of his goodness, might, and power to transform what seems impossible into reality. We can achieve this through our unwavering faith that God will do what he promised us throughout his Word.

God calls us each for a purpose that no one else can fulfill. Too often, we wimp out on our Lord. We become timid and complacent, feel ill-equipped or unworthy, and fall for the sneaky tactics of Satan. But when we partner with our Lord and are covered by the power of Jesus, an aura of protection surrounds us.

Jesus of gentleness, we pray for renewed strength as we depend on you to work through us as your ambassadors every day. Help us draw others toward you and work in partnership with you to expand your kingdom.

Scan To Branch Out

Let's Always Hope in Jesus

SCRIPTURE WHISPER

The poor will not always be forgotten, nor the hope of the burdened perish forever.

PSALM 9:18 AMP

It's prudent to recall the many times God has intervened when we felt burdened with no hope and time seemed to be running out, but he showed up in his perfect way and precise timing to catch us before we crashed. That is a reflection of God's character, goodness, and faithfulness to never forget us when we feel poor in spirit. He is orchestrating intricate moments behind the scenes even when it seems he's gone silent. Jesus has our back in every situation when we let him.

Even when we experience the hardships of life, like poverty and hopelessness, God's Word assures us that the Lord sees us and remains with us. We can depend on that when we invite him into our messes. That's when he builds a testimony for us to share, attracting others into his kingdom. That's our purpose as we allow him to live through us moment by moment.

Jesus of self-control, help us reflect on the many times throughout the Bible and throughout each of our lives when you came through in miraculous ways to save and rescue your people. You did it before, and we boldly expect that you will do it again.

Scan To Branch Out

Let's Emulate Paul

SCRIPTURE WHISPER

Though free from all human control, I have made myself the slave of all in the hope of winning as many converts as possible.

1 CORINTHIANS 9:19 WNT

Paul is an example for us today by his willingness to conform to whatever would attract an audience to the gospel of Jesus as the only way to salvation. Paul did whatever he could to fulfill the plan of God. Shall we consider our motives? What drives our way of life? Is it our career that drives us toward money or the power to accumulate more worldly gain, none of which satisfy or deserve our entire focus or allegiance?

Instead, as Christ followers, our highest ambition should be focused on others as we interact throughout the day with lost souls who need the hope of Jesus. We should be a mirror of Paul's dedication. When we grasp the true depth of God's incomprehensible love for his children, our passion should be channeled toward serving him so we can win lost souls through the way we live.

Jesus of love, help us evaluate our motivation and bring to light our life purpose. We pray that we become more like Paul, letting nothing distract us from being used as your voice of hope to those who need you.

Scan To Branch Out

Let's Witness by Our Lifestyle

SCRIPTURE WHISPER

He immediately started to preach about Jesus in the synagogues, saying, "This is the Son of God."
ACTS 9:20 ISV

Anyone who walks around bragging about being filled with the Spirit without bearing testimony to Jesus Christ is a walking contradiction. When Paul had his life-changing encounter with Jesus, he immediately stopped persecuting Christians and started proclaiming the truth about Jesus.

Has our encounter with Jesus filled us up in the Spirit, as evidenced by the walk we walk and the talk we talk? Has the Scripture come alive in our lives? Are we living the fruit of his Spirit? Is he living in and through the moments of our lives, leading the way? If not, we are living a contradiction of our devotion and service to our Savior.

Jesus of joy, we ask that you unveil any areas of our lives that we live differently from what you intended when you created us. We pray that others know us by our fruit, that we live in the example of your love, joy, peace, patience, kindness, goodness, faithfulness, gentleness, and self-control. May every aspect of our lives be devoted to the service of fulfilling your plan.

Scan To Branch Out

Let's Know Jesus Hears

SCRIPTURE WHISPER

While I was speaking in prayer, the man Gabriel, whom I had seen in the vision at the beginning, being caused to fly swiftly, reached me about the time of the evening offering.

DANIEL 9:21 NKJV

God hears our prayers and wastes no time in replying, as promised in our Scripture Whisper. That's great assurance. God helped Daniel understand that he hears and answers, but sometimes God's answers may seem delayed.

Often there are reasons for which we are not aware and beyond our control for the delay of his answer. The answer could depend on the choices of others who need to get in alignment with God's plan. Also the prayer may be answered in a different way from what we expect, but as Jesus' followers, we can be assured that in God's hands, it will unfold in his perfect timing and in his perfect way for our good and for his glory.

Jesus of peace, help us become more aware that every word we pray reaches your heart. May we be more eager to align our desires with your desires as we pray so that our prayers are aligned with your plans. Let us rest in the expectancy that you will accomplish your purpose in us.

Scan To Branch Out

Let's Cherish Answered Prayers

SCRIPTURE WHISPER

Jesus, turning and seeing her, said, "Daughter, take courage; your faith has made you well." And at once the woman was made well.

MATTHEW 9:22 NASB

Jesus places miracles throughout our days. We are just too hurried to notice. Too often, our faith is hopeful, but we're not intentional about noticing them or expectant that God will do what he promised. That's not faith. The woman who touched Jesus' cloak in Matthew 9 expected Jesus to heal her, and he did.

We are masters at taking things for granted. Even the slightest bits of favor go unnoticed, but if we realize that the hand of God carefully arranges every detail of our lives out of his pure love and tenderness for us, we might take more notice.

Jesus of patience, we pray that we become more keenly aware of the little things you do to make our lives smoother rather than failing to acknowledge that you are involved in the details of our days. Forgive us for the times when we have taken for granted the blessings you arrange. We are grateful to you for the miracle moments you have provided. Let us make you smile as we pause throughout the day and say, "Thank you, Jesus." We are grateful for all you do.

Let's Believe in Miracles

SCRIPTURE WHISPER

Jesus said to him, "If You are able? All things are possible to the one believing."

MARK 9:23 BLB

Do we pray with unwavering faith, or do we tend to prepare a backup plan in case our prayers are not yet answered or not answered in ways we envisioned? When our hearts are aligned with the heart of God, his desires and our desires are weaved together, and nothing is impossible. If we are devoted to the plan of God being fulfilled, we can be assured he will always catch us when we are hanging on by our last thread. He is looking for that kind of faith, the kind where we are doomed if he doesn't show up.

When we choose joy in the storms, that's the testimony he wants us to share to draw others to him. If it doesn't require a miracle, it's just another story that fades into conversations, but when we can passionately tell our God stories, lives change, and people pay attention.

Jesus of kindness, help us eagerly seek moments when you can demonstrate your miraculous ways for others to see. We pray these miracle moments become a brilliant light to overcome the darkness over our land. One miracle at a time can change one life at a time.

Let's Be a Model of Jesus

SCRIPTURE WHISPER

Christ did not enter a man-made copy of the true sanctuary, but He entered heaven itself, now to appear on our behalf in the presence of God.

HEBREWS 9:24 MSB

Do we live a lifestyle worthy of Jesus' suffering and sacrifice for our wrongdoings, wrong choices, wrong feelings, and wrong actions that separated us from the character that God designed for and expects from his children? That's quite a serious thought we should take to heart.

How it must grieve our Lord when we frivolously go about our days without including him in a relationship for which he died. As his sons and daughters, heirs to all he has, how dare we not become more intentional and honored and even delighted to include Jesus in a daily walk together? Life is so much more peaceful and joyful alongside the tenderness of his care.

Jesus of goodness, we want to engage with you in the moments of our lives as the very best friend we could ever hope for. You want only the best for us and extend your outstretched hand to guide us through the maze of life, which you have already arranged. Help us share this message through the way we live alongside you every day.

Scan To Branch Out

Let's Be Disciplined for Eternity

SCRIPTURE WHISPER

All athletes are disciplined in their training. They do it to win a prize that will fade away, but we do it for an eternal prize.
1 Corinthians 9:25 NLT

Too often people pretend their motives are aligned with the heart of God, but instead they work for worldly gain that will fade away. Authentic believers, disciplined in their training in God's Word and devoted to prayer, work out of love for Jesus toward an eternal prize. It's all about the condition of their hearts and the fruit of their spirits. These types of evidence determine the prize for which they are striving. Is it from a heart for others and God's glory, or is it the pride and selfish gain within their soul that proves their heart?

Where are our hearts? When we have opportunities to achieve a return on investment to save lives for the kingdom of God, is that our focus? Do we invest our time to bestow that salvation blessing on others? Where are our hearts in reaching the lost and hopeless, navigating believers toward a more intimate relationship with Jesus, and turning a worrisome way of life into a faithful trust in him?

Jesus of faithfulness, help us evaluate our hearts and focus on making a difference for you.

Scan To Branch Out

Let's Forgive Ourselves

SCRIPTURE WHISPER

He would have had to suffer many times since the foundation of the world. But now he has appeared one time, at the end of the ages, for the removal of sin by the sacrifice of himself.

HEBREWS 9:26 CSB

We don't have to ask for forgiveness over and over for our past mistakes. If we do, we have to ask ourselves if we're questioning whether Jesus' death and resurrection were enough to forgive us and wipe our slate clean. He even forgets our past, so why don't we live like we are forgiven?

Not forgiving ourselves is a sneaky but very effective tool for Satan's army. Those guilt-inducing demons play in our minds a recording that tells us that we are not worthy, that we should feel shame, and that our past sins are unforgivable and unforgettable. Those lies are inhibiting the blessings of favor that Jesus died to bestow upon his children. Jesus suffered in agony once and for all. His blood is sufficient to cover the sins of those who sincerely and deeply ask for forgiveness. Let's forgive ourselves as we have been forgiven.

Jesus of gentleness, we pray that we live a life worthy of your death for us, with a renewed self-forgiveness, because you have forever shattered that record of the past.

Scan To Branch Out

Let's Fulfill Our Purpose

SCRIPTURE WHISPER

I tell you of a truth, there be some standing here, which shall not taste of death, till they see the kingdom of God.

LUKE 9:27 KJV

What if before the end of your life, you could meet the person you could have become? This thought should prompt us to evaluate who we are today and what our future holds. How have we allowed the journey of our life to frame our identity and how others perceive us? Do others dread to see us walking in the door? Or do they feel inspired and encouraged when we leave?

It's never too late to change. In fact, our journey in life, although rough through many seasons, is meant to equip us to be the person God designed us to become. He takes what Satan tried to disrupt and molds us into his useful vessel with the character of his Son. What good would it do to gain everything you want on earth yet lose the real you? Those who choose to use their challenges to fulfill their God-ordained purpose by living in partnership with Jesus right here on earth are going to see with their own eyes the kingdom of God.

Jesus of self-control, we pray that we become the person you created us to be to fulfill your kingdom purpose.

Scan To Branch Out

Let's Be Ready

SCRIPTURE WHISPER

Christ died only once to take away the sins of many people. But when he comes again, it will not be to take away sin. He will come to save everyone who is waiting for him.
HEBREWS 9:28 CEV

Our Scripture Whisper reminds us that death isn't the end, but we often live as if death is the last word. People typically want to fulfill all their desires before they reach their death. However, death is just a transition, not a conclusion, because Jesus is coming back for those who believe and put their trust in him.

Jesus came the first time to take away our sins so he can engage in a personal relationship with his children. He's coming a second time to take us to an indescribable home in heaven, where there will be no more broken hearts and no more pain. We are now just living in the interim between Christ's death and his return, waiting, and in our waiting, he appoints us to encourage as many as we can to join us on that great day when we will be transformed for eternity.

Jesus of love, we pray that we will never give up during these tumultuous times and will continue moving forward in faith, knowing you are coming back soon. Help us be ready.

Scan To Branch Out

Let's Grow in Faith

SCRIPTURE WHISPER

He touched their eyes, saying, "It shall be done to you according to your faith."
MATTHEW 9:29 LSB

Faith, trust, and confidence grow like a muscle when we are faced with challenges. Our faith muscles stretch and develop whenever we depend completely on God to show up and our faith does not waver.

Satan attempts to make us feel unworthy, fearful, regretful, and shameful to inhibit our next level of faith by causing us to question our trust and confidence that God will come through. Satan wants to send us back to the starting line to go through the journey again. When we doubt God's ability as the maker of the universe to save the day every time, just in time, we fail to pass our faith tests. So when we reflect on the times when God came through before, why do we ever allow the gut-wrenching, worrisome thoughts to hijack our faith? When we are weary and woeful and it seems our faith stretch will never end, we must choose joy; it transfers the weariness to Satan, who loses the battle. Victory is won when we call out the name of Jesus and become joyful in the storm.

Jesus of joy, we pray that our testimony will be that you are God of the impossible.

Scan To Branch Out

Let's Open Blinded Hearts

SCRIPTURE WHISPER

The man replied to them, "That's amazing! You don't know where he's from. Yet, he gave me sight."
JOHN 9:30 GW

We know that God amazingly responds and delights to work through those who love him, depend on him, and partner with him along life's path. What more motivation do we need to daily engage in prayer and worship than desiring to live in the purpose of our creation?

Our Scripture Whisper proves Jesus gives sight to the blind. What a shout-out to the world to follow the way of Jesus in everything, giving him glory because nothing is impossible for those who ask with unwavering faith for God to give sight and new birth into a way of life devoted to our Lord. Jesus came into the world to amaze us with his grace and mercy, forgiving and forgetting our transgressions and embracing us in a willing relationship with him. He opens blind eyes so people receive him in their hearts and join us in his heavenly kingdom.

Jesus of peace, we pray that you open blinded eyes through us, bringing glimmers of hope to the hopeless so others see the light of your Spirit living in us.

Scan To Branch Out

October

Let's Be Devoted to God's Word

SCRIPTURE WHISPER

Jesus said: I tell you for certain only thieves and robbers climb over the fence instead of going in through the gate to the sheep pen.
JOHN 10:1 CEV

The master thief and robber is Satan. He climbs into the vulnerable places in our lives where we've left the gate opened. When we are devoted to God's Word, we can discern his voice more distinctly so Satan cannot camouflage himself. We can easily recognize the trickery of his evil intentions by clearly seeking the voice of our Lord.

Sheep know their shepherd and follow him because they are familiar with his voice. They won't follow a stranger but will scatter because they aren't used to the sound of another's voice. This should instill within us an insatiable desire to continue learning every day to clearly recognize the voice of Jesus. We would encounter less turmoil because we will no longer hear negative influences over the one who cast the stars in the sky.

Jesus of patience, help us delight in seeking the clarity of your voice, eliminating the confusion and trickery of the camouflaged voice of the Evil One. We pray that the voices of darkness throughout our land will be overtaken by the voice of light found in you.

Scan To Branch Out

Let's Think Sensibly

SCRIPTURE WHISPER

Sensible thoughts lead you to do right; foolish thoughts lead you to do wrong.

ECCLESIASTES 10:2 CEV

Solomon says that fools make their foolishness known; there's no hiding it. It takes only a foolish moment to contaminate a stellar reputation, and Satan is a master at that. The Evil One dangles temptations in our minds and works through the open doors of foolishness in our lives. And then he can use our foolish thoughts, like jealousy and contempt, to influence others to act foolishly in the same manner. Even a Christian can be tempted to obey their foolish thoughts because of insecurity, guilt, and pride.

A wise person's heart seeks what's right and is aware of the lurking areas of foolishness. One's wisdom may go unnoticed or unseen and even forgotten by everyone but God, but what does that matter? The one whom we are to please is the only one who matters. Fools are blinded to the fact that their foolishness is apparent to everyone else, but seeking God's wisdom opens our eyes to his truth.

Jesus of kindness, we pray that we carve out more time each day to seek your wisdom so we can be equipped to do what is right in the days ahead.

Let's Share God's Amazing Grace

SCRIPTURE WHISPER

Not knowing about God's righteousness and seeking to establish their own, they did not subject themselves to the righteousness of God.

ROMANS 10:3 NASB

Some of us have grown up with a religious background that didn't teach about a personal relationship with Jesus based on his gift of grace. This may have caused us to think our works earned his love and acceptance. We were taught to establish a point system of good deeds and follow the rules of religion that establish our scorecard of righteousness.

Those who follow biblical laws and think they will go to heaven if only they swirl around doing good works miss the purity of the gospel. Not by works but through a relationship with Jesus are we saved. God demands absolute perfection to be in his presence in a relationship; therefore, we must live a life without sin. Of course, we are all sinful. The Word tells us there's been only one perfect life, and that life was Jesus. But because of his sinlessness and sacrificial grace, taking on our sins to death, we can enter heaven when we accept Jesus in our hearts and involve him in our life.

Jesus of goodness, we pray that we share your message that there is no need to strive and toil our way to salvation. May we encourage others to invite you into their lives to be blanketed with your amazing grace.

Scan To Branch Out

Let's Lay to Rest Offenses

SCRIPTURE WHISPER

If the spirit of the ruler rises up against you, don't leave your place; for gentleness lays great offenses to rest.

ECCLESIASTES 10:4 WEB

We should be calm as we emulate Jesus, but sometimes our anger controls our actions. Satan has ways to evoke anger in those of us who struggle to heal from our past, which can marinate and transform into an uncontrollable rage. The tricks of Satan in this area of our lives interfere with family dynamics and office environments and friendships. A tone of voice, an accent, a smell, a look-alike person, or a setting may be a reminder of unresolved emotions, hurt, and rejection. This may set off our anger when the scars of our pasts haven't yet healed.

When we encounter someone's anger, we must remember that the resulting display often was not meant toward the one with whom they lost control. Instead of responding with our own anger, let's respond with gentleness, remembering that Jesus can lay all offenses to rest and heal us as we abide in his faithfulness.

Jesus of faithfulness, we pray for those who struggle to get past their past and for those in our lives who keep trying to remind us of ours. Help us forget the past as you have and find healing.

Scan To Branch Out

Let's Give Jesus Our Thoughts

SCRIPTURE WHISPER

Overthrowing arguments, and every high thing lifting itself up against the knowledge of God, and taking captive every thought into the obedience of Christ.

2 CORINTHIANS 10:5 BLB

When we start each day by giving our minds to Jesus, then there's no second-guessing. Our thoughts become his thoughts when we ask Jesus to think through us. And we can rest in assurance that Satan can't hijack our thoughts because Scripture tells us that the spiritual weapons we fight with are "divinely powerful toward the demolition of strongholds" (v. 4).

First thing each morning, we should be intentional to cast our minds to Jesus. He can capture any interference from Satan by bringing our thoughts into obedience to Jesus' way of thinking. We can think as Jesus does and make choices in the ways he chooses throughout the day. Offenses, arguments, rejections, jealousy, and hurt will pass right into the care of Jesus when we begin our day surrendering our minds to his management.

Jesus of gentleness, we pray that we become mindful each morning of the freedom we gain from surrendering our minds and full communication to you. It's freeing to know things that others say and thoughts that they provoke are no longer our responsibility once we cast them to you and leave them in your care.

Scan To Branch Out

Let's Depend On Jesus

SCRIPTURE WHISPER

Lord, there is no one like you; you are mighty, and your
name is great and powerful.

JEREMIAH 10:6 GNT

Who can possibly compare to our almighty, powerful
God, whom Jeremiah so wonderfully described in today's
Scripture Whisper? Who shouldn't depend on Jesus? How
can the world not acknowledge him? The evil forces can be
so deceptive about the true and mighty one who created
all things. Even Christ's followers find themselves being
deceived each day. They put God on a mighty throne but
don't include him in the moments of their lives as a personal
confidant.

If we were offered an expert in every field to handle all
situations we encounter, would we not access their knowledge?
Well, that's what Jesus offers. Turning to him for all things,
both small and large, will result in our lives unfolding more
seamlessly. Jesus is our everything, and we should invite him
into our moments and live together with him.

Jesus of self-control, you long for personal involvement in
our lives, which is the reason you went to the cross. We pray
that we never take for granted your gift of being our Lord and
that we honor you and love you as our best friend.

Scan To Branch Out

Let's Make Jesus Our Gatekeeper

SCRIPTURE WHISPER

Jesus said, "Truly, I tell all of you emphatically, I'm the gate for the sheep."

JOHN 10:7 ISV

Jesus emphatically described himself as our gatekeeper. In this verse, Jesus is the Shepherd, and he also became the sacrificial Lamb on the cross. Jesus made all sin sacrifices and burnt offerings unnecessary, offering eternal life in heaven for those who accept him in their hearts.

There are many who pretend to be a shepherd but allow Satan to climb over the fence. They are wolves disguised in sheep's clothing with no concern for the well-being of the sheep. They enter in slyly for their own gain. We must stay sharp in our awareness by studying God's Word so we can identify the counterfeits, those who pose as Christians but are far from what authentic Christ followers are all about. And as we engage in continual prayer, we can better recognize Jesus' voice, just like sheep recognize their shepherd's voice.

Jesus of love, we pray to devote more time in our days to hearing your still, small voice and aligning our hearts with your desires in obedience to your plan.

Let's Refrain from Revenge

SCRIPTURE WHISPER

One who digs a pit may fall into it, and one who breaks through a wall may be bitten by a snake.

ECCLESIASTES 10:8 NET

The Enemy is lurking, waiting to pounce on any vengeful thoughts that surface from the harsh words and actions of others. We tend to allow anger and emotions to establish a time bomb within our spirits for Satan to exploit with thoughts of revenge. When we strategize ways to get back at others, it may boomerang right back to us.

That's not the way of God. Instead, he instructs us to give bread to our hungry enemies and a drink if they are thirsty, treating others as we would want others to treat us. God's wisdom of self-control offers us an edge that we don't want to be without. It is foolishness on our part not to seek wisdom from the one who knows the future and wants the very best for us. Just imagine how many consequences we would avoid by asking Jesus to carry us through each decision and every choice. It's just a matter of pausing, asking, listening, obeying, and then leaving everything in Jesus' care.

Jesus of joy, help us engage you at the hint of a volatile situation brewing so that you can diffuse the temptation for us to react in ways that are not of you.

Scan To Branch Out

Let's Give Jesus Our Door Keys

SCRIPTURE WHISPER

I am the door: by me if any man enter in, he shall be saved, and shall go in and out, and find pasture.

JOHN 10:9 KJV

Jesus is our doorkeeper when we invite him in to manage our moments. So why do we often leave the door of our lives swinging back and forth for Satan to sneak in? Jesus tells us clearly that anyone who enters through his door will be saved and will live with him in eternity. He is the only way to eternal life. He promises that we will find a pasture, a place of peace and spiritual security, where we can abide in his care.

We must turn over the keys to our door to Jesus, trusting that he will navigate those he arranges to enter our lives and lock the door to those who cause harm.

Jesus of peace, we join in unity to become your dedicated ambassadors. Help us influence others to prevent Satan's entry into the door of their lives with your sacrificial seal and open the door to expand your kingdom, one life at a time.

Let's Mend Relationships

SCRIPTURE WHISPER

"A thief comes to steal, kill, and destroy. But I came so that my sheep will have life and so that they will have everything they need."

JOHN 10:10 GW

When there is a disruption in our peace, let it be known that Satan has come to destroy the work of Jesus within us. There are so many challenges these days in relationships. That's an area where Satan sneaks in chaos, confusion, and dissension. We are in the midst of a spiritual warfare running rampant throughout our world. Asking Jesus to fight the battle for us will return peace to a volatile conflict.

Jesus desires for his children to enjoy life, and he offers everything they need in abundance until it overflows. When that's not happening, then we must realize that the thief has come to steal and kill and destroy. Through Jesus' power, we can call on legions of angels to fight the battle so we can return to the enjoyment of life amid the storms we encounter every day.

Jesus of patience, we pray for relationships to heal throughout our land. Lord, you suffered and died and rose again so we can engage in a relationship with you. Please bring peace to our relationships.

Scan To Branch Out

Let's Not Be Disappointed

SCRIPTURE WHISPER

The Scriptures say no one who has faith will be disappointed.
ROMANS 10:11 CEV

Our expectations should remain high when we adhere to, trust in, and rely on Jesus to navigate our moments throughout each day. We will never be disappointed. That's what the Bible says.

Oh, we may be disappointed that things don't unfold in our specific ways, according to our timing or in our strategic plans, but we can be assured that God's plans far exceed what we can even envision. Scripture says Jesus only wants the best for us, and since only God knows the future, it's futile for us to ever be disappointed.

Jesus of kindness, we ask to become more intentional about making your plans our heart's desire and that peace will overtake disappointments when things don't go as we intended. Your plans are far greater than we could ever imagine, so teach us to depend on you, the only one who knows the future and creates individualized plans for each of us each moment of every day.

Scan To Branch Out

Let's Overlook Faults

SCRIPTURE WHISPER

Hate starts quarrels,
but love covers every wrong.

PROVERBS 10:12 GW

Forgiving and overlooking others' faults are often challenging. As Christ followers, we have the blessing of loving with the unconditional love of Jesus when we intentionally involve him in matters that cause us a sense of hatred. Anger fuels disagreements, which create discord in relationships, but love calms rebellion and creates an atmosphere of peace.

Forgiveness requires a big dose of Jesus' patience as we encounter hatred throughout the world. Battles of evil warfare overtake the spirits of those lost without a relationship with Jesus to depend on. Let's love like Jesus, which covers every wrong.

Jesus of goodness, we pray that love over hatred, gentleness rather than rebellion, and peace instead of discord cover our land. We pray for each other, that we carry the fruit of your Spirit to extinguish the darkness. May your brilliant light overtake our land with a renewed spirit of revival.

Scan To Branch Out

Let's Be Authentic to the Message

SCRIPTURE WHISPER

No temptation has come upon you except what is common to humanity. But God is faithful; he will not allow you to be tempted beyond what you are able, but with the temptation he will also provide the way out so that you may be able to bear it.

1 CORINTHIANS 10:13 CSB

We are faced with an ever-changing world with radical technological advances. Some areas of technology enhance our ability to read the Bible and access numerous translations and commentaries that expand our knowledge of God's wisdom and help us learn of his way. On the contrary, the same technology opens a wider door to the world of evil. It's our choice to allow ourselves to become more vulnerable to sin or to use technology to strengthen our relationship with Jesus.

We must depend on God's guidance to provide a way out of our temptations. We can accept Jesus' way of escape or succumb to the snares of the Evil One. Jesus suffered for our moments of temptations, and he asks us to cast them into his care. We must share of God's faithfulness to those who are drowning in Satan's evil schemes so that they turn to Jesus to intervene.

Jesus of faithfulness, thank you for providing a way out of temptations when we turn to you. May we always remain faithful to your message.

Scan To Branch Out

Let's Always Turn to Jesus

SCRIPTURE WHISPER

You do see; you take notice of trouble and suffering and are always ready to help. The helpless commit themselves to you; you have always helped the needy.

PSALM 10:14 GNT

God sees all things: everyone and all their actions, every detail of every moment, even what we say or think in our hearts. God sees trouble when we are afflicted and brokenhearted and offers us his caring hand. The goodness of the Lord is all around, but too often, we ignore his presence and his compassionate heart that longs to guide us through our troubles and suffering.

Jesus is waiting to help us, bring hope to our hopeless souls, and heal our broken hearts. God promises to help us in our time of need, but we must ask and depend on him to provide in his perfect way and in his optimum timing.

Jesus of gentleness, we pray that we will always rely on you in our moments of helplessness. In your presence, troubles will flee, and the evil forces are powerless.

Scan To Branch Out

Let's Share the Good News

SCRIPTURE WHISPER

How can people tell the Good News if no one sends them? As Scripture says, "How beautiful are the feet of the messengers who announce the Good News."

ROMANS 10:15 GW

Many are confused about whom they can trust these days. How can they know whom to trust if they haven't heard of the only one whom they can truly trust? And how can they know of the one in whom to trust if nobody tells them? And how will anyone tell them unless someone is sent to tell the good news of Jesus, who saves our souls? And who is there to be sent if we, his followers, don't listen and heed his call?

Jesus has called us to be his ambassadors of truth by the way we live our lives and express our stories of his trustworthiness. We must be an army of unity as we share all the good things about our loving Savior. But not everybody is ready to listen and act. Before they can trust, they must listen, but unless we share Christ's words, there's nothing to listen to.

Jesus of self-control, we pray to be bolder in living out your message, not aggressively turning people away from you but, rather, gently living the lifestyle of your character.

Let's Remain Wise and Pure

SCRIPTURE WHISPER

"Behold, I am sending you out as sheep in the midst of wolves, so be wise as serpents and innocent as doves."
MATTHEW 10:16 ESV

We live in a culture where others question our motives. Some will attack our reputation, calling us Jesus freaks who are weak, frail, and spineless. How that must sadden our Lord! The opposite is true of Jesus' strength, which surpasses any understanding. If only the lost would realize how tenderly Jesus can turn around their chaotic and confused lives.

But the Evil One operating within them radically twists the truth with ridicule and sneers about Jesus followers, who freely live in the Holy Spirit's protection by inviting Jesus to walk through life with them. When others ridicule us for our faith, they offer us a platform for sharing God's kingdom news. And we should never fret or worry about what to say or how we say it. The right words will be there. Jesus will supply every wise and pure word to share.

Jesus of love, we pray that we, as your sheep, never fear when we are daily sent into the world's pack of wolves. We are always covered with an anointing of your wisdom and protection.

Let's Make Jesus the Majority

SCRIPTURE WHISPER

Faith comes from hearing the message, and the message is heard through the word about Christ.

ROMANS 10:17 NIV

Many don't believe in Jesus even though they've been told about him. All through Bible times, people rejected the words of God through Scripture and the prophets. It's so heart-wrenching that Jesus followers have always been in the minority. After all, Jesus suffered for us so that he could engage in a personal relationship with his creation, and it's a tragedy when we turn our backs on his loving goodness.

God's purpose is to extend grace to all people, even those who are not searching or asking to be introduced to his saving grace of sacrifice, his mercy, and his unconditional love. When believers are faced with injustice, frustration, and pain, God uses what Satan meant to sidetrack and harm us and brings us back into his loving care. Our Lord is brokenhearted at our disobedience, but he will show us mercy and grace and immeasurable patience when we return to him.

Jesus of joy, we pray that others hear our faith and that what they hear comes with the message of your love, mercy, and grace through the opportunities you divinely arrange for us to share.

Scan To Branch Out

Let's Filter Our Words

SCRIPTURE WHISPER

You can hide your hatred by telling lies,
but you are a fool to spread lies.

PROVERBS 10:18 CEV

There's such hatred throughout our land, and many don't
realize why people react so harshly and in horrific ways.
Satan rants and rages through the world to beat down God's
chosen ambassadors, attempting to weaken our testimony
of the grace of Jesus. When never-ending slander is tearing
down Jesus' name, succumbing to weariness is easy, but God
has called us to stand firm in unity, upholding the Word of
God as the foundation of life and Jesus as the only way out of
worldly confusion.

Let's share the hope found in Jesus, whose suffering and
death rescues those who have invited him into their hearts
to live in a relationship together. It's a choice to either allow
hatred and revenge to overtake us, spreading slander like a
fool, or to control our emotions and speak righteous words
with a tongue as pure as silver. When we speak without
thinking, sin is unavoidable, and Satan sneaks in and crafts
our words in evil ways. It's our choice to carefully choose the
words we speak so that we ensure they advance the kingdom.

Jesus of peace, we surrender our words to you
so we can build others up with inspiration and
encouragement.

Scan To Branch Out

Let's Defeat the Enemy

SCRIPTURE WHISPER

I have given you the power to trample on snakes and scorpions and to defeat the power of your enemy Satan. Nothing can harm you.

LUKE 10:19 CEV

Jesus left his children with the authority and power described in our Scripture Whisper today, so why don't we use it against the snares of the Enemy all around us? The tricks of Satan become more apparent as we study God's Word and engage the Holy Spirit to navigate our moments. We have the power to seal the door shut so Satan cannot enter any areas of our lives. All we must do is to intentionally stay alert and call on Jesus to fight the battles life brings.

Jesus said in his Word to just ask him, and he will handle things when we cast them into his care. But why don't we always call on him, no matter how trivial our concerns may seem? Many small, seemingly insignificant decisions open the door to evil sneaking in, allowing Satan to hijack God's plan in our lives.

Jesus of patience, help us become more aware of your outstretched hand and that you long to live alongside us so that we can automatically default every moment into your almighty care.

Scan To Branch Out

Let's Be Jesus' Voice

SCRIPTURE WHISPER

"It won't be you speaking, but the Spirit of your Father speaking through you."
MATTHEW 10:20 ISV

The great promise that our Scripture Whisper presents is a priceless gift from our Lord. To never second-guess our words while depending on the Spirit of Jesus to speak through us is an assurance we can count on in our conversations. We must do our part and train and temper our mouths to pause and surrender to Jesus before we speak. That's challenging since Satan is lurking to grab every word and turn it to evil.

A great way to start our day is to ask Jesus to blanket us with his protection while we surrender our communication to him, asking Jesus to be our wordsmith and to speak his wisdom and insight through our voices. Then we can expect him to say the words that others need to hear. He often speaks through our voices.

Jesus of kindness, we regift our mouths to be your voice, even when what we are saying is out of our comfort zone. We remain confident that you will never allow us to be without the words you choose to speak through us. Remind us to pause before we speak and pray for a breath of your anointing.

Let's Call on Angels

SCRIPTURE WHISPER

I (Gabriel) will tell you what is inscribed in the writing of truth. There is no one who stands firmly with me and strengthens himself against these [hostile spirit forces] except Michael, your prince [the guardian of your nation].

DANIEL 10:21 AMP

There's no denying that Satan is hostilely interfering with God's plans in the lives of his children, and sometimes it takes archangels to destroy Satan's forces. Jesus has given us authority, transferred over from Jesus' shed blood on the cross, to call on his army of angels, to tear down strongholds, and to gain victory.

That's the victory we have because of Jesus' suffering for us, his death, resurrection, and ascension to the throne of God. So we do have the power to call on legions of angels to fight the battles. We must simply use the power bestowed upon us and call on them. Satan is running rampant, but we must stand strong together as Christ's followers, supporting one another and praying for each other in desperate times.

Jesus of goodness, we pray in unity for your warrior angel army to act in one accord. May legions of angels fight the battles in our lives and throughout the world.

Scan To Branch Out

Let's Get Past Our Pasts

SCRIPTURE WHISPER

Let us draw near to God with a sincere heart and with the full assurance that faith brings, having our hearts sprinkled to cleanse us from a guilty conscience and having our bodies washed with pure water.

HEBREWS 10:22 NIV

Why is it so difficult to get past our past, forgiving ourselves for our past sins and forgetting as Jesus did through his sacrifice? The regret of our past is a crafty tool of Satan, and we must be keen to recognize that twinge of regret bubbling up. It's like a volcano that rumbles slowly at first and then becomes explosive. The accumulation of frustrations that results from not forgiving ourselves can erupt into bouts of anger that can become unmanageable.

Our Scripture Whisper gives us a solution: to draw near to God so he can cleanse our hearts from a guilty conscience and wash us pure and clean. By the blood of Jesus, we are no longer in chains of bondage but free to live in the blessings of the life for which Jesus died.

Jesus of faithfulness, when Satan brings up our past, help us engage your power to close and seal that door shut by living in your presence.

Scan To Branch Out

Let's Unwrap Blessings

SCRIPTURE WHISPER

Let us hold tightly without wavering to the hope we affirm, for God can be trusted to keep his promise.

HEBREWS 10:23 NLT

A promise is a declaration or assurance that one will do a particular thing or that something will certainly happen. Have you ever been disappointed when someone failed to keep a promise or felt joy when they did? Our Scripture Whisper tells us God can be trusted to keep his promises.

Too often, people see the fulfillment of God's promises as mere coincidences. It seems somewhat overwhelming to realize God fulfills so many promises for his children. Considering each promise is a gift-wrapped blessing from our Lord, we often leave blessings unwrapped. We don't take the time to cherish the many blessings from our Lord scattered throughout our day. It's exciting to unwrap gifts of blessings each day and apply them to our prayers in support of each other.

Jesus of gentleness, we prayerfully reflect on the many promises that you have fulfilled in our lives and in the lives of those around us. You answer more prayers than we even take the time to recognize. Thank you, Jesus, for your gift of kept promises each day.

Scan To Branch Out

Let's Encourage One Another

SCRIPTURE WHISPER

We should keep on encouraging each other to be thoughtful and to do helpful things.

HEBREWS 10:24 CEV

Encouraging one another is a purpose we each have embedded within our spirit. That's part of parenting, friendships, and most other relationships. Jesus is the ultimate encourager, and he left behind his Holy Spirit to cheer us on every day. However, life's busyness can muffle his voice and distract us from our purpose and daily goals. That leaves a vulnerable opening for Satan to overwhelm us to the point of paralysis, so by the end of the day, we feel weary.

Satan is great at convincing us to book an unattainable schedule that distracts from the things in God's plan. To avoid Satan's clever tool of weariness, we need to make Jesus our master scheduler. When we put him in charge every morning, he will prioritize what he intends to do through us that day and what can wait until the next day.

Jesus of self-control, we waste valuable energy by stressing over what you have already mapped out for each of our days. Show us what matters at the end of the day, what builds memories with no regrets, what emulates what you would do, and what we can shift to tomorrow.

Let's Gather in Support

SCRIPTURE WHISPER

We should not stop gathering together with other believers, as some of you are doing. Instead, we must continue to encourage each other even more as we see the day of the Lord coming.

HEBREWS 10:25 GW

Thousands of years ago, when these God-inspired words were written, God knew that we would need this wisdom today. Changes in society have resulted in fewer folks in the pews each week. Many are suffering from complacency and have lost their devotion to gathering and worshiping together.

It's vital that we engage in fellowship to strengthen our faith and to worship, pray, and focus on God's Word in relationships with other Christ followers. Worship should never end. It's not just for Sundays. We should worship every day, spending quiet, quality time with Jesus in praise and adoration. By filling up our souls with his presence, we can be better equipped to be all he intends us to be in relationships with others, to influence the lost, and to bring hope to the hopeless.

Jesus of love, we pray for creative and devout ways that we can gather and encourage one another, especially now that the day of your return is drawing near.

Scan To Branch Out

Let's Stop Sinning

SCRIPTURE WHISPER

Dear friends, if we deliberately continue sinning after we have received knowledge of the truth, there is no longer any sacrifice that will cover these sins.

HEBREWS 10:26 NLT

The sacrifice of Christ was a once-and-for-all event. Those who reject Jesus reject the only sacrifice that can save them. There is not and will never be any other means to remove sin but through the acceptance of Jesus as God's sacrificial Son, who took our sins upon himself, past, present, and future, into eternity.

We all sin, are tempted every day, and are often blinded and twisted by Satan's sneaky schemes. Through the compassionate and forgiving grace of Jesus, when we bring our grieving hearts to him, we are forgiven. He extends his mercy not only to forgive us but to forget our sins and embrace us in his loving arms. Our challenge is to forgive ourselves, forgive others, and refuse to let Satan seep back in with regrets and shame. We should see ourselves reborn to be all Jesus died and suffered for us to be.

Jesus of joy, help us leave no entryway for Satan's temptations. We pray for your protection, a blanket of your anointing to follow us wherever we go.

Scan To Branch Out

Let's Believe in Impossibilities

Peace

SCRIPTURE WHISPER

Looking at them, Jesus said, "With man it is impossible, but not with God, because all things are possible with God."
MARK 10:27 CSB

This is one of the most encouraging promises in the Bible when life gets unbearable and hope seems lost. When we are discouraged, Jesus says to come to him for comfort. When we feel alone, Jesus says to come to him for companionship. When we are at our wits' end, Jesus says to come to him for wisdom. When we are weary, Jesus says to come to him for rest. When we have messed up, Jesus says to come to him, and he will pick us up, brush us off, cleanse us, and refresh our soul. Jesus is our shelter in the storm, our very present help in trouble.

When Jesus tells us throughout his Word to come to him, that's all we need to cling to for strength that surpasses any understanding. When we don't know what to do, God promises that nothing, that's no thing, is impossible for our Lord who loves us so unconditionally and desires the very best for us.

Jesus of peace, we come to you believing in the impossible, and we boldly expect there is nothing you can't do. Help us align with your plan, which far exceeds our imagination or expectation.

Scan To Branch Out

Let's Be Found in Him

SCRIPTURE WHISPER

"I give them eternal life, they'll never be lost, and no one will snatch them out of my hand."
JOHN 10:28 ISV

How secure are those who receive eternal life through Jesus? He promises they cannot be snatched out of his hand. Believers are eternally secure not because of their grip on God but because of his grip on them. If we truly come to Jesus by faith, he's got us in his grip eternally. When we falter, God will still be hanging on to us. He's a God of mercy and patience who knows our heart when life trips us up. With grieving hearts, when we ask for forgiveness, he will tighten his grip of love because of his goodness and grace.

But what about those who once professed faith but don't any longer? The Bible is clear: we will know them by their fruit. If their ways are consistently not the ways of Jesus, then perhaps they never fully submitted to God. We must pray that God continues his work in them. Those who will never perish have been saved through a transformed heart, which is evident by their fruit.

Jesus of patience, we pray for those whose spirits are not in alignment with your ways. Open their hearts and turn them toward a transformed life so they will be with us in heaven.

Let's Abide in Jesus' Safety

SCRIPTURE WHISPER

To the upright, the way of the LORD is a place of safety,
but it's a place of ruin to those who practice evil.

PROVERBS 10:29 ISV

As God's children, living in the pattern of Jesus and planting
the fruit of his Spirit, we can count on our Lord to navigate
precisely each step of our way. How reassuring. Jesus
develops in us a desire and a thirst to learn his ways by
studying his Word, the road map to life.

Those who live apart from the ways of Jesus and who
allow Satan to lead their way will face consequences not just
in this life but also for their eternity. That's the truth found in
God's Word. Time is short, and soon there will be no more
time. God wants us to help him gather the lost into his arms.
The most effective way for us to shine his life is by simply
living in his character, drawing the hopeless to his calling
through the way we live our lives. Then Jesus does the rest.

Jesus of kindness, we pray that we become magnets of your
light by the power of prayer, shifting the atmosphere from
the evil darkness into a resurgence of hope found in you.

Let's Extinguish the Darkness

SCRIPTURE WHISPER

Good people will stand firm, but the wicked will disappear from the land.

PROVERBS 10:30 CEV

How encouraging this Scripture Whisper is when evil is prevalent throughout our land. These words bring assurance that God knows what he is doing and that the wicked will not remain in the land. Scripture tells us the righteous will not be uprooted. God provides hope amid life's chaos and confusion. He is a mighty fortress that can't be shaken. The wicked, however, live vulnerably with no protection and can expect nothing but destruction ahead in eternal life.

In this troubled world, we can find solace and comfort in God's words inspired long ago. The upcoming days are critical, and the power of prayer can ignite revival and renewal throughout the land. Let's start a movement of prayer for our nation by praying in unity at 1:11 p.m. each day. Praying especially for those who have not yet accepted Christ's salvation can change their lives for eternity. God hears his children, and in his hands, nothing is impossible.

Jesus of goodness, we pray we stand firm as your ambassadors to draw the hopeless and lost to you. May we live in ways that attract them to your love within us and illuminate the darkness of evil prevailing throughout our land.

Let's Live for God's Glory

SCRIPTURE WHISPER

Whether you eat or drink, or whatever you do,
do everything for God's glory.

1 Corinthians 10:31 hcsb

Everything we as believers do, whether on a stage or at the dinner table, we should do with a heartfelt desire to bring glory to God. God's reputation is at stake and vitally more important than our personal preferences or choices. We are called to represent the integrity and the truth of God.

Others notice the smallest choices we make as they evaluate the authenticity of our message of devotion and dedication to Jesus. A Christian who is living a self-centered, tainted lifestyle can do more damage to God's kingdom than those who don't believe in God at all. Our standing is attached to the reputation of Jesus, and others perceive the purity of who he is through the example of his presence in our lives. We can either draw others to know more about him or chase them away. In everything we do, let it be to God's glory.

Jesus of faithfulness, help us never seek our own benefit but rather become focused on others. May we seek with compassion the well-being of others and be an influence to save souls and encourage believers to embrace a more intimate walk with you.

November

Let's Grow Our Branches

SCRIPTURE WHISPER

A Shoot (the Messiah) will spring from the stock of Jesse [David's father], and a Branch from his roots will bear fruit.
ISAIAH 11:1 AMP

Jesus is the Shoot that sprang from the love of God to render us worthy to bear fruit. We are uniquely designed to be God's gardener to bear fruit for his kingdom.

The Lord divinely places the root of dreams within our spirit. The root produces a trunk, which produces branches and then blossoms of blessings. The way we live waters the roots for a harvest or creates a drought, and the dream that God chose us specifically to fulfill will either flourish or die. When God has a plan for our lives, Satan will be diligent to inhibit its growth. We must be determined to engage the Creator, who originated the dream to win victory in the battle for our branch of blessings and to draw others into heaven.

Jesus of gentleness, we pray that the roots in each of our lives grow branches into a harvest of lives to make a difference for your kingdom.

Scan To Branch Out

Let's Honor Jesus

SCRIPTURE WHISPER

The spirit of the LORD will give him wisdom and the knowledge and skill to rule his people. He will know the LORD's will and honor him.

ISAIAH 11:2 GNT

This is a prophecy God revealed to Isaiah many years before the birth of the Son of almighty God, Jesus, who became our Savior. Because of the cross, these powers are offered to us when we accept Jesus into our hearts, God's entry to eternal salvation.

The Spirit of the Lord lives right by our sides when we invite him, and he will give us understanding, wisdom, and insight when we live in daily alignment with him. We will gain the same power and anointing of Jesus, which is God's promise to his children. So as our Scripture Whisper says, let's honor the almightiness of our Lord.

Jesus of self-control, we want to honor you and empty ourselves of worldly ways so we can be filled with your understanding, wisdom, and insight every day.

Scan To Branch Out

Let's Be a Model of Integrity

SCRIPTURE WHISPER

The integrity of the upright guides them, but the crookedness of the treacherous destroys them.

PROVERBS 11:3 NET

Integrity is the quality of being honest and whole and undivided, with strong moral principles and moral uprightness. The evidence of integrity is doing the right thing when no one is looking. You will know the people of integrity by the goodness that comes from their heart. The Spirit of the Lord is our best guide, the only guide, to keep us on track to become people of integrity. And God provides the Holy Spirit to guide us twenty-four seven, through every step of life's journey.

The Holy Spirit speaks through the Word of God, which is a lamp to our feet, brightening our pathway with discernment before each footstep ahead. When we heed his voice, he provides a clear direction with no twists or turns of confusion. Crooked paths come from another voice, the sound of Satan attempting to veer us off course. The Holy Spirit provides a direct route.

Jesus of love, help us represent your image with the quality of our integrity, a character of honesty, and a righteous lifestyle, bringing peace and an overflow of joy to those around us.

Scan To Branch Out

Let's Not Wait

SCRIPTURE WHISPER

If you wait until the wind and the weather are just right, you will never plant anything and never harvest anything.
ECCLESIASTES 11:4 GNT

It's easy to wait for perfect situations before we act on what we know in our spirits we should do. If we watch for the ideal circumstance, waiting in the culture of complacency, we will never accomplish anything. When we're walking up to an automatic door, it appears to be closed, and if we stop, it will never open. But moving forward in faith, knowing that door will open, automatically takes us through the open door.

Our Scripture Whisper tells us if we wait for perfect conditions to plant seeds, the plants will never grow, and the hope for a harvest from our lives will never manifest. Planting seeds in the hearts that God positions to cross our paths each day is our life purpose. It may be a divine moment he arranges for us to share our story of how Jesus transformed our hearts from the seeds planted into our lives.

Jesus of joy, we pray for opportunities to plant seeds into fertile soil, for those seeking hope, that they will not pass us by. That moment might be their only hope for entering heaven. We pray we never miss those moments.

Scan To Branch Out

Let's Be Examined

SCRIPTURE WHISPER

The LORD examines the righteous and the wicked.
He hates the lover of violence.

PSALM 11:5 HCSB

God examines his children, just like school children receive examinations to confirm their readiness to go to the next level. God doesn't cause trials, but he uses them to improve our ability to do the incredible things that he designed us to accomplish.

When we endure times when our faith is stretched, we prove that we are well equipped for what he has ahead for each of us. God evaluates our righteousness to see if we have buried our pride and adopted a lifestyle of humility, to see if we have taken no credit but given all the glory to God, who makes all things possible. Without him, we can do nothing. Staying empty of the world and full of God living through us renders us righteous and of high value in his kingdom work.

Jesus of peace, we pray to be useful to you because you know what it takes for each of us to be righteous, equipped, and ready for whatever you have arranged. You are working in us; help us be all you created us to be.

Scan To Branch Out

Let's Encourage Peace

SCRIPTURE WHISPER

The wolf will live with the lamb, and the leopard will lie
down with the young goat; the calf and the young lion will
feed together, and a little child will lead them.
ISAIAH 11:6 CEB

As explosive as things can appear in these troubled times,
when the end of time and the fulfillment of biblical prophecy
of the coming of our Lord seem to be drawing near and
when unrest overshadows peace, we, as believers, can rest
peacefully because we know what's ahead, as our Scripture
Whisper describes.

Since God's plan of peace includes predatory animals at
peace with their prey, just imagine the peace for God's children
in eternity. That's our hope in days of turmoil. Peace is coming
for his people, as God's Word of promises assures us.

Jesus of patience, we pray for those who don't have your
hope of assurance and that peace will become their new way
of life, with no wars, no unrest, no fighting or arguing, no
broken hearts or relationship discord. We pray that their
lives will be transformed under a blanket of your everlasting
peace for eternity. Help us be ambassadors of that message,
sharing your light of hope.

Scan To Branch Out

Let's Speak Jesus' Language

SCRIPTURE WHISPER

"Come, let us go down and confuse their language so they will not understand each other."

GENESIS 11:7 NIV

The act of God creating different languages, as described in our Scripture Whisper today, was his way of interfering in the evil plans of humanity. He confused the language to make it more difficult for people to strategize evil schemes and exercise their control apart from the ways of God and the perfect plan he created.

We know Satan is the author of confusion, but two can play at that game, and God always wins. He used Satan's tool of confusion to bring havoc to Satan's evil schemes at the Tower of Babel. We speak different languages today. The message of our hearts is not in unity, and our words are as confusing as those described at the Tower of Babel. Let's allow the character of Jesus to be the language of our hearts even among people who speak different languages.

Jesus of kindness, may the language we use as your followers show others the message that we are living in the fruit of your Spirit so it's apparent to one and all that our lives are devoted to you. May our words and our lives draw them to your light of hope.

Let's Trust in God's Plan

SCRIPTURE WHISPER

As it is written: God gave them a spirit of insensitivity, eyes that cannot see and ears that cannot hear, to this day.

ROMANS 11:8 HCSB

There is an intricately designed purpose behind all our lives, but as God's plans unfold, we may not fully understand it. Still, when we trust that the almighty Creator is always up to something for his glory and our best interests, we can fall back into his arms with the assurance that we are in the best of care.

God has a motive for good when he hardens hearts. He hardened Pharaoh's heart because Pharaoh refused to allow God's people freedom to worship God. Israel's heart was hardened because they rejected Jesus, God's sacrificial Son. But God used their rejection to deliver salvation to us today. God used what Satan meant for harm through the nation of Israel to open the gospel to the entire world. So as life takes a turn that we don't understand, God is using it for his purpose to build a way for unbelievers to find eternal salvation through our Savior Jesus Christ.

Jesus of goodness, we rest in you through life's confusing moments, knowing you are up to something good, trusting it's all well in your almighty hands.

Scan To Branch Out

Let's Ask, Seek, and Knock

SCRIPTURE WHISPER

"I tell you, keep on asking, and you will receive what you ask for. Keep on seeking, and you will find. Keep on knocking, and the door will be opened to you."

LUKE 11:9 NLT

In our Scripture Whisper today, God invites us to seek him in prayer with boldness, not to be complacent or wait for things to happen. Jesus calls us to ask and to expect him to hear and answer because of our faith. The Lord continues to give good gifts to his children. Even in this fallen world, he does not change. The Holy Spirit is available and accessible twenty-four seven through our faithful prayers to draw others into his arms for his glory.

Only God knows the future, so when we feel our prayers are not being answered, it's because God has something better in mind than our finite minds can comprehend.

Jesus of faithfulness, we pray that the desires of our hearts and those for whom we pray align with the wishes of your heart. We pray for your plan to unfold, and we wait patiently with bold expectancy, knowing that what you will do is better than the best in our minds and above our highest hopes.

Scan To Branch Out

Let's Be Messengers

SCRIPTURE WHISPER

"This is the one about whom it is written:
'I will send my messenger ahead of you,
who will prepare your way before you.'"
MATTHEW 11:10 NIV

Our Scripture Whisper today speaks of John the Baptist, a cousin of Jesus. John was a kingdom-minded man, dedicated to sharing the message of Jesus as the only way to salvation and urging sinners to repent. John wasn't intimidated by ridicule or persecution, knowing he would face violent opposition. He accepted with enthusiasm that he was God's chosen messenger, as foretold in the Old Testament, to prepare the way for Jesus.

God has also handpicked us to be the messengers who share the gospel, planting seeds so he can harvest souls into his arms to live with him in heaven for eternity. It's quite a responsibility that we should take seriously. It doesn't require special skills. It's just telling the story of how our lives were transformed and forever changed when Jesus came to live in our hearts.

Jesus of gentleness, we pray that we never miss an opportunity that the Holy Spirit puts before us to allow Jesus to speak through us the words others need to hear.

Scan To Branch Out

Let's Await Jesus' Coming

SCRIPTURE WHISPER

At that time the Lord will again lift his hand to reclaim the remnant of his people from Assyria, Egypt, Pathros, Cush, Elam, Shinar, Hamath, and the seacoasts.

ISAIAH 11:11 NET

After a glimpse into God's heart, Isaiah prophesied that God would reclaim his remnant for his eternal kingdom, which will become a reality at Christ's second coming. Isaiah details that upon Christ's coming, the cow and bear will graze together in the same field, the lion shall eat straw like an ox, the nursing child shall frolic on a cobra's den, and the earth will be filled with the glory of God as the waters cover the sea (vv. 7–8).

Our Scripture Whisper reminds us that during these days, God will gather his remnants from the earth's four corners, rescuing his people. We live in tumultuous times, but in the promises of God's Word, we have tremendous hope that there will be an eternal world. Now that's hope that we can cling to during troubled days.

Jesus of self-control, we pray that we will stand in faithful unity in the coming days and share the hope of Jesus' coming with those who need to hear it so they, too, can invite Jesus into their lives.

Scan To Branch Out

Let's Choose Our Words

SCRIPTURE WHISPER

It is foolish to speak scornfully of others.
If you are smart, you will keep quiet.
PROVERBS 11:12 GNT

Our wisdom is known both by the words we speak and by the words we refrain from saying. A person with wisdom can keep silent and does not belittle others. A measure of a person's trustworthiness is if they can keep a secret. If they choose to be a gossip, they don't deserve our confidence.

We can't lasso back words we wish we had never spoken. Words can encourage and inspire or tear down and destroy. Many anger issues we deal with as adults are the result of a hurtful phrase from a peer on the playground or a devaluing comment from a coach, teacher, or parent that has marinated throughout our life, resulting in insecurity. Often, we blame this person through adulthood and never take responsibility to get past our past. We can decide to become bitter or better from hurtful words. May we rise above and become what God intended despite Satan's attempts to devalue our self-worth. Let's choose our words through the filter of Jesus.

Jesus of love, help us pause before speaking, allowing you to quiet our words or speak through us in your tender tone.

Scan To Branch Out

Let's Gift the Gospel to Others

SCRIPTURE WHISPER

"If you who are evil know how to give good gifts to your children, how much more will your Father in heaven give the Holy Spirit to those who ask Him!"
LUKE 11:13 BSB

Parents only want the best for their children. So how extraordinary is the gift of our heavenly Father, who also desires to provide the best for his children, and he did! God gave us the ultimate sacrifice of his only Son so that we could live in relationship with him while on earth as he guides us through life. Who would turn that down?

Many who allow Satan to confuse the simplicity of the gospel refuse the great gift of Jesus. Satan has brainwashed them with the lie that they must give up their fun. How much more fun is it to live without the consequences and heartaches that result from sin? How much more fun is it to live in peace and joy rather than the anxiety from the collateral damage of a sinful life? Let's return to Jesus our gift of living the fruit of his Spirit, drawing others to him.

Jesus of joy, we pray to live a life worthy to be called the children of God; your reputation is at stake.

Scan To Branch Out

Let's Seek Godly Counsel

SCRIPTURE WHISPER

Where there is no guidance the people fall,
but in an abundance of counselors there is victory.

PROVERBS 11:14 NASB

Our world is falling apart more every day. When we think it can't get worse, it does. Wise leadership comes from the one who created all things, but tragically, God has been removed from the hearts of people across the land.

Where do we go for advice? Foremost, as Christ followers, we seek the wisdom of our Lord, but he often grants us confirmation through godly advisers. How do we confirm that those advisers are authentic? Scripture tells us that we will know them from their fruit. Only Jesus is perfect, and we all stumble and fall, but that doesn't disqualify us from having godly wisdom. A heart sold out to Jesus equips us to discern wise guidance and counseling. Then the Holy Spirit may use us to advise someone else.

Jesus of peace, we ask for the wisdom to evaluate those we associate with and consider if their lifestyle reflects a yearning to live more like you. Help us choose those with like-minded spirits and strengthen our ability to clearly discern those who can advise us well along our journey. They should allow you, Lord, to live through them and speak words of true wisdom.

Scan To Branch Out

Let's Listen and Understand

SCRIPTURE WHISPER

"Anyone with ears to hear should listen and understand!"
MATTHEW 11:15 NLT

Words come at us from all directions, which leads to many voices sending mixed messages. Satan has fertile ground to grow confusion in our world. We certainly are not responsible for others' messages, but we must monitor what we allow our ears to hear and the message we voice to those who need to know Jesus. We can overlook the impact of casually spoken words, but Satan doesn't, nor does God. It's a choice and a responsibility we must take seriously.

There were many who heard Jesus when he was on earth, but only those with "ears to hear" understood the truth of what Jesus was saying and surrendered their hearts to follow him. Some people are continually resistant to the gospel because they are not open to listening with their hearts. We are called to present the gospel, live in Jesus' example, pray, and then let God do the rest.

Jesus of patience, help us be more responsible about what our ears hear and what others hear from our mouths. May we truly understand your truth.

Let's Focus on the Heavenly City

SCRIPTURE WHISPER

They aspire to a better country, that is, a heavenly one.
Therefore God is not ashamed to be called their God, for He
prepared a city for them.

HEBREWS 11:16 LSB

This verse points to the strength of our faith for things not
yet seen. We should not turn back on our faith but stand
strong in an unwavering belief in the unseen, believing
that God has prepared a better country for his children, a
heavenly one.

 If our focus is on the eternal things ahead, the
temporary things on earth fade in importance. Since we are
mere earthly vessels, how foolish it is for us to spend energy
trying to be the god of our lives when God has offered each
of us his Holy Spirit to walk alongside us while on this earth.
He will bring a glimpse of heaven on earth throughout
our days, taking our troubles and transforming them into
tremendous blessings when we ask him. There's just one
thing we need to do: stay out of his way!

Jesus of kindness, please help us aspire to be heavenly
focused since worldly things are temporary and distract us
from our mission on earth to draw others to the city you
have prepared in heaven.

Scan To Branch Out

Let's Depend On Help

SCRIPTURE WHISPER

"I will come down and speak with you there, and I will take some of the Spirit that is on you and put that Spirit on them. They will help you bear the burden of the people, so that you do not have to bear it by yourself."

NUMBERS 11:17 BSB

Have you ever felt alone in bearing a task that God put before you, like Moses, and it became so overwhelming and daunting that you were desperate for help? God's words to Moses are for us today; he will bring people to share the burden. God will never call us for a task for which he will not provide people to help and provisions to fulfill what he asks us to do. God designed each of us uniquely to do what no one else can do.

The bigger the potential impact, the greater the attacks from Satan to bring weariness and discouragement along the journey. It is our responsibility to stand firm in faith, believing Jesus will fight our battles. That's a promise in the Bible when we engage Jesus in partnership. May we never grow weary of his call when God appoints us to his divine plan.

Jesus of goodness, we ask for stamina, perseverance, and tenacity to never give up and to always depend on you to provide help.

Scan To Branch Out

Let's Sow Righteousness

SCRIPTURE WHISPER

A wicked person earns deceptive wages,
but the one who sows righteousness reaps a sure reward.
PROVERBS 11:18 NIV

As Christ followers, we do what is right not to be rewarded but rather to please Jesus because of our love of him and the meaning of his sacrifice.

It often seems the wicked gain in life when we are on the sidelines in the waiting game. That's far from the truth, as our Scripture Whisper tells us. Gaining from the evil ways of the world suggests you're headed toward an entrance into eternal hell, but following a path of right living is an indication that you've made the choice to follow Jesus, yielding rewards of eternal salvation and a home in heaven, where there will be no more evil. Life is about the wait, trusting in faith that God is working to train and equip us for great and mighty things ahead.

Jesus of faithfulness, thank you for allowing us to come to you in partnership and trust that you are always working for us, your children. Help our faith not to waver as we wait for your plan to unfold, understanding that you know the future and want the best for us.

Scan To Branch Out

Let's Be Sensitive to Jesus

SCRIPTURE WHISPER

"I'll give them a united heart, placing a new spirit within them. I'll remove their stubborn heart and give them a heart that's sensitive to me."

Ezekiel 11:19 ISV

This verse was written for the Israelites, but it should be our prayer for the world every day. Across our land, there are hearts of stone where evil has taken over. People are so divided, and it is difficult to find the unity for our fellow man and respect for those who devote their lives to service.

All facets of our lives have been affected by the ways of the world, yet God promises to give us a world with singleness of heart and a new, tender spirit. We must stand firm and become a beacon of light for those whose hearts are stony and cold. A tender response and a devotion to living the fruit of Jesus' Spirit can melt the most concrete hearts when Jesus works within us.

Jesus of gentleness, help us be your light today, an example for those who are not living in singleness of heart with you. Lord, take their stony, stubborn hearts and transform them into tender hearts, responsive to your Spirit moving within them. Use us as your beacon of light today and every day.

Scan To Branch Out

Let's Live Rightly

SCRIPTURE WHISPER

The Lord hates sneaky people,
but he likes everyone who lives right.
PROVERBS 11:20 CEV

We will reap the bounty of God's many promises when we love him, accept his Son as our way to salvation, and, as our Scripture Whisper tells us, live rightly. So what is the right way? It's spending time each day in God's Word, talking to God in prayer, engaging his Spirit in our everyday lives, and making a habit of living the fruit of his Spirit. Jesus will take great pleasure in those who follow the right way.

But there's more! A right way of living also prevents a host of consequences that bring heartache and frustration, despair and worry, discord and disillusion. Instead, right living prompts a life of peace and joy and puts up a barrier of protection against Satan's attempts to manipulate us away from God with his sneaky ways, crooked heart, and warped mind.

Jesus of self-control, please give us the desire to ring you up and chat with you through your Word, our cell phone to God. Help us influence others to know you as the only way to joy and peace and to be forever mindful of your presence.

Scan To Branch Out

Let's Be Productive Figs

SCRIPTURE WHISPER

Peter remembered what had happened and said to Jesus, "Look, Teacher, the fig tree you cursed has died!"
MARK 11:21 GNT

The fig tree had no figs in its season of harvest; therefore, Jesus used it to illustrate a life that bears no fruit, a life of opportunities withered away. We all know people who live in constant negativity. Not a positive or hopeful word comes out of their mouths. They seem to look for defeat and disappointment. The result is a trail of collateral damage, and that's the example in the story of the fig tree.

Instead, as Christ followers, we should live with hope, always seeking the best in others, knowing with full assurance that things will turn out better than we hoped or imagined in the care of Jesus, as Ephesians 3:20 tells us. As a result, we leave a trail of seeds from Jesus' character along our path. The harvest will be plentiful, and our lives will be productive as God intended when he masterfully created us to accomplish things for which no one else is designed.

Jesus of love, help us become better stewards of the opportunities you prearranged and predestined for us as your productive ambassadors.

Scan To Branch Out

Let's Have Faith in God

SCRIPTURE WHISPER

Jesus said to them, "Have faith in God."

MARK 11:22 NET

This is the most straightforward verse to memorize and to weave into our conversations. It's just eight words—and yet it's a powerful way to live. For us to fret when we think we can't go on is not trusting in God. There's no faith in that behavior. Trusting in God is believing without a shadow of a doubt that he will come through. What God calls us for, he promises to provide.

We often cannot fathom how we can get through another day, but Jesus knows all things and is our master provider, perfect in his ways and reasons. We are positioned to wait so that we learn to trust God more, and then God can trust us for greater things ahead. It's no different from the way we train and equip our children for adulthood. Jesus is preparing us for what he will call us to do ahead, and he promised to always provide when we trust him without wavering or questioning or jumping in his way.

Jesus of joy, thank you for preparing us for greater things and forgiving us when we jump in your way and complain about the wait. Your timing is always perfect.

Scan To Branch Out

Let's Move Mountains

SCRIPTURE WHISPER

If you have faith in God and don't doubt, you can tell this mountain to get up and jump into the sea, and it will.
MARK 11:23 CEV

Don't we trust the electric company to provide us with power if we adhere to the contract and pay the bill? We don't doubt that electricity is flowing when we turn on the switch. So why don't we have that same unwavering, vibrant faith in the God of the Bible, knowing that we will have the spiritual authority to access his divine power when we turn on the switch by the power of bold, expectant prayer?

God has already blessed us with every spiritual blessing in Christ. Through faith as believers in Jesus, we have access to a divine authority far greater than the light switch we depend on people to provide. God is our power provider.

Jesus of peace, you are our master provider of all things, which is far greater than we could ever conjure up in our finite minds. We ask that our faith will be strengthened through our journey so that we will believe without a doubt and trust that what you say will happen. Give us mountain-moving confidence.

Scan To Branch Out

Let's Believe to Receive

SCRIPTURE WHISPER

"I tell you, whatever you ask for in prayer, believe that you have received it, and it will be yours."

MARK 11:24 NIV

Often, as we wait on God's answers, we grow weary and frustrated and jump in the way, thinking, *It appears God's not doing anything. I must get involved and help him out!* That's a very effective strategy Satan has authored to tempt us to forget that God is arranging things, transforming lives, and managing our choices to align with his plan. We think we are waiting on God; just imagine how much he waits on us!

God will answer our prayers but often not in the way we envision. Still, God promises he will do many awe-inspiring things, immeasurably good things, greater than we could ever ask or imagine through the power of Jesus at work within us. Our part is the power of waiting in unwavering faith, no matter how grim and gloomy things appear, no matter how impossible things might look. But over time, our response to these tests will reflect not our gut-wrenching impatience but our assurance that Jesus always has our backs.

Jesus of patience, help us share our stories of your faithfulness to help others build a lifestyle of unwavering faith.

Scan To Branch Out

Let's Forgive as Jesus Did

SCRIPTURE WHISPER

"Whenever you stand praying, if you have anything against anyone, forgive him, so that your Father in heaven will also forgive you your wrongdoing."

MARK 11:25 HCSB

But what about those who make it so hard to forgive? We can simply bury our feelings and ignore them with our human hearts, or we can forgive anyone for anything by forgiving through the heart of Jesus. Just think of all the things for which God has so mercifully forgiven us. He endured the most brutal pain of all ages to forgive our sins so that we can walk in a relationship with him every day. How dare we not, in turn, do as he asks and forgive others?

Unforgiveness keeps us in the prison of bondage while those we refuse to forgive hold the prison door keys and walk in freedom. Let's take back our God-given, spiritual authority by doing what God has told us to do: praying and forgiving through the heart of Jesus.

Jesus of kindness, you gifted us with access to your power. Let us align our hearts with your heart and become empty vessels available for your power to live through us.

Scan To Branch Out

Let's Give Time to Jesus

SCRIPTURE WHISPER

"Everyone who lives and believes in Me will never die.
Do you believe this?"
JOHN 11:26 BSB

Jesus tells us that the one who believes in him will never die. According to our Scripture Whisper today, we will pass from physical life immediately into eternal life. The present tense also shows that Jesus is a right-now deliverer, not just a future one. He gives life in the blink of an eye to those who profess him as the Son of God, the only way to eternal life. To those who died thousands of years ago, it will seem like yesterday, as if we all went to heaven simultaneously.

God works on a different timetable. We feel that if something doesn't happen within a matter of moments, we may miss out. God is not limited by the same constraints of time. Time is not an issue with God. He has an unlimited amount of time for us. If God is working on a plan that could take ten thousand years, it's no different from a plan that he took ten seconds to accomplish.

Jesus of goodness, through your generous sacrifice, we never die, moving from this sinful, earthly world into your heavenly arms in the blink of an eye. Help us share that gift.

Let's Shut the Door on Trouble

SCRIPTURE WHISPER

The one who searches for what is good seeks favor,
but if someone looks for trouble, it will come to him.
PROVERBS 11:27 CSB

When trouble lurks, why is it so appealing to look for it
when, instead, we can search for Jesus' favor? We live in a
fallen world because Adam and Eve disobeyed God, and
Satan uses that as an open door to invite trouble for us today.

There's no doubt that Satan takes advantage of our
human nature. When we think we can't have something,
there's an insatiable desire to go to great extremes to get
it. We must be aware of the signs. Satan is very good at
camouflaging trouble, and we must become intentional to
prevent his evil entrance, realizing that trouble is not from
God but from Satan.

Parents often witness this in their children when they
are tempted to cause trouble and test the boundaries when
the parents say no. The most significant part of the battle for
us is becoming aware when trouble knocks on our door and
calling on Jesus to extend his gracious favor.

Jesus of faithfulness, thank you for heightening our senses
to recognize the first sign of trouble so that we can block it
from entering our lives. Help us seek the sweet
fragrance of your moments of favor throughout
our day.

Scan To Branch Out

Let's Find Rest in Jesus

SCRIPTURE WHISPER

"Come to me, all you who are weary and burdened,
and I will give you rest."
MATTHEW 11:28 NIV

Life can be wearisome and burdensome in every direction
we turn, but we must choose joy. It's Satan's practice to lurk,
seeking to attack a weary spirit to drag us down. But the
power of Jesus can break that stronghold and grant us rest. We
must be intentional about choosing joy in wearisome times.

As children of God, we are gifted the choice not to
be weary. We have the same power that Jesus had on the
cross to throw our burdens toward Jesus' army of angels,
gain victory, and defeat Satan's evil army. The forces of
evil become weary as the legions of angels fight the battle
victoriously. God's angel armies destroy Satan's demonic
army every time we call on them to fight our battles.

Jesus of gentleness, you suffered in agony to transfer your
power to your children so that legions of angels could fight
our battles in spiritual warfare and win in your almighty
name. Help us not to engage in the battle alone but to rest
with assurance that you have won the battle and covered us
with your mercy and grace.

Let's Take On Jesus' Yoke

SCRIPTURE WHISPER

"Take my yoke upon you and learn from me, for I am gentle and humble in heart, and you will find rest for your souls."
MATTHEW 11:29 NIV

How do we find that peace that surpasses any understanding when the storms of life rage and we hang on by our fingertips for dear life? We hop into the yoke of Jesus. He will take over the reins and give us soothing relief, ease of comfort, renewal of hope, and blessed quiet to restore our souls.

The gentleness of abiding in his yoke will give us the security of knowing that the Master, the creator of all things, cares for us and wants only the best for his children who surrender their will into his yoke. Let's share the beauty of his yoke with the many souls searching for a restful place to quiet their troubled souls.

Jesus of self-control, thank you for your patience when we find ourselves resisting your yoke. Help us never to miss that opportunity to become more Christlike in our nature so that the raging seas of life become calm in your care. Thank you for giving us the yoke of your peace.

Scan To Branch Out

Let's Plant a Life-Giving Tree

SCRIPTURE WHISPER

Live right, and you will eat from the life-giving tree.
And if you act wisely, others will follow.
PROVERBS 11:30 CEV

A meaningful life is well lived with purpose and value and with an epitaph that reads, "He loved God more than all others and was a life-giving tree to all." As Christ's followers, we have a purpose with two goals: to love God and help others. The questions for each of us are these: Does our lifestyle reflect a life-giving tree with branches of the fruit of Jesus' Spirit in all our ways? And are we affecting the lives of others for good?

The second commandment after loving God is to love others. The most loving thing we can do for another person is to help them live a Christ-centered life by leading them to Jesus. The highest measure of love is influencing others to live in a relationship with Jesus by living in ways that make others curious to understand that our light in the chaos of darkness comes from the Lord.

Jesus of love, help us plant seeds you will harvest. May we be life-giving trees for those whom you arrange for us to influence. We ask that our lives reflect the fruit of your Spirit and lead others to you.

Scan To Branch Out

December

Let's Find Life Pleasant

SCRIPTURE WHISPER

Don't let the excitement of youth cause you to forget your Creator. Honor him in your youth before you grow old and say, "Life is not pleasant anymore."

ECCLESIASTES 12:1 NLT

This verse is as real today as it was the day it was written. The evil days are upon us, and the pleasures of living in the rule of God have disappeared before our eyes. Our voices have been complacent for far too long. But as believers, we have assurance that God is unfolding his plan.

As ambassadors of God, our mission during troubling times is to ignite Jesus' light in the darkness and show joy in trusting in God, knowing he will manifest his promises in his Word. Our youth are surrounded by a world of evil confusion. Let's pray that we can be a hedge of protection around young people by being the voice of hope and drowning out the voice of Satan's confusion.

Jesus of joy, we ask that ears hear and hearts receive an understanding of the days to come, the days without evil. May we be those who trust in you and accept you as our hope of salvation. Lord, we are grateful for the pleasures you shower upon us in troubled times.

Let's Change the Way We Think

SCRIPTURE WHISPER

Don't copy the behavior and customs of this world, but let God transform you into a new person by changing the way you think. Then you will learn to know God's will for you, which is good and pleasing and perfect.

ROMANS 12:2 NLT

Ever since Adam and Eve fell into temptation, the world has had the interference of Satan running throughout the land. As a result, we are all born into sin. When we accept Jesus as our Savior, he provides a way of escape from our sinful pattern of living, our sinful way of thinking, and Satan's enticement.

When our flesh is not yet renewed, we have embedded within us old habits that run according to the evil principles of the world. For our old flesh to fall in line with our new spirit, our hearts and minds must be transformed by Jesus' Spirit within us. This is a result of our intentional efforts to learn from God's Word and make a habit of the fruit of Jesus' Spirit each day.

Jesus of peace, help us renew our minds through the knowledge of your Word so that when the trials of life test us, we can be pleasing to you, inspiring others to transform into a likeness of you too.

Let's Stay in Our Lane

SCRIPTURE WHISPER

Because of God's gracious gift to me I say to every one of you: Do not think of yourself more highly than you should. Instead, be modest in your thinking, and judge yourself according to the amount of faith that God has given you.

ROMANS 12:3 GNT

We must never fail to consider that our gifts, talents, abilities, and knowledge are all from God and are not of ourselves. It is for each of us, in faith, to use them as the Lord leads for optimum results in his plan.

And it is important that we realize that we should not veer into or be jealous of the tasks God has given someone else. They may have similar gifts, but we are to stay focused on our unique gifts as we encourage and inspire others in the areas in which they excel. Otherwise, we dilute what God created us to do and may interfere with others who are living to their potential. Let's humbly celebrate what God is doing to expand his kingdom through each of our lives.

Jesus of patience, help us stay in our lane and celebrate those who excel in areas beyond our capabilities, knowing that you weave each of our lives together for your glory and to draw others into your kingdom.

Scan To Branch Out

Let's Say Hallelujah Together

SCRIPTURE WHISPER

At that time you will say, "Praise the LORD. Call on his name. Make his deeds known among the nations. Make them remember that his name is highly honored."
ISAIAH 12:4 GW

There's no better way to remember and make known God's glorious actions than to pray in community. As we pause in prayer together, we strengthen each other and our world, calling on God in unity to make a difference. We can also make his character and works visible by living the fruit of Jesus' Spirit, weaving God's words into our conversations, and taking a moment to memorize our daily Scripture Whisper when we see the date throughout the day.

Let's send praises to our Lord as he shines through us like a beacon of light, opening the door to tell everyone what Jesus has done to transform our lives and the wonders of his goodness and grace for his children.

Jesus of kindness, please take away from us any inhibitions that keep us from being your voice in this troubled world. Forgive us for our complacency that has brought harm to your name. Help us share your wonders each day.

Scan To Branch Out

Let's Reunite in Harmony

SCRIPTURE WHISPER

In the same way, even though we are many individuals,
Christ makes us one body and individuals who are
connected to each other.

Romans 12:5 GW

As Christ's followers, we are a collective group intended to
operate as one body in Christ. There are countless people
in many other places with vastly different jobs, talents, and
gifts. Still, together we are to be unified as we devote our
individuality toward a united purpose.

Conflict, competition, and pride have no place in the
unity of Christ. We must all work as God has directed,
complementing one another and serving each other together
with the same goal in mind: expanding God's kingdom and
bringing lost souls and hopeless hearts into Jesus' arms.

Jesus of goodness, we don't always live according to the
unity of your ways. We ask that you inspire us to do our
part to break down those barriers and reunite in harmony.
Help us pause and notice that you are weaving our gifts and
talents together to fulfill your plan when we live in unity.

Let's Accomplish Our Tasks

SCRIPTURE WHISPER

There are different abilities to perform service, but the same God gives ability to all for their particular service.

1 CORINTHIANS 12:6 GNT

It's freeing and reassuring to know that God created our differences to accomplish various tasks and that he is masterminding every intricate detail. We often don't understand why we go through certain troubles in life, but God has a purpose. He equips us to have an impact on others' lives, whether through a group discussion or caring for someone after a personal tragedy. We are not to question or judge the distinctive ways of others but to seek ways for God to use us more effectively.

Knowing that God is working his purpose through us brings meaning to our heartaches and hope to our hopelessness. We are blessed to have a master scheduler in our midst who frees us by taking the pressure off the start of each day when we hand over our moments to Jesus.

Jesus of faithfulness, help us become more mindful that our life experiences are training us and equipping us for the days ahead. Show us how to walk in the confidence that you are living through us to achieve your ultimate divine purpose.

Let's Shelter from Evil

SCRIPTURE WHISPER

You, LORD, will protect them; you will continually shelter each one from these evil people.
PSALM 12:7 NET

There's evil all around, but God provides hope. He positions himself as a shelter of protection from evil people; that's his promise. Just as he protected Noah and his family from the flood and Daniel in the lion's den and the Israelites when he parted the Red Sea, he will do it for each of us today and every day. We must simply ask.

Even if the future might seem grim, we can rest in our Scripture Whisper today that says we, as Christ's followers, are protected and sheltered by our Lord. Jesus calls us to be his ambassadors of truth to those who don't know our Lord and are not living under his tender care. Living in the character of Jesus, reacting in his ways, and displaying the fruit of his Spirit in our lives are beacons of light for those who need hope. Let's attract the lost and downhearted to the hope we have in Jesus.

Jesus of gentleness, help us do our part to be your light in the darkness for those who need hope. Show us how to walk in alignment with your plan and to live in a way that attracts others to the salvation we have in you.

Scan To Branch Out

Let's Give from Our Gifting

SCRIPTURE WHISPER

If your gift is to encourage others, be encouraging. If it is giving, give generously. If God has given you leadership ability, take the responsibility seriously. And if you have a gift for showing kindness to others, do it gladly.

ROMANS 12:8 NLT

God has gifted each of us with an exceptional thirst deep within our souls to fulfill the gifts he created within us. Our Scripture Whisper encourages us to live to the fullest. The worries, pressures, confusions, and temptations disappear as we become more and more intentional about being devoted Christ followers and living in the ways of Jesus.

The mark of an authentic Christian is to love genuinely with friendly affection. Detest evil and live a lifestyle of goodness. Outdo each other in humble service. Remain in hope, be patient in tribulation, and constantly talk to Jesus in prayer. Show hospitality and bless others with kindness. Rejoice with those who rejoice and weep with those who weep. Live in harmony with one another. When we live out the gifts God has given us, we become a light for Jesus in this dark world.

Jesus of self-control, engrave a smile in our hearts because we have participated in the fulfillment of your plan by using our unique gifts.

Let's Glory in Our Weakness

SCRIPTURE WHISPER

He hath said unto me, My grace is sufficient for thee: for my power is made perfect in weakness. Most gladly therefore will I rather glory in my weaknesses, that the power of Christ may rest upon me.

2 Corinthians 12:9 asv

When we are weak, we become strongest when we invite Jesus to bring his strength into our situation. But when we choose to do life on our own, there's no opportunity to live in oneness with the creator of the universe, who is the only one with the knowledge of the future. He will navigate our lives in his strength through our weak vessels.

What an assurance that we no longer must live on our own. The master of the world is ready and waiting to impart his strength to our weakness. That's why our Father sacrificed his only Son, Jesus, to suffer and die in such agony for our times of weakness when sin overtakes us. His shed blood on the cross wiped away all our sins so we can call on Jesus to be our strength in place of our weakness and frailty.

Jesus of love, help us be mindful of our weakness and remember that our weakness invites your strength. We only need to call on you.

Scan To Branch Out

Let's Make a Difference

SCRIPTURE WHISPER

Be devoted to one another with mutual love, showing eagerness in honoring one another.

ROMANS 12:10 NET

Being focused on others is the authentic lifestyle of a heart devoted to Jesus. The many stories in the Bible of Jesus' life on earth tell of his love and devotion to others everywhere he traveled. He sought out those opportunities to serve others.

The slightest act of kindness can transform someone's life. Searching for ways to make a difference is how Jesus lived. Only he knows the future and the needs ahead, which is a stark contrast to our lack of insight, but we can open our ears and listen for opportunities. With our eyes, let's seek opportunities to help fulfill God's plan. With our hearts, let's never miss a chance to make a difference.

Jesus of joy, we ask you to help us embrace your ways so that we will see others through your eyes and hear others as you do. Help us act on the needs you put before us and never miss an opportunity to show your loving goodness, your kindness, your tenderness, your gentleness, and your generosity to those you arrange in our pathway every day.

Scan To Branch Out

Let's Serve with Devotion

SCRIPTURE WHISPER

Work hard and do not be lazy. Serve the Lord with a heart full of devotion.

ROMANS 12:11 GNT

It's easy to lose our enthusiasm when it seems the world gets worse daily; our zeal for doing good diminishes. But we have appointed times on God's divine calendar to serve him in ways for which no one else has been equipped. Those times are, possibly, the only moments God has arranged for someone to have an opportunity to know Christ and join us in eternity.

The Bible says we should choose joy when we feel like giving up in despair. God shows us mercy, so we can be joyful. In God's grace, there's a spring of renewed vigor deep within the well of our souls that will bubble up the zeal we need to be all Jesus requires for us and to seize the opportunities he arranges. All we must do is call on him to live through us.

Jesus of peace, we pray that our enthusiasm never wanes and that we continue seeking your grace and mercy with fervent zeal in serving others. May we always walk alongside you as ambassadors of your goodness, mercy, and grace.

Scan To Branch Out

Let's Be Joyful in Affliction

SCRIPTURE WHISPER

Be joyful in hope, patient in affliction, faithful in prayer.
ROMANS 12:12 NIV

These three lifestyle instructions should resonate throughout our thoughts each day. When we feel like curling up in the fetal position and burying our situation in the depths of the sea, we're not often good at being joyful in hope. Still, we can call on Jesus, casting our every care into his transforming hands, and he will give us his patience in our affliction as we faithfully pray. Jesus asks us to depend on him in all circumstances.

Afflictions, pain, and suffering to varying degrees are often caused by our choices and those of others but are sometimes entirely out of our control. What a perfect time to relinquish our control to Jesus so he can manage the situation! We should expect that there are lessons to learn that will equip us for what he has in store ahead. What afflicts you in this present time? How freeing will it be to hand it over to the only one who knows the future and can arrange the very best for us in every way!

Jesus of patience, help us involve you in times of suffering, concern, and confusion and be prayerfully joyful and patient in all our afflictions.

Let's Respect and Obey God

SCRIPTURE WHISPER

Everything you were taught can be put into a few words:
Respect and obey God! This is what life is all about.
ECCLESIASTES 12:13 CEV

Life isn't over when it's over on earth. Our actions, both
good and evil, are all recorded. And while we can't erase past
recordings, we can create new and better recordings of our
journey ahead. It's an intentional effort we must consider as
Christ's followers so that our life is pleasing and meaningful
for our Lord.

As long as we draw a breath, the recorder is still
running. Therefore, we should not waste a moment before
choosing to live a lifestyle that mirrors Jesus, making a habit
of the fruit of his Spirit and maximizing the time God has
given us.

Jesus of kindness, help us seek your perspective in our
choices and daily decisions. We want to make our life count
toward fulfilling your kingdom's purpose for our lives,
which are uniquely and intricately created so we can live
as ambassadors of your kingdom. Help us make our lives
pleasing to you. And when you call us home, you will listen
to our recording and say, "Well done, my faithful servant."

Scan To Branch Out

Let's Pause before Speaking

SCRIPTURE WHISPER

Your reward depends on what you say and what you do;
you will get what you deserve.
PROVERBS 12:14 GNT

Jesus tells us throughout Scripture that our words matter and
to be careful about what we say, not to speak in haste but
to pause and allow him to formulate the words he intends
others to hear. How awkward it may seem to pause before
each word. But not really; we can pause before a thought
with a deep breath, asking the Holy Spirit to formulate his
words through our lips.

And we can do something important to design our own
private dictionary of words in each of our minds, and that is
to study the words in the Bible, engraving them deep within
our heart and soul. A simple pause before speaking will
soon become automatic as we pull out words from our heart,
words we have collected in the dictionary of our souls.

Jesus of goodness, before we speak, help us pause for a
clearer understanding of the importance of choosing words
that represent you to the world. May we be your voice to
share the words others need to hear to draw them to you
with a curiosity to know you more.

Scan To Branch Out

Let's Share Meaningful Gifts

SCRIPTURE WHISPER

He told the people, "Be careful to guard yourselves from every kind of greed. Life is not about having a lot of material possessions."

LUKE 12:15 GW

During these days of holiday shopping and collecting gifts, it's often hard not to sporadically accumulate things for ourselves. Many of those things we really don't need, and if we think about it honestly, we often don't even want them when we get home. Buying stuff is in the air, part of the season of consumerism. Equally so, when choosing gifts for others, are they meaningful? Will they enhance or enrich their lives? Or are they for show and accolades, which is an indication of a greedy spirit?

Gifts should make a difference, and buying a gift just to have a gift to give is not what the Christmas season is all about. This time of year should be about Jesus' birthday, a day to remember the greatest gift ever given, God's only Son, the Savior of our lives. He offers eternity for those who accept his gift as the only way to salvation. We can offer many meaningful gifts and acts of kindness as our gifts to others throughout the year. Let's give meaningful gifts this year.

Jesus of faithfulness, help us not to get caught up in the commercialism of the season but instead to share with others the true meaning of your birthday.

Scan To Branch Out

Let's Live in Harmony

SCRIPTURE WHISPER

Live in harmony with each other. Don't be too proud to enjoy the company of ordinary people. And don't think you know it all!

ROMANS 12:16 NLT

Let's be honest. We all have relationship conflicts. We all are wired with different perspectives, life experiences, hurts, and broken hearts that frame who we are. Therefore, expect disagreements and conflicts. We can't control others' reactions, and we aren't meant to. We can only genuinely control ourselves. The art of self-control is reacting through the fruit of Jesus' Spirit, transforming relationship conflicts into meaningful relationships that last. As representatives of Jesus, how do others perceive us in situations of conflict?

We live in a world full of selfishness, brokenness, and pettiness, yet in our Scripture Whisper today, Paul said we should live in harmony with one another, finding common ground in agreement as believers. Agreeing to disagree is an alignment in unity. God desires that we take our differences, personalities, backgrounds, and journeys we've traveled and blend them to make something that is beautiful and harmonious with an impact.

Jesus of gentleness, help us live in the spirit of harmony.

Scan To Branch Out

Let's Return Goodness for Evil

SCRIPTURE WHISPER

Never repay evil for evil to anyone. Respect what is right in the sight of all people.

ROMANS 12:17 NASB

There's no healing in evil; there's healing only in loving forgiveness. There's healing in knowing past pain and heartache are often the reasons behind the evil actions of others. Often if we repay evil for evil, we will end up hurting ourselves. That should motivate us to return goodness instead of evil.

It should give us pause to realize that when we depend on Jesus, we have risen above the effects of the evil treatment others may have inflicted on us, knowing Jesus is in the middle of it all. We must invite him to repay evil with his goodness as his unconditional love lives through us.

Jesus of self-control, we pause in prayer together today, asking you to help us focus on what is right and gracious and proper in your sight. Please help us realize that others' unkind actions are often a result of the hurt and pain they have experience but not yet resolved. Help us rise above and, instead of returning evil for evil, love others through your heart and live peaceably with everyone. Deep down, others just need to know we will be a friend. Help us be friends through you.

Scan To Branch Out

Let's Live in the Unity of Peace

SCRIPTURE WHISPER

If possible, so far as it depends on you,
be at peace with all people.

ROMANS 12:18 NASB

We have all misinterpreted this Scripture Whisper as if it says to be patient for as long as we can, but once our patience runs out, enough is enough, and we have the right to lose it. But what Paul meant is that it is our choice to control our side of the relationship. We should live at peace and do everything we can to get along with everyone.

Sometimes just being silent is the most challenging part, but silence speaks from the depths of our soul, leaving room for Jesus to work in the situation. And if the other side continues berating and harboring a grudge, it's on them. It's no longer our battle. It takes two to fight, so they are fighting with themselves. And we should pray for their inner turmoil. It's not often us they are fighting. It's Satan within them.

Jesus of love, help us return a kind and gentle spirit to others, a reaction they least expect. That leaves room for you to begin their healing. And one day we may experience a moment of kindness from them when we least expect it.

Scan To Branch Out

Let's Leave Room for Jesus

SCRIPTURE WHISPER

Friends, do not avenge yourselves; instead, leave room for God's wrath, because it is written, Vengeance belongs to me; I will repay, says the Lord.

ROMANS 12:19 CSB

Our Scripture Whisper prompts two questions: How long do we love and forgive our enemies? If we keep loving our enemies and they never change, isn't that unfair?

God has a clear answer. He cares deeply and wants to handle things for us. So when we feel like nothing is happening, that people are continually getting away with their behavior, and that their fighting spirit is lurking, our display of the fruit of his Spirit opens the door to their vengeful heart and leaves room for God to enter to begin their healing. One of the reasons God hasn't dealt with our enemies yet could be that we are still in the way. And remember that God promises to repay us with blessings.

Jesus of joy, you are the one who conquers evil and gains the victory. Help us be willing vessels to do our part to live the fruit of your Spirit. It's your battle to fight, not ours. Help us do our part and allow you to be God in others' lives today.

Scan To Branch Out

Let's Start Anew

SCRIPTURE WHISPER

Samuel replied, "Don't be afraid. Even though you have committed all this evil, don't turn away from following the LORD. Instead, worship the LORD with all your heart."
1 SAMUEL 12:20 CSB

It's never too late to turn from evil ways and start anew. That's what God is waiting for and the reason he provided a way out of a sinful life through the sacrifice of his only Son.

But we must have a change of heart with a desire to live in the pattern of Jesus' ways. That doesn't mean we never sin again. Instead, we have a transformed heart and a yearning to live in the paths of righteousness, learning from our sinful choices to become more conformed to the likeness of Christ. Many feel they've sinned too much and are unworthy to come before Jesus, but sin is sin, and God can cleanse a lifetime of evil ways, washing us clean and transforming our heart to follow in Jesus' ways.

Jesus of peace, help us be your voice for those who feel unworthy to come into your presence and ask for forgiveness. Your love conquers all for those with a heart that desires to relinquish evil ways and turn to you.

Scan To Branch Out

Let's Overcome Evil with Good

SCRIPTURE WHISPER

Do not be overcome by evil, but overcome evil with good.

Romans 12:21 NKJV

The only way to conquer evil is with good. We cannot overcome evil by being evil although that's the natural worldly reaction. We must not fail to remember that God sent his Son, Jesus, who knew no sin, to declare those who accept Jesus as their Savior to be sinless.

Only the light of Jesus can drive out darkness. Evil cannot drive out evil; only love can do that. To be God's light of goodness is to live the fruit of his Spirit, making this a daily habit to conquer evil in our hearts while influencing those we encounter. When we are kind to those who seek to hurt us, peaceful when tempers are heightened, and joyful when we are heartbroken, we can overcome evil with good. If we all make a habit of living the fruit of the Spirit each day and reflecting Jesus' character in our ways, then the world will be different.

Jesus of patience, we ask you to help us devote more time each day to living the fruit of your Spirit so that your goodness overcomes evil. May we bring others to a knowledge of your love and goodness.

Scan To Branch Out

Let's Illuminate God's Work

SCRIPTURE WHISPER

He reveals mysteries from the darkness and brings the deepest darkness into the light.

JOB 12:22 HCSB

God is behind the scenes today just as he was when these words were written in Job. True wisdom is from God, from whom we learn how to live and what to live for. Strength and success belong to God, and he longs to shower these blessings upon his obedient children.

The richness and depth of our Scripture Whisper give us hope that God is at work. Even when situations worsen, he is maneuvering ahead for the good of his children and for his kingdom to come. God uses us to be the light that extinguishes the darkness. With one flicker of his light, darkness diminishes.

Jesus of kindness, as we go about our day and encounter many disturbances throughout our land, help us not to be blinded but to see the opportunities you put before us to be your light in this world of darkness. We know you have a plan, and we stand firm in our belief that the power of prayer will bring a wave of your light to the hearts of the hopeless. Let us be all you intend for us to be, making a difference as your light in the darkness.

Let's Sync with Jesus' Timing

SCRIPTURE WHISPER

Jesus answered them, "The hour has now come for the Son of Man to receive great glory."
JOHN 12:23 GNT

Jesus operates on a divine clock. He can because he knows the future. And today, when we place our moments in his care at the start of our day, he will masterfully schedule every second to fulfill his plan in each of our lives.

How freeing it is when we ask God to become our master scheduler. What a gift he has given that so many never unwrap! God has complete knowledge of the past, present, and future and has appointed times in every moment for all mankind. But do we seek those moments throughout our days? Do we obey when he leads us? There's no better way to begin our day than by asking God to direct our steps.

Jesus of goodness, what a gift we so often take for granted as you wait for us to surrender the moments of our lives to fulfill your plans. It's exhilarating to experience your perfect timing and to look back and see how you have intersected our lives with others at the right moment. Let us be aware of how vital it is to seek your divine timing to make a difference along our journey.

Scan To Branch Out

Let's Die to Self

SCRIPTURE WHISPER

"I tell you the truth, unless a kernel of wheat is planted in the soil and dies, it remains alone. But its death will produce many new kernels—a plentiful harvest of new lives."
JOHN 12:24 NLT

It's a law of nature: a seed must die for a plant to grow and produce more seeds, and then one seed multiplies into many. Our lives, too, mirror this multiplying principle. The Light of the World gave us a new life, a reborn and transformed eternal life, through his sacrificial death. We are to die to self and worldly ways and burst forth, grow up, and multiply into a spiritual harvest.

It's a lifelong process. It can happen sooner for those who understand this principle of life: when we die to self and take on the character of Jesus, the fruit of Jesus' Spirit within us multiplies as Jesus arranges divine appointments for a harvest.

Jesus of faithfulness, we pray together today that we bury any ways that are not of you and close any opened doors that Satan can creep in to stain our character and inhibit others from seeing the light of your presence within us.

Let's Focus on Others

SCRIPTURE WHISPER

"Those who love their life in this world will lose it. Those who care nothing for their life in this world will keep it for eternity."
John 12:25 NLT

Living a self-centered, entitled lifestyle is the way of the world and seems to be more prominent than ever. The others-focused principles described throughout the Bible are lost in our culture today, which is much of the reason there is so much conflict, chaos, and turbulent lifestyles.

But Jesus modeled an opposite lifestyle that leads to a life filled with peace and contentment that far surpasses our imagination. Trying to grab hold of a me-style existence will cause us to lose the very things we are trying to hold on to. If our lives are solely focused on self-centered goals, we will never find the true value of life apart from a selfish pursuit. We are to put off worldly, self-centered ways and, instead, welcome a transformation into a servant's heart, continually seeking ways to make a difference for others.

Jesus of gentleness, we pray that you make us aware of our ways that are not of you, that favor ourselves rather than serving others first. You gave us your life. Help us share with others the fruit of your Spirit each day, especially today, as our gift to you. Happy birthday, Jesus.

Scan To Branch Out

Let's Serve Obediently

SCRIPTURE WHISPER

"Anyone who wants to serve me must follow me, because my servants must be where I am. And the Father will honor anyone who serves me."

JOHN 12:26 NLT

As ambassadors for Jesus, we are to serve him by loving those whom he loves and for whom he gave himself, which is all mankind. This is evidence of Jesus living and loving through us.

This world is full of people who are somewhat hard to love, and many are even hard to like. But Jesus loves everyone, even those who have allowed Satan in by living a sinful lifestyle. But we are to surrender our worldly love to his unconditional, supernatural love. It's documented many times how the evilest heart can melt and be transformed through the compassionate love of Jesus.

Jesus of self-control, help us serve you by loving others as you do. Show us how to become your melting pot for hearts of stone, broken hearts, and open doors of darkness in many souls, which have allowed Satan a foothold in their hearts. Help us show that living in the past keeps us from living in your future. It's a ball and chain that we must sever to live our best-intended life. Let us serve you by loving others through your unconditional love.

Scan To Branch Out

Let's Live Our Purpose

SCRIPTURE WHISPER

"My soul is troubled, and what shall I say? 'Father, save Me from this hour'? No, it is for this purpose that I have come to this hour."

JOHN 12:27 BSB

Jesus' soul was troubled. He was God, but he was Man, and because he foresaw the suffering that would be required of him, he cried out to his Father for help; it's a human reaction. Jesus chose to die for our sins to save us from the fallen world. Throughout Jesus' earthly ministry, God was glorified through miracles. Still, the ultimate glorification was forthcoming at the cross and resurrection when Jesus saved the world.

If we could look at life as Jesus did, we would know full well that when we face heartaches and difficulties ahead, God has a purpose in them and will bring the best from our challenges. God doesn't cause trouble. We live in a fallen world, but he has the power to restore and redeem what's broken and equip us to handle great things he has in store for us.

Jesus of love, help us look at days ahead not in dread but in your glory. You don't intend for us to do life alone, so why do we? Help us unwrap your beautiful gift, the present of your presence.

Scan To Branch Out

Let's Shake Loose from the World

SCRIPTURE WHISPER

We should be grateful we were given a kingdom that cannot be shaken. And in this kingdom we please God by worshiping him and by showing him great honor and respect.

HEBREWS 12:28 CEV

God's kingdom cannot be shaken. No matter the trouble, we are just passing through to life ahead in the heavenly realms without Satan, the way God intended in the garden of Eden before the fall of humanity.

But until then, Satan's hold was severed at the cross. We have the same power to crush Satan's hold on us. God gives this power to his children when we accept his Son as the only way to salvation, inviting Jesus to live in a relationship with us until the day we are called to eternity. To accomplish this purpose, God shakes us loose from anything that's not part of his kingdom plan. So instead of grasping earthly things that are temporary and unstable, let's learn to be grateful for what God has in store.

Jesus of joy, live through us to make a difference in this world, living the fruit of your Spirit in all we do.

Scan To Branch Out

Let's First Hear

SCRIPTURE WHISPER

Jesus replied, "This is the most important of all the commandments: 'Hear O Israel, the Lord our God, the Lord is One.'"

MARK 12:29 MSB

If we love God and live out our love for him, it becomes a joy and honor to follow his commandments, which are meant for our good and his glory. After the most important commandment, that we are to love God, Jesus said we are to love others. But it's intriguing that the greatest commandment doesn't start with the word *love* but with the word *hear*.

The first principle we need to obey is to hear and understand and accept that the Lord is our God. The rest of Scripture means nothing if we do not hear and then understand who God is.

Jesus of peace, we know that you long for our empty vessels to be your light in this dark world. We ask that we will demonstrate our love for you in ways that will ignite a movement of dependence on you and bring hope to the hopeless. May we extend a branch to hope and create a shelter of your amazing grace and unconditional love, drawing others to hear you too.

Let's Love God

SCRIPTURE WHISPER

"'Love the Lord your God with all your heart and with all your soul and with all your mind and with all your strength.'"
MARK 12:30 NIV

The very nature of God is his love, and this permeates all his other qualities. This commandment to love the Lord our God is the root of all the fruit of his Spirit. Love displays the depth of our soul. When we love like Jesus, our hearts speak. Scripture says, "These three remain: faith, hope and love. But the greatest of these is love" (1 Corinthians 13:13).

God desires that we love him to the very heart and core of our being so that the deepest affections of our soul are centered on our love for him and his love for us. God also desires that we love him with every fiber of our understanding so that our moment-by-moment thoughts ponder him and manifest his way of loving others.

Jesus of patience, we ask that our very nature be permeated with the atmosphere of your life, casting an aura that allows others to see the purity of our relationship bond with you every day, in every way, and in all we do. Help us speak your love through our lives.

Scan To Branch Out

Let's Love Others as Jesus Does

SCRIPTURE WHISPER

"The second most important commandment says:
'Love others as much as you love yourself.' No other
commandment is more important than these."
MARK 12:31 CEV

How do we love our neighbor as ourselves? A great model is
the Golden Rule: treat others as we would like to be treated
and never in ways that we would not like to be treated. What
we wish for others is what we wish for ourselves.

It's often hard to love others, especially when anger
prevails and tempers are heightened. How do we love the
unlikeable? By loving God first and foremost with our
whole heart, then loving others through his way of loving,
unconditionally. Making a habit each day to live the fruit of
Jesus' Spirit is a way to love others as we go about our days.

Jesus of kindness, help us love as you love, bring joy into
others' lives as you would, and be patient, peaceful, and kind
to others. May we be examples of your spirit of goodness
when tempers are heightened, remain faithful to your ways,
and be gentle in your spirit as we exercise your self-control,
especially when we feel tempted to live any other way but
your way. Help us always model your behavior and love
others as you do.

Scan To Branch Out

Acknowledgments

To Jesus, foremost, the Author, who chose me for this blessing.

To everyone Jesus has woven into the tapestry of my life. His voice is heard because of you! If I mentioned everyone's name who helped write this book, it would take another book. I would like to mention the ways many contributed and made this book possible. I hope you will hear your name in the following.

- Connecting me to BroadStreet Publishing

- Inspiring me behind the scenes

- Architecting and developing our Branch to Hope app, which inspired the book

- Proofing the daily Branch to Hope messages so masterfully

- Providing gourmet meals when I never left my writing desk

- Editing to make me look like the author I'm not

- Devotedly praying to uplift my soul with encouragement and support

About the Author

Bobbie Cox is a never-say-never entrepreneur with a biblical counseling certification. She is an ambassador of encouragement with a passion for inspiring people to intentionally change their habits for a better way of life by living the fruit of the Spirit, walking with Jesus in their everyday lives, and modeling his character. These small changes transform not only our lives but the lives of others, reaping blessings that far exceed our imagination.

To amplify her mission, Bobbie is devoted to pen the whispers of Jesus' heart each day. Her soulful longing is to encourage others to be diligent, daily prayer warriors and for millions to pause and pray in unity each day at 1:11 p.m., igniting a prayer movement that can transform our land and establishing that the power of praying together can make a difference.

Bobbie lives in the quaint town of Grapevine, Texas, and has one daughter, Ashley; a son-in-love, Blake; and two adorable granddogs.

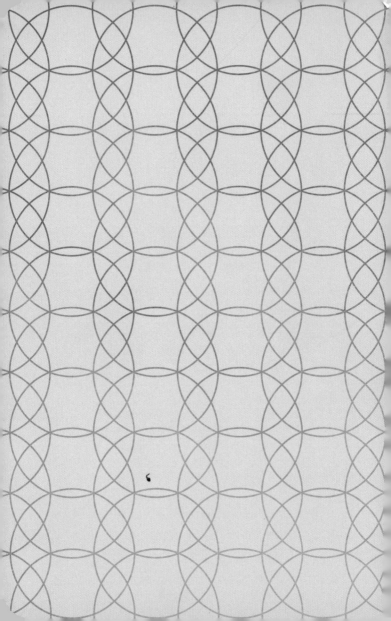